MICROSOFT CERTIFIED SYSTEMS ENGINEER

MCSE Windows® 2000 Professional Lab Manual, Student Edition

MCSE Windows® 2000
Professional Lab Manual,
Student Edition

Jane Holcombe
Chuck Holcombe
Walter Merchant

McGraw-Hill/Osborne
New York Chicago San Francisco
Lisbon London Madrid Mexico City Milan
New Delhi San Juan Seoul Singapore Sydney Toronto

McGraw-Hill/Osborne
2600 Tenth Street
Berkeley, California 94710
U.S.A.

To arrange bulk purchase discounts for sales promotions, premiums, or fund-raisers, please contact **McGraw-Hill**/Osborne at the above address. For information on translations or book distributors outside the U.S.A., please see the International Contact Information page immediately following the index of this book.

MCSE Windows® 2000 Professional Lab Manual, Student Edition

1234567890 CUS CUS 0198765432

ISBN 0-07-222300-6

Publisher Brandon A. Nordin	**Acquisitions Coordinator** Athena Honore	**Illustrator** Michael Mueller
Vice President & Associate Publisher Scott Rogers	**Technical Editor** Lee Cottrell	**Series Design** Roberta Steele
Acquisitions Editor Chris Johnson	**Production and Editorial Services** Anzai!, Inc.	**Cover Series Designer** Greg Scott
Senior Project Editor Betsy Manini	**Illustration Supervisor** Lyssa Wald	

This book was composed with Corel VENTURA™ Publisher.

We fondly dedicate this book to the students who will use this manual in pursuing a career in Information Technology. We wish each student a long career, rich with rewards and growth.

ABOUT THE AUTHORS

Jane and Charles Holcombe are consultants, trainers, and authors with decades of experience. They now write technical books and creative non-fiction (which is sort of the same thing) as a team.

Jane's career in writing computer courses and teaching classes in computer technology began in 1984. She taught both basic and advanced computer networking and operating system topics. Jane was a pioneer in PC support training in the mid-'80s when she co-founded a successful national training company and authored numerous technical-training courses, then taught them coast-to-coast. She has been a Microsoft Certified Trainer (MCT) for a number of years, and has earned the Microsoft Certified Systems Engineer (MCSE) certification for Windows NT 3.51, Windows NT 4.0, and Windows 2000. She also holds CNA for NetWare 3, A+, Network +, and CTT+ certifications. Her current focus is on the Windows 2000 and Windows XP operating systems.

Chuck was a pioneering computer programmer, sales analyst, salesman, sales manager, and computer-based training product manager for a super-computer manufacturer. For the past 23 years he has been an independent trainer and management consultant, during which time he authored and delivered training courses worldwide. His focus has been on human interaction: sales, customer relations, negotiation, and teaching inter-personal skills to technical people. He is now returning to his first love: computer technology.

Dr. Walter Merchant, currently CIS Department Chair at ECPI College of Technology, has been teaching for over 20 years. He is Microsoft, Cisco, UNIX, and Novell certified; an experienced instructional designer; and the author of *MCSE Windows 2000 Accelerated Instructor's Pack* (McGraw-Hill/Osborne, 2001), *MCSE Windows 2000 Professional Instructor's Pack* (McGraw-Hill/Osborne, 2001), and *Networking: A Beginner's Guide Second Edition Instructor's Pack* (McGraw-Hill/Osborne, 2001).

CONTENTS

ACKNOWLEDGMENTS

We greatly appreciate the help and contributions of the following people:

- The people at **McGraw-Hill**/Osborne who originated and managed this project. They include Chris Johnson, Athena Honore, and Betsy Manini among many others we met through our countless e-mails.

- Our technical editor, Lee Cottrell, who made significant and valuable suggestions throughout the book. His considerable experience especially showed in scenarios he described to us, which resulted in several lab hints.

- Tom Anzai and his entire team, who all, once again, took a greater interest in this project than their assigned tasks required. We especially thank Lee Musick, whose sense of humor and technical knowledge made him a copy editor extraordinaire. Sorry, Lee, we ran out of Thin Mints, too.

INTRODUCTION

Welcome to the *MCSE Windows 2000 Professional Lab Manual*. This manual contains 50 lab exercises designed to give you hands-on, practical experience in your preparation for Microsoft's Exam 70-210, Installing, Configuring, and Administering Microsoft Windows 2000 Professional. Use the exercises in this lab manual to reinforce the concepts you learn in the *MCSE Windows 2000 Professional Study Guide* (McGraw-Hill/Osborne, 2000).

The lab exercises are presented in the context of real-world situations to prepare you for on-the-job experiences. Learning objectives align with the exam topics of Exam 70-210. The labs have grown out of decades of field and classroom experience with the topics.

You have a great deal of flexibility in how you use these labs, because each individual lab lists the materials and setup required. In each lab you are presented with a scenario that you might encounter on the job. It may be a task that must be accomplished or a problem that must be solved. You will then go through the steps to accomplish the task or solve the problem. You will find these lab exercises engaging because they do involve real-world situations that have either happened directly to us or to someone we know.

We strove to provide exercises that teach the concepts and skills needed without providing each mouse click of instruction. To that end, the lab exercises guide you through the tasks step-by-step rather than click-by-click. In some labs we do provide more detail, but only because we judged that someone preparing for their 70-210 exam might not have the experience to perform the task without such detail.

You can test your grasp of the concepts and skills practiced in the lab exercises by taking the Lab Analysis Test that follows the labs in each chapter. And the Key Term Quiz will test your ability to "talk the talk" relevant to each chapter. You'll find solutions to all the questions, and insights and helpful hints abound. Also watch for lab warnings, lab hints and cross-references that are sprinkled throughout.

In addition to the lab exercises, each chapter includes the following sections:

- ■ Lab Analysis Test which contains essay questions.
- ■ Key Term Quiz which builds vocabulary and gives you the confidence to "talk the talk."

■ Lab Solutions, found at the end of each chapter, which provide answers to the Lab Analysis Test and Key Term Quiz. You will also find more detailed instructions for the more complex lab exercises.

■ Lab Hints that provide additional information relevant to the lab exercise, including alternative methods or tips for using the technologies involved.

■ Lab Warnings that draw attention to potential pitfalls.

■ Cross-references that direct students to relevant information in the *MCSE Windows 2000 Professional Study Guide* (McGraw-Hill/Osborne, 2000).

MICROSOFT CERTIFIED SYSTEMS ENGINEER

1

Introduction to Installing, Configuring, and Administering Windows 2000 Professional

I magine that you are a Desktop Support Analyst in an organization that is planning a desktop migration from Windows 98 to Windows 2000 Professional. Before you can accomplish this migration, there is much you need to learn about Windows 2000. Chapter I of the *MCSE Windows 2000 Professional Study Guide* gives you an overview of the topics covered in that book, and how you can use the book to prepare for Microsoft's Exam 70-210, Installing, Configuring, and Administering Microsoft Windows 2000 Professional.

Chapter 1 of the Study Guide also describes administrative tools you will be using in the following chapters. In this first chapter of the lab manual you will work with some of the administrative tools in order to familiarize yourself with them, beginning with the Microsoft Management Console (MMC), a graphical user interface (GUI) that Microsoft uses for many administrative tools.

Then you will review a set of GUI tools with which you may already be familiar: the applets of the Control Panel. Next you will review the use of Device Manager, and you will follow that with a review of some registry basics. These labs can be completed with Windows 98 or Windows 2000. Each lab has a few optional steps that you can complete if you are using Windows 2000. Don't be concerned if you are starting out with Windows 98—you will install Windows 2000 in the following chapter.

LAB EXERCISE 1.01

Exploring the Microsoft Management Console

30 Minutes

As a member of the Desktop Support team, you are preparing for the rollout of Windows 2000 Professional to the client desktops in your organization. You have learned that many of the administrative tools that you will be using are MMC snap-ins. You want to become familiar with the MMC interface, but you are still using Windows 98 on your desktop computer. And while the MMC can run on any version of Windows since Windows 95, it was not included with Windows 95 or Windows 98. However, it is available for download at the Microsoft web site.

Learning Objectives

By the end of this lab, you'll be able to

- Install the latest version of the MMC
- Explore the MMC Interface
- Add a Snap-in to the MMC (Windows 2000 only).

Lab Materials and Setup

The materials you need for this lab are:

- A PC with Windows 98 or Windows 2000 installed
- A browser (Internet Explorer preferred) and a connection to the Internet (if Windows 98 is installed)

cross
Reference *For an overview of the Microsoft Management Console, read the section titled "Using the MMC" in Chapter 1 of the* **MCSE Windows 2000 Professional Study Guide.**

Getting Down to Business

In the following steps, if you are using Windows 98, you will download the MMC installation program, install it on your computer, and familiarize yourself with it. If you have Windows 98, use this lab to become familiar with the MMC interface. Don't worry, you will install Windows 2000 in the next chapter and soon be working with MMC snap-ins. If you already have Windows 2000 installed on your lab computer, you can experiment with creating a custom console that has some tools you will use later in the class.

lab
Warning *Note that you may not be able to add any administrative snap-ins, because they are only available on your computer if you also install the supporting services.*

Step 1. *This step is only necessary if you are using Windows 98 (or even Windows 95). If your lab computer has Windows 2000 Professional, go to Step 2.*

Use your Internet browser to connect to the download page for the Microsoft Management Console (MMC). At the time of this writing this page was at the following url: http://support.microsoft.com/support/mmc/mmcdown.asp. If this URL does not work for you, connect to http://support.microsoft.com/support/mmc and browse to the download site using the link titled MMC Downloads (near the bottom of the page). Follow the instructions to download and install the MMC. When prompted, restart your computer.

Step 2.   Run the command **MMC** from the Start | Run box. You will see the empty MMC Console, as shown in Figure 1-1. Familiarize yourself with the "look and feel" of the MMC console window.

Step 3.   Leave the MMC console open on your desktop and use the top menu bar to select Help | About Microsoft Management Console. This window will display the version of Microsoft Management Console, the version of Windows, licensing information, and physical memory available to Windows, as shown in Figure 1-2. Version 1.2 was included with Windows 2000 when it was introduced. Version 2.0 was included with Windows XP. Click OK to close the Window.

Step 4.   Return to the MMC Help menu and select Help Topics. This will open a Microsoft Management Console containing Help information for the Microsoft Management Console. Notice the How To section where you can learn how to work with the MMC, and the Concepts section where you can learn more about the MMC. Read through these two sections—it will make working with the MMC consoles easier for you.

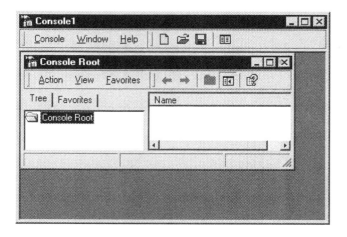

FIGURE 1-1

The MMC
Console

FIGURE 1-2

Help | About
MMC Display

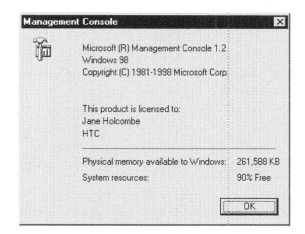

lab
(i)int
If you enjoy using keyboard shortcuts, you will find plenty of them in Help under Accessibility for MMC.

Step 5.   *If you are using Windows 98, close the console and skip the remaining steps in this lab. If you are using Windows 2000 or Windows XP, leave your console window open and complete the remaining steps.*

Step 6.   *Complete this step only if your lab computer has Windows 2000 or Windows XP.*
Following instructions in Help, add the Group Policy snap-in. You can find these instructions in the topic titled "Add a published snap-in to a new MMC console" under How To Author an MMC Console File, selecting Local Computer for the Group Policy Object. Using the Save As choice from the Console menu, save this console as GPEditor.msc in the root of your current drive. The MSC file extension indicates that this file is a Microsoft saved console file. Remember this location. If your current drive is C:, this location is C:\. You will use this saved console in Chapter 9.

Step 7.   *Complete this step only if your lab computer has Windows 2000 or Windows XP.*
Extensions are discrete portions of a snap-in that cannot stand alone, but must be installed as a subtree of a snap-in. Typically, when you install a snap-in that includes extensions, all the extensions are installed unless you deselect some. In this step you will view the extensions that were installed with the Group Policy snap-in.

With the GPEditor console open, select Console | Add/Remove Snap-in. Notice that the Add/Remove Snap-in dialog box has two tabs—the Standalone tab and the Extensions tab. The Standalone tab displays the Local Computer Policy (because you chose to focus the Group Policy Editor on your local computer), while the Extensions tab contains the extensions to Group Policy. If you wanted to create a console for someone who is only responsible for administering logon scripts, you could deselect all the extensions except Scripts (Logon/Logoff).

Step 8.   Close the GPEditor Console window.

lab
Ⓗint

An ordinary user can create MMC consoles. All that is needed is permissions to the MMC.EXE file and the supporting snap-in files, but you must have the appropriate permissions and rights to access and make changes to users, groups, computers, and other objects while using a console. To learn more about the MMC, read all of the Microsoft Management Help topics or point your Internet browser to http:/msdn.microsoft.com and search on "MMC."

LAB EXERCISE 1.02

Using Control Panel

30 Minutes

You have learned that Windows 2000 continues to use the Control Panel as a GUI container for a variety of applets used to configure, manage, and administer a Windows computer. Some of these applets are MMC consoles, others are wizards, and some are the conventional property dialog boxes you have used in the past. You have worked with the Control Panel applets in the past, but would like to review their use before participating in the Windows 2000 rollout.

Learning Objectives

By the end of this lab, you'll be able to

- Identify Control Panel applets
- Access Control Panel applets outside the Control Panel.

Lab Materials and Setup

The materials you need for this lab are:

■ A PC with Windows 98 or Windows 2000 installed

Review the section titled "Windows 2000 Control Panel" in Chapter 1 of the **MCSE Windows 2000 Professional Study Guide**.

Getting Down to Business

In the following steps you will explore the Control Panel to see some of the tools available there. You will also try accessing some of these applets from locations outside the Control Panel.

Step 1.   Start Control Panel and look at each of the applets, noticing the form that the individual applets take, such as properties sheets, wizards, and MMC consoles.

If you are using Windows 2000 for this lab, you may notice that a few applets have been transformed from property sheets to a new, more functional, look. Other applets are wizards that walk you through multi-step tasks. While some applets have remained much the same, others have been greatly changed and/or combined. For example, the former Network applet is now Network and Dial-up Connections and includes the Dial-up Networking capabilities that were previously in a special folder under My Computer. Also, the former Modems applet has been combined with the Telephony applet in the new Phone and Modem Options. Windows 9x has a Users applet, which enables you to have different profiles for users, but is not involved in actually creating or modifying user accounts as the new Users and Passwords applet in Windows 2000 is. It allows an administrator to create and manage local user accounts that reside in the registry of the local computer. There are also completely new applets, such as Administrative Tools, Folder Options, and Scheduled Tasks.

Step 2.   Compare the Windows 98 Add/Remove Programs applet in Figure 1-3 with the same applet in Figure 1-4. This applet has been greatly enhanced in Windows 2000. Also notice that on your lab computers, these application lists may be completely empty. Only installed applications that were not part of the Windows source files will appear in the boxes shown. On the Windows 98 computer used to create

Windows 98
Add/Remove
Programs Applet

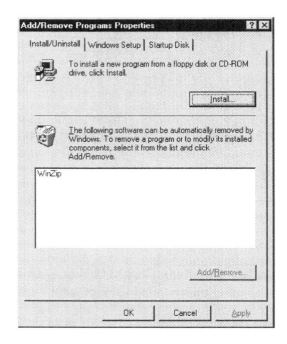

Figure 1-3, WinZip is the only such application, while on the Windows 2000 Professional computer, there are many additional applications.

Step 3. In both Windows 98 and Windows 2000, many of the Control Panel applets are available through other options in the desktop. See how many of them you can find, and list them below.

lab
Hint

Right-clicking will get you a long way in the Windows interface! Also, finding the files that end with .cpl and double-clicking on them can start Control Panel applets.

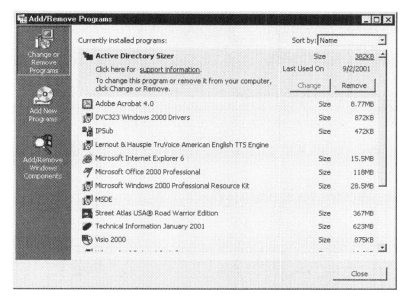

FIGURE 1-4

Windows 2000
Add/Remove
Programs Applet

LAB EXERCISE 1.03

Using Device Manager

30 Minutes

Another tool you can expect to use when supporting Windows 2000 Professional is the Device Manager. While it was not included with Windows NT, it was part of Windows 95 and 98, and continues to be included with Windows 2000 and Windows XP. This is a handy tool for troubleshooting hardware and device driver problems. Using Device Manager, you can view hardware configuration information, update device drivers, disable devices, and remove devices. With this in mind, you will examine this tool in order to prepare yourself for the pending rollout of Windows 2000 Professional.

Learning Objectives

By the end of this lab, you'll be able to

- Run Device Manager
- View devices and system resources in Device Manager.

cross
Reference   *For an overview of the Windows 2000, read the section titled "The Windows 2000 Registry" in Chapter 1 of the **MCSE Windows 2000 Professional Study Guide.***

Lab Materials and Setup

The materials you need for this lab are:

- A PC with Windows 98 or Windows 2000 installed

Getting Down to Business

Device Manager has been included in Windows since Windows 95. In both Windows 98 and Windows 2000, Device Manager can be found through the System applet. However, where it was previously simply a tabbed sheet in the System Properties dialog box, it is now an MMC snap-in, and opens up into a separate console window when launched from System Properties | Hardware | Device Manager.

Step 1.   Open Device Manager. If you are using Windows 2000, compare the old Device Manager GUI with that of Windows 2000, shown in Figure 1-5.

lab
Hint

Windows 9x does not have true local security. For instance, anyone can install and modify drivers in Windows 98, but you must have administrative level rights to do that in Windows 2000 (also in Windows NT and Windows XP). Therefore, if you are logged on as a non-administrative user and start Device Manager on one of these more secure operating systems, you will receive a warning that you do not have sufficient privileges to install or modify device drivers. However, if you click the OK button on this warning box, Device Manager will open. Basically, a non-administrative user is allowed to look but not touch!

Step 2.   With the aid of the Help program (if necessary), explore the Device Manager, performing the following:

- View devices by type
- View devices by connection
- View resources

FIGURE I-5

Windows 2000
Device Manager

Step 3. Close Device Manager.

LAB EXERCISE 1.04

Viewing the Windows 2000 Registry

30 Minutes

The MMC snap-ins, Control Panel applets, Windows setup program, and application setup programs are the most common tools that you will use for administration, installation, and configuration. All of these tools perform operations that usually result in changes to the registry—that hierarchical database of operating system and application settings, configuration settings, and user preference settings. Changes to the registry are most properly made through the use of these tools. However, as you may know from past experience with Windows, occasionally you have to manually make changes to the registry. For this reason, you will review the differences between the registry editors in Windows 98 and Windows 2000.

Learning Objectives

By the end of this lab, you'll be able to

■ Describe differences between the REGEDIT.EXE (Windows 98) and REGEDT32.EXE (Windows 2000).

Lab Materials and Setup

The materials you need for this lab are:

■ A PC with Windows 98 or Windows 2000 installed

cross
Reference

For an overview of the Windows 2000 registry, read the section titled "The Windows 2000 Registry" in Chapter 1 of the MCSE Windows 2000 Professional Study Guide.

Getting Down to Business

The registry editor is a tool we hope to never have to use, because changing the registry is like performing brain surgery on your computer—you must be absolutely sure you are doing the right thing. This means that editing the registry is something you will only do as a last resort, and with explicit, well-tested instructions. So, just in case you are faced with such a situation, you are now going to look at the tool you would use. As it turns out, there are two registry editors that come with Windows 2000. REGEDIT.EXE is the same registry editor that came with Windows 98, and REGEDT32.EXE is nearly the same registry editor as that which comes with Windows NT. What are the differences, and why do you care? In the following steps you will examine each of these tools. If you are using a Windows 98 computer, you will look at REGEDIT.EXE and compare it to a screen print of REGEDT32.EXE.

Step 1. Start the Windows 98 registry editor by using its executable filename in Start | Run.

Step 2. Compare the user interface of REGEDIT (Windows 98) with that of REGEDT32 (Windows 2000), as shown in Figure 1-6. If your lab computer has

FIGURE 1-6

Windows 2000
REGEDT32.EXE

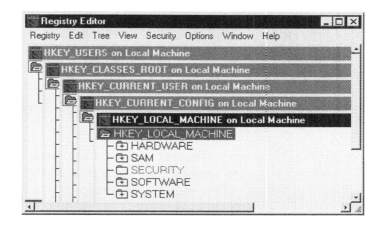

Windows 2000 rather than Windows 98, simply run the REGEDIT program.
Answer the questions below:

1. How would you describe the fundamental difference between the user interfaces of REGEDIT and REGEDT32?

   _____

   _____

   _____

2. What differences do you see on the main menus of these two programs?

   _____

   _____

   _____

3. What is the effect of not having a Security menu in REGEDIT in Windows 2000?

   _____

   _____

   _____

4. Which registry editor gives you some protection from accidentally editing the registry?

_____

_____

_____

lab
Hint

Although you often encounter warnings against directly editing the registry, on the job you will discover that many solutions to software problems require a registry fix. A proven strategy for doing this is to edit the registry on a test computer. Ensure that the change has had no adverse effects, then export the modified key from the test computer and import it to any desktop computers requiring this change. You can check out the Help topic "Import or Export Registry Keys" in REGEDIT.EXE.

LAB ANALYSIS TEST

1. The Desktop Support team will be among the first to have Windows 2000 Professional on their desktops. You have experience with the administrative tools available to you in Windows 98. What is the major difference you will see in administrative tools that you will use in Windows 2000?

_____

_____

2. While working on a Windows 2000 computer in the lab one day, you notice that you can create an MMC, even when you are logged on as a user with no administrative rights. Does this mean that ordinary users will be able to cause damage to their computers using these powerful administrative tools? Explain your answer.

_____

_____

3. The Desktop Support team has created a test lab to test the proposed user desktop configurations. One of your co-workers finds that in Windows 2000 the Dial-Up Networking folder is missing from the My Computer folder. Tell him where he can find dial-up networking settings in Windows 2000.

_____

_____

4. You have installed Windows 2000 Professional on a test computer that includes a non-Plug and Play sound card. This is not the optimum configuration you hope to have on the desktop, but some of your client computers have these old sound cards, and you have been asked to test them with Windows 2000. Although you installed the proper driver for this card, you do not hear sounds. You have checked out the power to the speakers, volume control on the speakers, and connection from the speaker to the sound card. What tool can you use to troubleshoot a non-functioning device?

_____

_____

5. One of your team members has been reading about the Windows 2000 registry and has recommended that the team make some registry changes to the computers as they configure them. What advice would you like to add to this suggestion?

_____

_____

KEY TERM QUIZ

Use the following vocabulary terms to complete the sentences below. Not all the terms will be used.

> Control Panel
>
> Device Manager
>
> extensions
>
> Folder Options
>
> MMC
>
> MSC
>
> REGEDIT
>
> REGEDT32
>
> resources
>
> snap-in

1. In Windows 2000 the new _____ Control Panel applet allows you to control the appearance of folders when opened and what triggers a folder to open (single-click or double-click).

2. When you add the Computer Management snap-in to an MMC console, many _____ are installed by default.

3. When you create a custom console, you save it as a Microsoft Saved Console file with a/an _____ extension.

4. Formerly a page in the System Properties dialog box, _____ is now an MMC snap-in and opens in its own window.

5. _____ has a menu that allows an administrator to set permissions on individual registry keys.

LAB WRAP-UP

In this chapter, you first explored some of the administrative tools, beginning with the Microsoft Management Console (MMC), which is not in itself so much a tool as it is a GUI container for one or more tools. As you continue through the lab manual, you will work with the MMC using both the set of consoles that come with Windows 2000 Professional, and consoles that you create yourself, using the snap-ins and extensions provided by Microsoft. Computer Management is an example of a preset console you will frequently use with Windows 2000 Professional, while the Group Policy Editor is an example of a console that you will create in a later chapter when you add the Group Policy snap-in to an MMC console.

LAB SOLUTIONS FOR CHAPTER 1

In this section, you'll find solutions to the lab exercises, Lab Analysis Test, and Key Term Quiz.

Lab Solution 1.01

Step 1.   The version of the MMC that we downloaded was 1.2, and the file name was IMMC.EXE. This may change with a newer version of the MMC. Rather than run the install from the Microsoft web site, we saved it to our computer, then browsed to the location on disk, and double-clicked on the file to execute it. After the reboot we were ready to proceed to Step 2.

Step 2.   No additional instructions are required for this step. You should observe that the console window includes two panes. The left pane has two tabs, Tree and Favorites. Until you add one or more snap-ins, the Tree tab only contains the Console Root; future snap-ins will appear as expandable branches from this root. When a snap-in is loaded into a console, the window on the right will contain the content, and the titles on that window will change for the content. Snap-ins will only appear if you have installed one or more services that can be administered by MMC snap-ins. If you are running Windows 98, we will assume that you do not have such a service installed.

Step 3.   No additional instructions are required for this step.

Step 4.   When you add one or more snap-ins to your console, the Help Contents will include both Microsoft Management Console and the topics for the snap-ins that are installed.

Steps 5 through 8.   No additional instructions are required for these steps.

Lab Solution 1.02

Step 1.   Select Start | Settings | Control Panel. Open the Accessibility applet. This applet is not significantly changed between Windows 98 and Windows 2000, except that in the former it is labeled Accessibility Properties, while in Windows 2000, it is labeled Accessibility Options. After studying the details of the Accessibility applet, continue to look at each of the other available applets.

Step 2.   No additional instructions are required for this step.

Step 3.   Answers will vary, but should include some of the following, and perhaps others we have overlooked:

1. Right-click on My Computer and select Properties to open the System applet.

2. Right-click on My Network Places and select Properties to open the Network and Dial-up Connections applet.

3. Right-click on any empty space on the desktop and select Properties to open the Display applet.

4. Right-click on the Internet Explorer icon, and select Properties to open the Internet Options applet.

5. From the Start Menu select Settings | Folder Options to open the Folder Options applet (Windows 98).

6. Double-click on My Computer and select Tools | Folder Options to open the Folder Options applet (Windows 2000).

7. From the Start Menu select Settings | Network and Dial-up Connections (Windows 2000) to open the Network and Dial-up Connections applet.

8. From the Start Menu select Settings | Printers to open the Printers applet.

9. Locate and right-click on the speaker icon in the tray portion of the Task Bar and select Adjust Audio Properties to open the Sounds and Multimedia applet.

lab
ⓗ**int**   *You say you've never heard of the tray? It's the right-most portion of the Task Bar containing icons where the time usually appears.*

Lab Solution 1.03

Step 1.   Windows 98 instructions: Open the System applet, and click on the Device Manager tab.

Windows 2000 instructions: Open the System applet, click on the Hardware tab, then click on the Device Manager button.

Step 2.   The Device Manager displays the options described in the table below.

To View	In Windows 98	In Windows 2000
Devices by type	Click on the radio button View Devices By Type. (This is the default initial view of Device Manager.)	Use the Console menu and select View	Devices By Type. (This is the default initial view of Device Manager.)
Devices by connection	Click on the radio button View Devices By Connection.	Use the Console menu and select View	Devices By Connection.
Resources	Click on the properties button, then use the radio buttons to view the different types of resources: interrupt request (IRQ), direct memory access (DMA), input/output (I/O), and Memory.	Use the Console menu and select View	Resource By Type or select Resources by connection. (The resource listings will be organized based on which of these you display.)

Step 3.   No additional instructions are required for this step.

Lab Solution 1.04

Step 1.   Select Start | Run and enter the command REGEDIT.EXE in the Open box and then click OK.

Step 2.   Answers will vary. The answers below include some advice and opinion.

1. The fundamental difference between the user interfaces of REGEDIT and REGEDT32 is that REGEDIT has a two-part window. On the left is the tree pane that contains a hierarchical view of the registry, and on the right is the contents window. REGEDT32 has multiple child windows like the user interface of Windows 3.x. Each window contains a subtree of the registry, and it is not a visually pleasing tool to use.

2. The REGEDIT menus consist of Registry, Edit, View, Favorites, and Help. The Favorites menu is not included with REGEDT32. It allows you to save the location of a registry key so that you can quickly jump to it without having to navigate to it. However, REGEDT32 includes the other menus of REGEDIT, as well as the additional menus Security, Windows, and Options.

3. Not having a Security menu in REGEDIT means that an administrator cannot modify security settings on the registry keys. It does not mean that you are immune to security settings when you are using this tool.

4. REGEDT32 gives you some protection from accidentally editing the registry with the Read Only Mode, found in the Options menu. It is not turned on by default, but you should be in the habit of turning this setting on, so that you must take an extra step and turn off Read Only mode before modifying the registry.

ANSWERS TO LAB ANALYSIS TEST

1. In Windows 2000 most administrative tools are MMC snap-ins. The MMC is a GUI container for these tools, giving a standard interface for administrators. Actually, there were some MMC tools available before Windows 2000. Microsoft had several network services that used MMC administrative snap-ins, including Exchange Server and Systems Management Server. Remember that older clients may be able to run the MMC console, but the availability of the appropriate snap-in depends on the ability to install the supporting services into an operating system. You will have support for more snap-ins with Windows 2000.

2. Any user can create an MMC, as long as they have permissions to run the MMC.EXE executable file and the files relating to the snap-ins that they wish to add to the console. However, what a user can actually do with these snap-in tools depends on their permissions and rights to perform such action. So, the user will not be permitted to perform tasks that the snap-in provides which require special permission or rights, such as formatting a hard drive or creating new users.

3. You can tell your co-worker that the settings which were previously available in the Dial-Up Networking folder in the My Computer folder are now combined with the networking settings in the Network and Dial-up Connections applet in Control Panel. You can also show him that it is available from Start | Settings or by right-clicking My Network Places.

4. You can use Device Manager to troubleshoot device problems.

5. It is important to remember that it is dangerous to directly edit the registry, and this should not be considered routine. As a rule, changes to the registry should only be done through the GUI tools of the Control Panel applets, or by installation programs. Perhaps the co-worker's suggested changes could be done by some method rather than directly editing the registry with the registry editor. If not, consider the strategy suggested in the Lab Hint at the end of Lab 1.04.

ANSWERS TO KEY TERM QUIZ

1. Folder Options
2. extensions
3. MSC
4. Device Manager
5. REGEDT32

MICROSOFT CERTIFIED SYSTEMS ENGINEER

2

Performing an Attended Installation of Windows 2000 Professional

I n Chapter 1 of the *MCSE Windows 2000 Professional Study Guide* you were given an overview of the contents of the book, as well as Exam 70-210, and you explored some of the software tools you will be using in Windows 2000.

Now it is time to get down to more serious work. Recall the scenario introduced in Chapter 1 of this lab manual in which you are a desktop support analyst in an organization that is planning a desktop migration from Windows 98 to Windows 2000 Professional. Imagine, at this point in the planning process, that you are exploring tasks that must be performed before installing Windows 2000. Then you consider performing an attended installation. By attended, we mean that someone pays attention during the entire installation process, answering all the questions asked by the Setup program, as opposed to an unattended installation in which the questions asked during setup are answered via a script (which we'll cover in Chapter 3).

Whether an installation is attended or unattended, there are variations of installations. The two major types of installations are usually described as *upgrade* or *clean*. An upgrade is an installation literally on top of the previous operating system (into the same installation directory), which will retain your configuration settings for installed hardware and preferences for installed software. When you perform a clean installation, you are installing to a new (hence, clean) computer or at least into a new location on a computer that is already running DOS or Windows. In the latter case, the result is a dual-boot configuration. In this case, you can dual boot (or choose) between Windows 2000 and your previous operating system (as long as it is DOS or Windows) if you wish to be able to continue to dual boot to your previous operating system. This is fraught with potential problems, so avoid doing this if you can. However, you might do it for yourself if you must support several operating systems, but only have a single computer. (It is hard to talk to an end user about an operating system that is not right in front of you.)

The *MCSE Windows 2000 Professional Study Guide* has several excellent labs (2-1 through 2-4) that guide you through an attended clean installation. Exercise 2-5 in *the MCSE Windows 2000 Professional Study Guide* provides the steps to begin an installation over the network, connecting to a network share that holds the Windows 2000 Professional source files. To supplement these exercises, the lab exercises in this chapter of the Lab Manual first have you run the Readiness Analyzer on a computer running Windows 98 in order to determine if it is compatible with Windows 2000, then have you perform an upgrade to Windows 2000.

Chapter 2 of the *MCSE Windows 2000 Professional Study Guide* discusses deploying service packs and has you determine the version and service pack level of Windows 2000 in Exercise 2-7. In this chapter of the Lab Manual you have a lab exercise in which you apply the latest service pack to your Windows 2000 lab computer.

The final topic in Chapter 2 of the *MCSE Windows 2000 Professional Study Guide* is Troubleshooting Failed Installations. It discusses common problems and describes the Setup Log files, which you explore in Exercise 2-8. In this chapter of the Lab Manual you are presented with several scenarios describing the symptoms of failed installations, and you are given a resource to use to determine what steps you would take to troubleshoot the failure.

LAB EXERCISE 2.01

Using the Readiness Analyzer Before Upgrading to Windows 2000

30 Minutes

In an ideal situation, when planning to roll out a new operating system to the desktop and laptop computers in an organization, you simply wait until the end of the lease cycle on the present equipment, and order new equipment with the new operating system already installed. However, not all situations are ideal, and there is no Santa Claus, Virginia. Perhaps your company does not lease end-user computers, and/or there is existing equipment that must be upgraded. Even in these situations, you might still opt to do a clean install rather than upgrade the existing operating system. This is called a migration. You may even repartition and reformat the hard drive in the process. However, before you take such drastic measures, you should determine the compatibility of the hardware and software. We suggest that you run the Readiness Analyzer utility under the existing operating system. This will tell you if the hardware is sufficient, and if the installed applications need to be modified or removed and reinstalled before they will run under Windows 2000. Once you discover what hardware and software may not be compatible, you can do further research at the web sites of the vendors of these products. They may have developed newer drivers or written update scripts to make modifications to the registry of file locations for better compatibility between their product and Windows 2000.

Learning Objectives

By the end of this lab, you'll be able to

■ Run the Windows 2000 Readiness Analyzer

■ Save the results of the Readiness Analyzer

■ Determine what actions you must take.

Lab Materials and Setup

The materials you need for this lab are:

■ A PC with Windows 98 installed

■ The Windows 2000 Professional CD (or a local or network location containing the contents of the i386 directory)

For an overview of Performing an Attended Installation of Windows 2000 Professional, read the section titled "Certification Objective 2.01" in Chapter 2 of the MCSE Windows 2000 Professional Study Guide.

Getting Down to Business

In the following steps, you will run the Readiness Analyzer, review and save the upgrade report.

At one time, Microsoft made the Readiness Analyzer available as an executable file, downloadable from their web site. This is no longer true. They recommend that you check their web site for hardware and software compatibility. However, you can still run the analyzer by running winnt32.exe with a special command line switch that you will use in this lab exercise.

Step 1. Place the Windows 2000 CD in the drive. If your computer is set up for AutoPlay, the message box in Figure 2-1 will appear.
Click No. You do not want to upgrade now.

Step 2. Open a command prompt and enter the following command (replace D with the letter of your CD-ROM drive):

```
D:\I386\WINNT32   /CHECKUPGRADEONLY
```

FIGURE 2-1

Microsoft
Windows 2000
CD Message

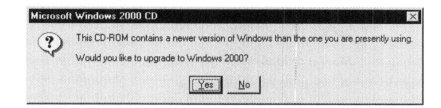

If you are running Windows 98, a screen similar to Figure 2-2 will appear. This screen shows a progress bar that moves as the analysis process runs. In a heavily loaded system, that has many application programs, analysis can take a while as it examines all the system files and all installed applications.

When the analysis is complete a window like that in Figure 2-3 appears which contains the upgrade report. Note the scroll bar indicating that the report is quite lengthy. It includes sections on:

■ Hardware

■ Software Incompatible with Windows 2000

■ Software That Must Be Uninstalled

FIGURE 2-2

Microsoft
Windows 2000
Readiness
Analyzer (while
executing)

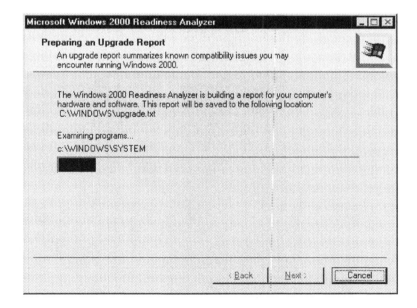

■ Software to Reinstall

■ Program Notes

■ General Information

■ Upgrade Pack Information

lab
Hint *Note that in this instance (see Figure 2-2) the upgrade report is automatically saved to C:\WINDOWS\UPGRADE.TXT, but you can also use the Save As button to save it to another location and filename (recommended) and/or you can print it out. If you're running Windows NT the process will run much faster and you won't see a progress screen.*

Step 3. In the next lab you will be doing an upgrade to Windows 2000. So if you plan to do that lab, you should take any steps that the Upgrade Report indicates are necessary.

Step 4. Click Finish to close the Upgrade Report window.

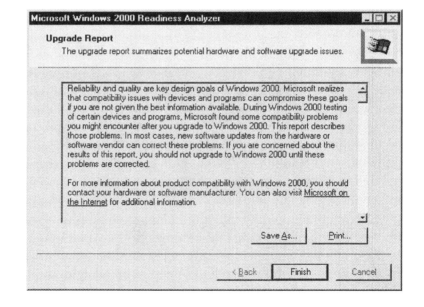

FIGURE 2-3

Microsoft Windows 2000 Readiness Analyzer Upgrade Report

LAB EXERCISE 2.02

Upgrading to Windows 2000 Professional

100 Minutes

Whenever possible, it is desirable to do a clean installation of a new operating system. However, sometimes you will be required to upgrade a previous version of Windows to Windows 2000 Professional, which means that you are installing on top of the old version in order to acquire the existing settings and preferences. To prepare for that event, you will do an upgrade of Windows 98 on your lab computer, because it is always good practice to try any procedure in a test environment before you have to do it on a client's desktop.

lab

Warning *Windows 2000 will not upgrade from Windows 98 if the system is dual booted. In this case you need to remove the other OS, upgrade to Windows 2000, then reinstall the other OS.*

Learning Objectives

By the end of this lab, you'll be able to

■ Upgrade Windows 98 to Windows 2000 Professional.

Lab Materials and Setup

The materials you need for this lab are:

■ A PC with Windows 98 installed

■ A Windows 2000 Professional CD or a location on the local hard drive, or a network share, where the source files have been copied.

■ The Windows 2000 Professional Product Key (a 25-character code on the envelope or box)

■ Any parameters that your instructor wants to change during the upgrade

cross
Reference   *For an overview of Upgrading to Windows 2000 Professional, review the section titled "Certification Objective 2.02" in Chapter 2 of the* **MCSE Windows 2000 Professional Study Guide**.

Getting Down to Business

In the following steps, you will perform an upgrade from Windows 98 to Windows 2000. In the previous lab, you ran the Readiness Analyzer, which will be automatically run again during this upgrade. If the Upgrade Report from the previous lab indicated that you need to remove certain applications for reinstallation after upgrading, or that other steps needed to be taken prior to upgrading, you should accomplish those things before doing this lab.

Before doing this lab exercise, we recommend that you complete Exercise 2-6 in Chapter 2 of the *MCSE Windows 2000 Professional Study Guide.* That exercise has you check out the current TCP/IP configuration. Do that, and also ask your instructor if there are any TCP/IP configuration settings in the existing operating system that should be changed when you upgrade.

Step 1.   Insert the Windows 2000 Professional CD into the CD-ROM drive. If AutoPlay is turned on, you will see a small dialog box stating that the CD-ROM contains a newer version of Windows than the one that is presently installed, and asking if you would like to upgrade now. If this appears, select Yes, and continue. If this dialog box does not appear, you will have to manually start the upgrade process. To do so, enter the following command from Start | Run (replace D with the letter of your CD-ROM drive):

```
D:\I386\WINNT32
```

lab
Hint   *If the source files have been copied to your local disk or to a network share, you will need to give the correct path to the WINNT32.EXE program, such as \\SERVER1\W2KSOURCE\WINNT32.*

Step 2.   On the Welcome screen to the Windows 2000 Setup Wizard, select Upgrade To Windows 2000 (Recommended) as shown in Figure 2-4.

Step 3.   Continue through the first few screens, reading and accepting the License Agreement, and providing the information requested in subsequent screens, including

FIGURE 2-4

Welcome to the
Windows 2000
Setup Wizard

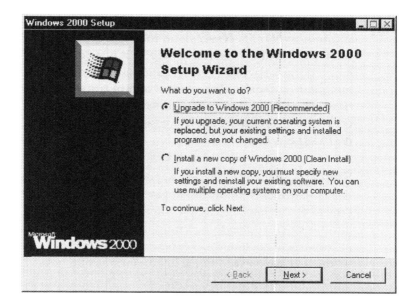

the 25-character product key. Stop at the Provide Upgrade Packs page and take the appropriate action if you found that upgrade packs were required in lab exercise 2.01.

lab ⓗint *If you had acquired upgrade packs from software vendors, you would select Yes, I Have Upgrade Packs, and provide a list of packs at this point. If you did not, you will select No, I Don't Have Any Upgrade Packs. You then select Next to continue.*

Step 4. Pause at the Upgrading to the Windows 2000 File System page and select Yes, Upgrade My Drive. Since you are upgrading from Windows 98, the most advanced file system you could have had was FAT32 (which stores files more efficiently than FAT16), but does not hold a candle to any version of NTFS when it comes to file and folder security.

Click Next to continue. The Wizard will display a page containing a status bar while it prepares the Upgrade Report. At this point it is running the Readiness Analyzer.

lab
Warning

When you install Windows 2000, it will automatically upgrade all local NTFS volumes to NTFS5. Never mind that you thought you had a choice to upgrade to NTFS5 (the new version of NTFS), it is a done deal. If you plan to dual-boot a computer between Windows 2000 and Windows NT 4.0, NT must be at a minimum of Service Pack 4 level before the upgrade. This is the service pack that allows NT 4.0 to read and write to an NTFS5 volume, although it cannot create one, nor can it use the new features. In Chapter 4 you will work with NTFS5 features.

Step 5. When the Upgrade Report is complete, select Next to continue. The Ready to Install Windows 2000 page will appear, which gives you the estimated time to do the upgrade and the number of times the computer will restart. It also informs you that everything from this point on is automatic, and you will not have to answer any questions. Click Next again to continue.

You do have one additional important function however, so pay attention for a few more minutes. The next page only appears during the copying of files. As soon as the copying is finished, the Restarting page appears, indicating that the computer will reboot automatically in 15 seconds. You must remove the CD before the computer restarts!

lab
Warning

If you do not remove the CD from the drive before the reboot, it might boot from the CD and you will find yourself doing a clean install; all the choices you made for the upgrade will be ignored.

Step 6. After the reboot, the text mode boot menu will appear, as in Figure 2-5. The first choice will take you to Windows 2000 Professional Setup, while the second choice will return you to your old operating system. When you select Setup, a blue text-mode setup screen will appear and prompt you to insert the CD into your drive. Follow the instructions and continue. Windows 2000 setup will perform the upgrade, based on the choices you made before the reboot. You will see some differences between this upgrade and the clean install described in Exercises 2-1 through 2-4 in the *MCSE Windows 2000 Professional Study Guide.*

Describe the differences you observe between the clean install and this upgrade:

_____

_____

_____

FIGURE 2-5

Windows 2000
Boot Menu

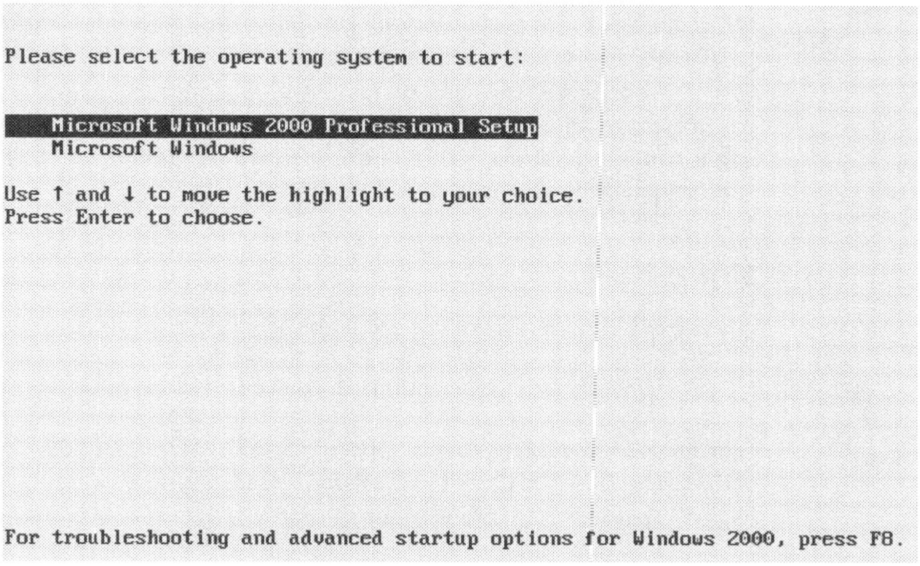

```
Please select the operating system to start:

     Microsoft Windows 2000 Professional Setup
     Microsoft Windows

Use ↑ and ↓ to move the highlight to your choice.
Press Enter to choose.




For troubleshooting and advanced startup options for Windows 2000, press F8.
```

LAB EXERCISE 2.03

Installing Service Packs

40 Minutes

A *service pack* is a bundled collection of patches to fix problems with the code in
an operating system or application program. Microsoft releases service packs on a
regular basis. In most organizations service packs are not routinely applied as soon
as they are released. The more common practice is to test the latest service pack on
computers representative of the computers in the organization—desktops, laptops,
and servers. Then, when the IT staff is satisfied that there are no hidden problems
or incompatibilities, the service pack will be rolled out to the desktops and/or servers.

As a member of the help desk support team, you must know how to install service
packs. In your organization, once a service pack is approved for use it will probably
be copied to a network share on the corporate network so that it is always available.
However, you have been told that sometimes you will be at a site where the service
pack source share will not be available. For such a situation you can either carry the
service pack in on CD or download it from the Microsoft web site.

lab
Ⓗint

Microsoft is constantly working on fixing reported bugs and problems in their software. Previously, service packs would contain both tested and certified patches to fix bugs as well as software upgrades, and they would be released at arbitrary times when the quantity justified a release. Now service packs only contain patches, and will be released at regular intervals. Software updates will be released in a different manner.

Learning Objectives

By the end of this lab, you'll be able to

- Upgrade Windows 2000 with the latest service pack.

cross
Ⓡeference

For an overview of deploying service packs for Windows 2000, read "Certification Objective 2.03" in Chapter 2 of the **MCSE Windows 2000 Professional Study Guide**.

Lab Materials and Setup

The materials you need for this lab are:

- A PC with Windows 2000 installed
- The source files for Windows 2000
- Internet access *or* the source files for a Windows 2000 Service Pack

Getting Down to Business

In the following steps you will access the Microsoft web site, download the latest service pack, and then apply that service pack to your lab computer.

Step 1. If you do not have an Internet connection from the classroom lab, your instructor may provide you with the latest service pack on your local hard drive or on a network share.

Connect to the Windows 2000 home page at www.microsoft.com/windows2000. From this page browse to the Windows 2000 Professional page and select the link to download the latest service pack (Service Pack 2 at the time of this writing). Read the information about the service pack and follow the instructions to download the

Express Installation version. Use this version when you want to quickly apply the service pack to a single computer.

lab
ⓗint   *Choose the Network Installation download when you want to download the entire service pack to a directory from which you can apply it to many computers on your network. You can also perform an Integrated Installation from the service pack source files. This type of installation allows you to update the Windows 2000 source files (the I386 directory from the CD) with the latest service pack. To learn more about this type of installation, search the Microsoft site for the readme file for the version of the service pack that you would like to use, and then search that document for the installation options.*

Step 2.   After the file is downloaded, execute it. The Service Pack Setup wizard will display a licensing agreement, as shown in Figure 2-6. Read and accept the terms and continue with the installation.

Step 3.   Service Pack Setup will display a progress screen, as shown in Figure 2-7.

Step 4.   At conclusion of the Service Pack Setup, you will see a small message box, with only one choice, as shown in Figure 2-8. Click Restart.

FIGURE 2-6

Windows 2000
Service Pack
Setup Licensing
Screen

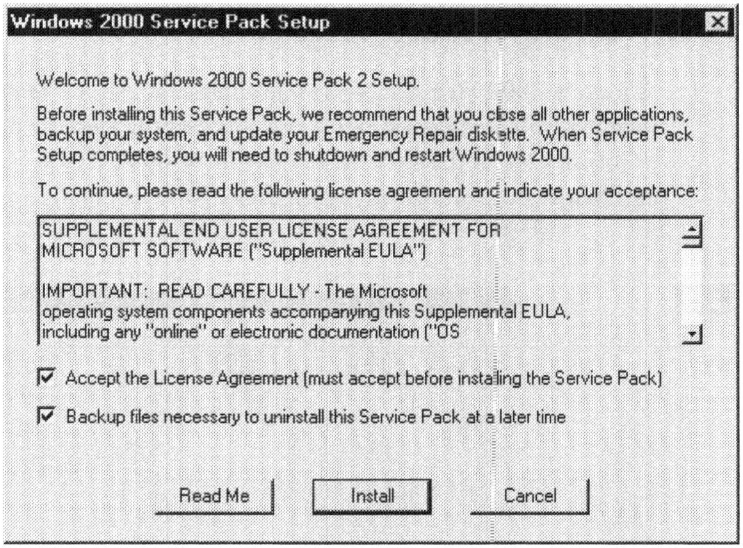

Windows 2000 Service Pack Setup

Welcome to Windows 2000 Service Pack 2 Setup.

Before installing this Service Pack, we recommend that you close all other applications, backup your system, and update your Emergency Repair diskette. When Service Pack Setup completes, you will need to shutdown and restart Windows 2000.

To continue, please read the following license agreement and indicate your acceptance:

SUPPLEMENTAL END USER LICENSE AGREEMENT FOR
MICROSOFT SOFTWARE ("Supplemental EULA")

IMPORTANT: READ CAREFULLY - The Microsoft
operating system components accompanying this Supplemental EULA,
including any "online" or electronic documentation ("OS

☑ Accept the License Agreement (must accept before installing the Service Pack)

☑ Backup files necessary to uninstall this Service Pack at a later time

Read Me   Install   Cancel

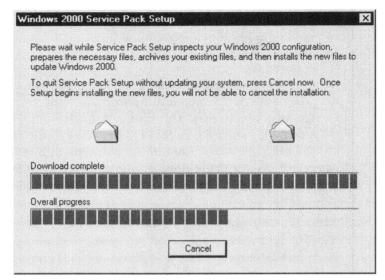

LAB EXERCISE 2.04

Troubleshooting a Failed Windows 2000 Installation

60 Minutes

Windows 2000 Help has various Troubleshooters. A *Troubleshooter* is a set of screens in which you answer questions, and progress through the possible solutions to your problem. One of the Troubleshooters in Windows 2000 Help is titled System Setup, and helps you work through Windows 2000 installation problems. To prepare for troubleshooting failed Windows installation, your boss has given you three hypothetical scenarios that could happen in real life.

Learning Objectives

By the end of this lab, you'll be able to

■ Troubleshoot failed Windows 2000 installations.

Lab Materials and Setup

The materials you need for this lab are:

■ A PC with Windows 98 or Windows 2000 installed

For an overview of troubleshooting Windows 2000 installations, read the section titled "Troubleshooting Failed Installations" in Chapter 2 of the MCSE Windows 2000 Professional Study Guide.

Getting Down to Business

Using the System Setup Troubleshooter in Windows 2000 Help, find and describe the solutions you would apply to each scenario below.

Scenario One.   Setup fails during the file copy phase. You have opened the computer, and you notice that the hard disk drive and the CD-ROM drive are on the same channel in a master/slave arrangement, although a secondary channel is present and enabled.

_____

_____

_____

Scenario Two.   You are attempting to install Windows 2000 on ten identical new computers with no previous operating system (OS). Your company uses a local vendor who delivers computers to specification, but without an operating system. The hardware vendor assured you that all the hardware was compatible with Windows 2000. However, when you attempt to install, you have intermittent problems. You actually succeeded in installing the OS on one of the computers, but not on the others. Someone suggested that you disable the system cache (using the system setup program) just for the duration of the installation, and then enable it again once the operating system has been installed. You tried this, but still cannot run Setup.

Scenario Three. If your computer will not boot from the CD-ROM drive, and does not already have a previous version of Windows from which you can run the setup program, you can create a set of four Setup floppy diskettes from which to initialize the Windows 2000 setup program. In this scenario, you have attempted to use these diskettes, but Setup is failing on the second diskette.

LAB ANALYSIS TEST

1. In your planning sessions for the Windows 2000 Professional rollout, there has been discussion about how to determine if the existing hardware is compatible with Windows 2000. Some of the other members of the team have not had the benefit of testing the Readiness Analyzer as you have in your test lab. Explain in a few sentences the type of information you will receive in a Readiness Analyzer report.

---

2. The upgrade planning committee has identified several computers that must be upgraded rather than being replaced by new machines. You have run the Readiness Analyzer and completed all the research. As a result, you have three upgrade packs that must be installed. At what point do you apply these? Must you apply these to the old operating system before running the upgrade program?

---

3. When preparing for an upgrade to Windows 2000, what must you do if the Readiness Analyzer determines that the computer has a virus scanner that is incompatible with Windows 2000?

---

4. You have about 50 computers that must have the latest service pack applied. What strategy can you use to efficiently apply the service pack to these computers?

---

5. You are performing an upgrade on a client's computer. But after answering the questions for the upgrade, the computer rebooted. It is now running setup from scratch, requesting information from you that you had already provided—such as asking where you want to install Windows 2000, and what file system you want to use. You are sure that you should not have to answer such questions after this first reboot. It is as if it has forgotten all your answers. What may have happened?

KEY TERM QUIZ

Use the following vocabulary terms to complete the sentences below. Not all the terms will be used.

       Express Installation

       migration

       Network Installation

       Readiness Analyzer

       service pack

       slip stream

       Troubleshooters

       upgrade

       Upgrade Report

       UPGRADE.TXT

1. The _____ allows you to test the Windows 2000 compatibility of the hardware and software on a computer that is running a previous version of Windows.

2. The default name of the file in which the Upgrade Report is saved is _____.

3. When you install a new operating system into the same location as a previous version in order to save preferences and settings, this type of installation is called a/an

    _____.

4. The process of performing a clean installation of Windows 2000, then reinstalling all your applications is called a/an _____.

5. If you wish to install a new service pack on many Windows 2000 computers on your network, you will download the version of the service pack that is described as a/an

    _____.

LAB WRAP-UP

In this chapter you first ran the Readiness Analyzer on a Windows 98 computer and examined the report it produces. Then you upgraded your Windows 98 computer to Windows 2000. Once you had Windows 2000 installed, you applied the latest service pack. And you then followed these labs by using the Help Troubleshooters to suggest solutions for failed installation scenarios. These experiences have prepared you for the next logical step: automated installations. These will be covered in the next chapter.

LAB SOLUTIONS FOR CHAPTER 2

In this section, you'll find solutions to the lab exercises, Lab Analysis Test, and Key Term Quiz.

Lab Solution 2.01

Steps 1 through 4.   No additional instructions are required for these steps.

Lab Solution 2.02

Steps 1 through 5.   No additional instructions are required for these steps.

Step 6.   Among the differences between this upgrade and the installation described in Exercise 2-1 through 2-4 in the study guide, is that it is truly hands-off except that you are prompted to remove any disks before the reboot. In addition, setup displays a message about deleting files from the previous operating system—something that would not be necessary in a clean install with no previous operating system present. After this, it proceeds through the installation process, detecting and installing devices.

Lab Solution 2.03

Step 1.   Once at the Windows 2000 home page, we selected the link to Windows 2000 Professional. On the Windows 2000 Professional page we selected the link titled Download Service Pack 2. On this page we selected the link titled Windows Service Pack 2 Download and Information Page. Then we selected the link titled Get SP2 Now. And, we weren't quite there yet, because we then had to select the link titled Download Windows 2000 SP2, then we had to make sure the correct language was selected and click Go. Finally, you are at the page where you can select between the SP2 Express Installation and the SP2 Network Installation. Selecting the Express link brought up the File Download dialog box. You can choose between Run This Program From Its Current Location or Save This Program To Disk. We chose to save the program to disk, and saved the program file (SP2express.exe).

When you choose the Express Installation option, it downloads a much smaller file than when you choose a Network Installation. This smaller file for Service Pack 2 was only 540 KB, and was named SP2EXPRESS.EXE. We copied it to our local hard drive and ran the program from there.

lab
①int *The file which is downloaded if you choose Network Installation is much bigger—over 100MB for Service Pack 2. This file was named W2KSP2.EXE.*

Step2. We ran the program SP2EXPRESS.EXE from the saved location.

Steps 3 and 4. No additional instructions are required for these steps.

Lab Solution 2.04

Scenario One.

1. Open the Help Program.
2. In the Contents tab of the left pane select Troubleshooting and Maintenance | Windows 2000 Troubleshooters. In the details pane on the right scroll down and select System setup.
3. In the Windows 2000 System Setup Troubleshooter click the radio button for Setup Fails When My Computer Tries To Copy Files. Then click Next.
4. At the top of this page it asks the question, Are All Of Your IDE Hard Disk And CD-ROM Drives Controlled By The Appropriate Device?
5. It suggests that you print out this page, so that you have it available to you while you shut down the computer and check out the drive jumper settings physically as well as the computer setup settings saved in CMOS RAM.
6. It recommends that if both drives are on the same channel, and a secondary channel is physically available and enabled in CMOS, you should move the CD-ROM drive to the secondary channel and configure it as a master. The actual configuration of the CD-ROM drive will vary, but we have found that newer CD-ROM drives can often be moved without physically reconfiguring them, and we have often placed CD-ROM drives alone on the secondary IDE channel. On this page, select No, I Can't Run Setup in response to the question, Can You Run Setup When All Of Your Drives Are In A Master/Slave Arrangement? Then click the Next button.
7. Since this is theoretical, we will assume that this solved the problem, and on the next page select Yes, I Can Run Setup in response to the question, Can You Run Setup After You Correct Any Hardware Conflicts? When you click Next the Troubleshooter ends, because the problem has been resolved.

Scenario Two.

1. Open the Help Program.

2. In the Contents pane select Troubleshooting and Maintenance | Windows 2000 Troubleshooters. In the details pane on the right scroll down and select System Setup.

3. After you open the System Setup Troubleshooter, select the radio button by I'm Having Intermittent Problems Running Setup and then click Next.

4. The resulting page asks the question, Do You Need To Make Your System Cache Memory Unavailable During Setup? You have already tried this and Setup still failed, so select the radio button by No, I Can't Run Setup and click Next.

5. The following page suggests that you test for RAM problems. You would take all the actions suggested here, testing the Setup program after each action. When you find a solution that allows the Setup program to run, test it more than once (remember, it was an intermittent problem), then consider the problem solved.

6. Real world: get in touch with this vendor. This would be a very undesirable situation. Either they have mixed RAM modules that should not be mixed, or they have a batch of bad RAM. Whatever the situation, they should be involved in correcting it.

Scenario Three.

1. Open the Help Program.

2. In the Contents pane select Troubleshooting and Maintenance | Windows 2000 Troubleshooters. In the details pane on the right scroll down and select System Setup.

3. In the Windows 2000 System Setup Troubleshooter click the radio button for Setup Fails When My Computer Tries To Read From The Windows Setup Floppy Disks. Then click Next.

4. At the top of this page it asks the question, Are Your Setup Disks Damaged Or Corrupted? It suggests that you attempt to read the disks. If there is a problem with just one diskette, you still must recreate the entire set of four.

lab
Hint

On this last page, the Troubleshooter has expansion buttons for the instructions for creating the diskettes. Look at these instructions now. There is an error in the second and third set of instructions. The Help program describes a batch file that is not found in the location described (in the BOOTDISK directory of the CD-ROM), although other files for creating the diskettes are located in that directory. If you are using Windows 95, Windows 98, or Windows NT, you can use the 32-bit version of the program for creating these diskettes. The correct name for this program is MAKEBT32.EXE. The 16-bit program, MAKEBOOT.EXE, is for running under DOS or Windows 3x. Both of these programs will run under Windows 95, Windows 98, Windows NT, and Windows 2000, but the MAKEBT32.EXE takes advantage of the 32-bit support in these operating systems and is faster.

5. If a problem is discovered with the Setup disks, use the instructions found in the Troubleshooter, but substitute the program filenames described in the Lab Hint. If this solved the problem, you would select the radio button by Yes, I Can Run Setup, and click Next to complete the troubleshooter.

6. Close the Windows 2000 Help window.

ANSWERS TO LAB ANALYSIS TEST

1. The analysis report contains information about the compatibility of the hardware, as well as information about what software is incompatible, what software must be uninstalled before upgrading and then reinstalled after an upgrade. The report will also contain information about known upgrade packs that will be required. To get the most up-to-date information, you will want to check out the web sites of the vendors of the hardware and software that is indicated as being incompatible.

2. You do not apply the upgrade packs to the old operating system. Rather, you copy them to the source location or have them available on a network share. Then, during the information gathering stage of the upgrade, you will be asked if you have update packs, and be given a place to list them.

3. If the Readiness Analyzer determines that you are running a virus scanner that is incompatible with Windows 2000, you should disable it before the upgrade, then obtain and install a version that is compatible with Windows 2000.

4. First of all, you will need the Network Installation version of the service pack. Then, you will place this on a network share from which it can be installed to the various computers. You have further options for making this more efficient, but this would get us into a discussion that is beyond the scope of this chapter (and possibly of the *entire MCSE Windows 2000 Professional Study Guide*) and into looking at topics such as Microsoft's System Management Server and Group Policies.

5. If you did not remove the CD, the computer may have booted from the CD-ROM drive and gone directly into a new install. We have experienced this in our lab—on a computer that normally requires that you press a key at the correct time in order to boot from CD. It is quite curious—especially since, on this same computer when we remove the CD before the reboot, Setup resumes the upgrade, prompts you to insert the CD into the drive, and does not request any additional information. Then, on the subsequent reboots, it does not make the same mistake again. If we leave the CD in, it will not reboot from the CD unless we press a key. We have tested this repeatedly with the same results.

ANSWERS TO KEY TERM QUIZ

1. Readiness Analyzer

2. UPGRADE.TXT

3. upgrade

4. migration

5. Network Installation

MICROSOFT CERTIFIED SYSTEMS ENGINEER

3

Performing an Unattended Installation of Windows 2000 Professional

LAB EXERCISES

In Windows 2000 Microsoft has added new tools and improved on the previous tools for automating installations. The Setup Manager now allows you to create four different types of scripts, including unattended scripts for network or CD installations, scripts to use Sysprep images, and scripts to use with Remote Installation Services (RIS) installation. Exercises in Chapter 3 of the MCSE Windows 2000 Professional Study Guide provide practice using these tools for some of their intended functions.

As a member of the planning and implementation team for the roll out of Windows 2000 Professional to the desktops in your organization, you have completed the exercises in Chapter 3 in the *MCSE Windows 2000 Professional Study Guide,* but there are some variations on using Setup Manager and Sysprep that you have not yet tried. You have decided to return to the lab and practice these variations, because they fit some of the scenarios for the rollout. The following labs will lead you through a multi-step process. First, you will use Setup Manager to create a script to be used by the Mini-Setup that runs when an image prepared by Sysprep boots up for the first time. In the second lab exercise, you will ensure that the script file is in the correct folder on the machine to be imaged, then prepare the image with the Sysprep utility. Finally, in the third lab, you will boot up the image, as you would on a new computer, and observe as the Mini-Setup runs, noting how it accepts the information provided in the script, and how it requests information not provided in the script.

cross
Reference

To best prepare for these labs, read Chapter 3, "Performing an Unattended Installation of Windows 2000 Professional," of the **MCSE Windows 2000 Professional Study Guide** *in its entirety and perform all the exercises.*

LAB EXERCISE 3.01

Using Setup Manager and Sysprep

75 Minutes

As a Desktop Support team member you know that in most departments of the company there are dozens, or even hundreds, of desktop computers with common hardware and software needs. The best solution for installing new operating systems and applications into these computers is to use one computer, identical to the many desktop computers, as a "template." You install and configure the operating system and all necessary application software onto the template computer. When you have finished the entire required configuration, you test the template computer. Once you are convinced that it contains the perfect image for the purpose, you use software such as Symantec's Norton Ghost or PowerQuest's Drive Image to copy this as a master image and save it on a network share. In this context, a network share is a shared folder on a server. The specific purpose of this share is to be a source location for the image files.

The Sysprep utility allows you to do just one last thing to this installation before using the imaging software to copy it to a network share. Sysprep strips out the identifying information, such as the product key, username, company name, administrator password, network configuration, domain or workgroup name, and date and time zone information. It also modifies the behavior of the operating system so that the next time it starts up, it runs a special Mini-Setup Wizard.

After you run Sysprep, you shut down the computer. In practice, you would then boot the computer with the boot diskette from a disk-copying program and copy the disk image to a network share on your network. Then you would use the imaging software to bring these images down to multiple client machines. The next time that image "wakes up" will be after it has been copied to each of the computers to which you want to apply this image. As it boots up on each computer, it runs the Mini-Setup Wizard. The job of this wizard is to ask the installer (user) to accept the End-user License agreement (EULA) and provide the other information that was stripped out of the master image.

Now, this is a great way to install identical images quickly (operating system, applications, and settings) onto many computers, but if someone must physically respond to the questions from Mini-Setup, this is not truly a completely automated installation. With a little effort it can at least be partially automated. You can use Setup Manager to create a special script to answer the questions asked by Mini-Setup. Your team will be doing this, so you want to practice it in this lab.

Learning Objectives

By the end of this lab, you'll be able to

- Use Setup Manager to create an Automation Script for the Sysprep Mini-Setup Wizard
- Use Sysprep to prepare an image.

Lab Materials and Setup

The materials you need for this lab are:

- A PC with Windows 2000 installed
- The Windows 2000 Professional CD (or a local or network location containing the contents of the I386 directory)
- The Administrator password for your lab computer
- A unique name to use as the computer name
- A workgroup or domain name to use in the lab
- Any custom network settings that are needed for the class lab computers
- The share name of a network printer (optional)

lab
ⓗint

Exercise 3-1 in Chapter 3 of the **MCSE Windows 2000 Professional Study Guide** *shows the use of Setup Manager to create a different type of script. Some of the screens are the same ones you will see here, but you will often be making different choices.*

Getting Down to Business

In this lab exercise you will use Setup Manager to prepare for a different installation than those you practiced with the exercises from the *MCSE Windows 2000 Professional Study Guide*. First, you will expand the Deployment Tools from your Windows 2000 Professional CD, if you have not done that already. Then you will use the Setup Manager to create a Sysprep script.

lab
ⓗint

Exercise 3-12 in the **MCSE Windows 2000 Professional Study Guide** *contains instructions for creating a different script—an Unattended Installation script. However, it has several screenshots in common with the procedure you will do in this lab. For that reason, we only include screen shots here that will enhance this lab without unnecessarily repeating the screen shots shown in Exercise 3-12. You will find it helpful to complete that exercise and review the screens before doing this lab exercise.*

Step I.   Log on as an administrator and extract the Windows 2000 Professional Deployment Tools from your Windows 2000 Professional CD to a folder you create on C: named DEPTOOL, using the instructions in Exercise 3-1 in Chapter 3 of the *MCSE Windows 2000 Professional Study Guide.* At the conclusion of that exercise it mentions that seven files are copied to the DEPTOOL folder. List those files here:

_____

_____

_____

Step 2. Use Windows Explorer to browse to the DEPTOOL folder you created in Step 1, and double-click the SETUPMGR.EXE program file. The Welcome page of the Windows 2000 Setup Manager Wizard will appear, as shown in Figure 3-1. Click Next.

Step 3. On the New or Existing Answer File page select Create A New Answer File and then click Next.

Step 4. On the Product to Install page (see Figure 3-2) select the radio button by Sysprep Install and then click Next.

FIGURE 3-1

Welcome page of the Windows 2000 Setup Manager Wizard

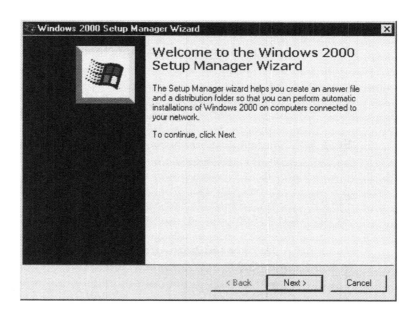

FIGURE 3-2

Product to Install
page of the
Windows 2000
Setup Manager

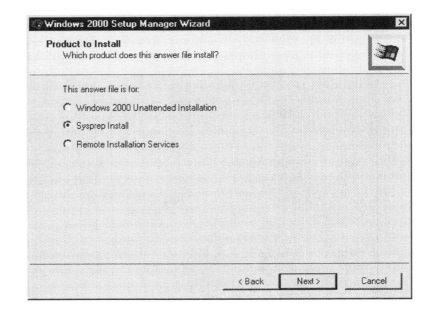

Step 5. On the Platform page select Windows 2000 Professional, and then click Next.

Step 6. On the License Agreement page (see Figure 3-3), select Yes, Fully Automate The Installation and then click Next.

Step 7. On the Customize the Software page (see Figure 3-4), enter the name and organization information, and then click Next.

Step 8. On the Computer Name page, enter a name for your computer that is unique on your class lab network, and then click Next.

Step 9. On the Administrator Password page, enter a new password (twice) for the Administrator account on the computer, and then click Next.

You must remember this password. You will need it to log onto the computer in Lab Exercise 3.03.

lab
☝int

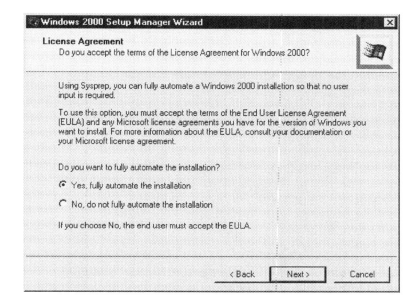

FIGURE 3-3

License Agreement page of the Windows 2000 Setup Manager

FIGURE 3-4

Customize the Software page of the Windows 2000 Setup

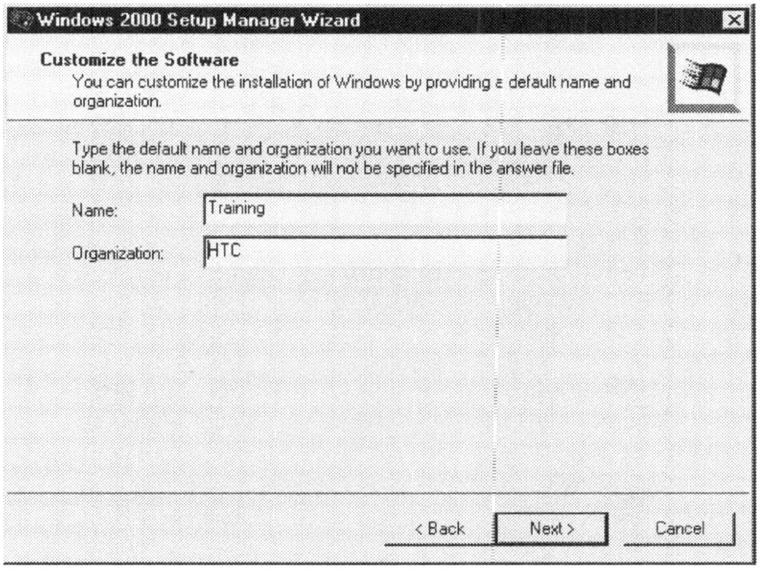

Step 10. On the Display Settings page, enter the default display settings that you wish to apply to the target computers. Be sure to select a combination that you have tested and that you know will work on the targeted PCs. Then click Next.

Step 11. On the Network Settings page, select Typical Settings, unless your instructor has given you special TCP/IP settings to be used in the classroom, and then click Next.

Step 12. On the Workgroup or Domain page, enter the information provided by your instructor, and then click Next.

Step 13. On the Time Zone page, select the correct time zone, and then click Next.

lab
Hint
Did you change your mind about a setting on a previous page of the Wizard? Remember that you are just using Setup Manager to create or edit a script. No action will take place until after you complete the script, save it, and the Mini-Setup program runs it. Therefore, you can use the Back button at any point in the Wizard and go back to any page you wish to change, without losing any intervening settings.

Step 14. On the Additional Settings page (see Figure 3-5), select Yes, Edit The Additional Settings and then click Next.

Step 15. On the Telephony page, leave the defaults as is and then click Next.

Step 16. On the Regional Settings page, leave the defaults as is and then click Next.

Step 17. Leave the additional languages unselected unless it is necessary to select some, and then click Next.

Step 18. On the Install Printers page, you may optionally add the share name of a printer on the lab network (or leave it blank) and then click Next.

Step 19. On the Run Once page, leave the text boxes blank and then click Next.

FIGURE 3-5

Additional
Settings page of
the Windows
2000 Setup
Manager

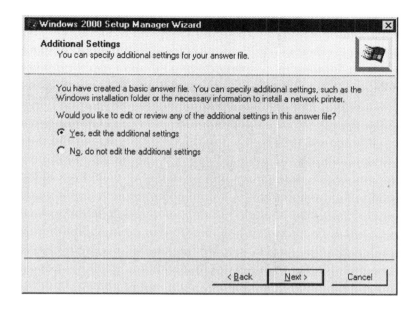

lab

Warning *You will only do the following step if you are running Setup Manager on the computer that will be imaged, because it creates the folder on the local machine. In this lab you will be running Setup Manager on the same computer that will be imaged, but on-the-job, you might be creating this script while working on your desktop computer (if it is running Windows 2000 or greater).*

Step 20. On the Sysprep Folder page (see Figure 3-6), select Yes, Create Or Modify The Sysprep Folder and then click Next.

lab

Hint *If you do not have Setup Manager create a Sysprep folder, you should manually do one of two things. Either create a Sysprep folder and copy the necessary files to this folder (see Lab Exercise 3.02 in which you will look at the files Setup Manager places in the Sysprep folder), or put the files on a diskette which you place in the computer as Mini-Setup is running. Read more about this in the DEPTOOL.CHM Help file in your Deptool directory.*

Step 21. On the Additional Commands page, leave everything blank and then click Next.

FIGURE 3-6

Sysprep Folder
page of the
Windows 2000
Setup Manager

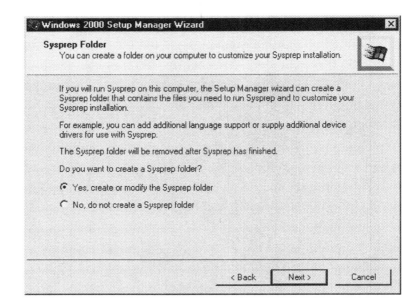

Step 22. Leave the entries blank on the OEM Branding page and then click Next.

Step 23. On the Additional Files or Folders page, do not make any changes and then click Next. You will be asked to supply the location of sysprep.exe, and an Open dialog box will appear. Browse to the DEPTOOL folder and then click Open.

Step 24. Leave the text box empty on the OEM Duplicator String page and then click Next.

Step 25. On the Answer File Name page, notice that the default location is the location from which you are running the Setup Manager program. The script file and other supporting Sysprep files are saved in this location, as well as in the C:\SYSPREP folder. For this lab, leave the default location as it is and then click Next. The final page of the Wizard will appear, as shown in Figure 3-7. Notice the files that it will create then click Finish.

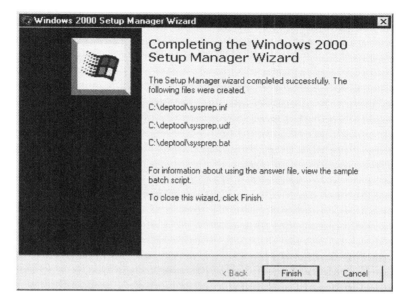

FIGURE 3-7

Final page of the
Windows 2000
Setup Manager
Wizard

LAB EXERCISE 3.02

Using Sysprep to Prepare a Master Image

30 Minutes

In the previous lab exercise you used Setup Manager to create an automated script
(SYSPREP.INF) for Mini-Setup. This file was saved in the Sysprep folder on your
computer. In this lab exercise you will verify that this file is in the correct location
and then use Sysprep to prepare your master image. After Sysprep is finished, it will
shut down your computer. Do not restart your computer until you are ready to
complete lab exercise, 3.03.

Learning Objectives

By the end of this lab, you'll be able to

- Use Sysprep to prepare a master image.

Lab Materials and Setup

The materials you need for this lab are:

- A PC with Windows 2000 installed
- The Windows 2000 Professional CD (or a local or network location containing the contents of the i386 directory)

For an overview of preparing for an unattended installation of Windows 2000 Professional, read the section titled "Certification Objective 3.01" in Chapter 3 of the **MCSE Windows 2000 Professional Study Guide.**

Getting Down to Business

This lab depends on the successful completion of Lab Exercise 3.01, in which you prepared a script for use with a Sysprep image. In the following steps you will use Sysprep to strip out the identifying information in your computer, and shut it down, leaving it ready to be imaged. On the job, you would then use a program like Ghost to copy this master image to a network share from which you would place the image onto multiple computers.

Step 1. Use Windows Explorer to browse to the Deptool folder. Notice the three additional files stored there. Then browse to the C:\SYSPREP folder. Notice that these same files, as well as other files needed for the Mini-Setup are saved in this location. This is the Sysprep folder that you requested be created back in Step 20 of Lab Exercise 3.01.

The SYSPREP.EXE, SYSPREP.INF, and SYSPREP.BAT files, as well as the program that calls up the Mini-Setup (SETUPCL.EXE) and the folders in which you would have placed Plug and Play drivers (I386\OEM) and additional language support files (I386\LANG), were all placed in the Sysprep folder by Setup Manager.

Open the SYSPREP.INF file (using Setup Manager or a text editor like Notepad) and see the changes you requested when you used Setup Manager to create this script file. Then close the file.

Step 2. Browse to the Deptool folder and run SYSPREP.EXE. An informational message (Figure 3-8) box will appear that is actually a warning about the changes that Sysprep will make. Click OK to allow Sysprep to run and to shut down your computer.

Step 3. Leave your computer off until you are ready to complete Lab Exercise 3.03.

LAB EXERCISE 3.03

Installing a Sysprep Image

45 Minutes

In the previous labs you prepared a script for use with a Sysprep image, then used Sysprep to strip out identifying information from an installation. Your lab computer should be shut down now. The "missing steps" are what you would do on the job: use disk duplicating software to copy the master image to a network share, then use it again in the mode for copying the image from the server to multiple computers. Imagine that you did those two steps, and now your lab computer is one of many that have had the master image copied to them. It is ready to restart and run the Mini-Setup and acquire its new identifying information.

Learning Objectives

By the end of this lab, you'll be able to

- Recognize and respond to the Mini-Setup questions from a new Sysprep image.

FIGURE 3-8

Windows 2000 System Preparation Tool Message

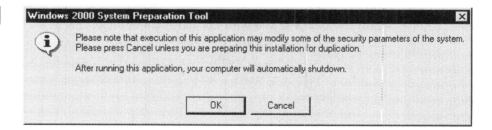

Lab Materials and Setup

The materials you need for this lab are:

- A PC on which you have successfully completed Lab Exercise 3.02

- The product key for your copy of Windows 2000 Professional

- The password you provided for the Administrator account when creating the Sysprep script in Lab Exercise 3.01, Step 9.

cross
Reference

For an overview of preparing for an unattended installation of Windows 2000 Professional, read the section titled "Certification Objective 3.01" in Chapter 3 of the **MCSE Windows 2000 Professional Study Guide.**

Getting Down to Business

In Lab Exercise 3.01 you used Setup Manager to create a script (SYSPREP.INF) to answer nearly all of the Mini-Setup questions (except product key). In Lab Exercise 3.02 you ran the Sysprep utility to strip out the identifying information on your lab computer. Let's assume that you then used an imaging program to copy this image to a server, and then copied it to one of many new computers. You are now ready to restart one of those computers and allow Mini-Setup to apply the information from the script to your computer.

lab
Hint

It is clear that this type of an installation can only be done as a clean install, because it replaces the contents of the drive to which it is copied. That drive must also be at least the same size as the one imaged. Most imaging software will allow you to adjust the size to a larger size on the receiving computer.

Step 1. Start up your lab computer. The Windows 2000 Professional start up splash screen will appear with the Starting up progress bar at the bottom. This will be a rather lengthy start up, but much, much faster than an ordinary installation!

A blue screen appears briefly, then a small Windows 2000 Setup box appears on the screen with the message, Please Wait…. It is running Mini-Setup and reading your answer file.

Step 2. When the Your Product Key page appears, enter your product key and then click Next.

lab
(h)int *The product key is a 25-character code that is usually found on a sticker on the CD case or envelope.*

Step 3.   Notice that this is the last piece of information you will have to enter. You will see the Network Settings, Workgroup and Domain, and a few other pages of the Setup Wizard. Click Finish on the Completing the Windows 2000 Setup Wizard page. A Windows 2000 message box will display (see Figure 3-9) for 15 seconds, and your computer will automatically restart.

Step 4.   After the reboot, log on as administrator with the password you provided in the answer script (Lab Exercise 3,01, Step 9).

Step 5.   Use Windows Explorer to examine your hard drive and answer the following questions with explanations:

   a. Is the C:\SYSPREP folder still there?

   _____

   _____

   b. Is the C:\DEPTOOL folder still there?

   _____

   _____

FIGURE 3-9

Windows 2000
Setup Message
Box

LAB ANALYSIS TEST

1. In your test lab, you have practiced using a script with a Sysprep image. Is such a script always necessary when using Sysprep images? Please explain.

   _____

   _____

2. You are working in the test lab, using Setup Manager to create a script. You are nearly done when you realize that you may have provided the wrong information about 5 pages back. You see that the Back button is active, but you are afraid that if you back up, you will lose all your responses on the intervening pages. What can you do?

   _____

   _____

3. You have used Setup Manager to create a script, and now you are ready to use Sysprep to prepare the image. Before you do this, you want to be sure that the script file is on the computer in the Sysprep folder, and you want to double-check your settings in the script file. How can you do this?

   _____

   _____

4. When Sysprep completes, it shuts down the computer on which it was run. Can you simply boot this computer up again and be back to life as it was before Sysprep?

   _____

   _____

5. In a planning meeting, a manager asked if you could use a Sysprep image to upgrade 50 Windows 98 computers in his department. Answer this question, explaining your reasoning.

   _____

   _____

KEY TERM QUIZ

Use the following vocabulary terms to complete the sentences below. Not all the terms will be used.

> Mini-Setup
>
> network share
>
> Remote Installation Service (RIS)
>
> Remote Installation Boot Disk
>
> script
>
> Setup Manager
>
> SYSPREP.EXE
>
> SYSPREP.INF
>
> UNATTEND.TXT
>
> Unattended Setup

1. The _____ program will allow you to create scripts for three types of Windows 2000 installations: unattended, Sysprep, and Remote Installation Services.

2. The script you create to be used with a Sysprep Mini-Setup is called _____.

3. You can use a/an _____ script for either a clean install or an upgrade.

4. After you prepare an image with Sysprep, you use a third-party imaging program (sometimes called disk copying or duplicating) to copy a disk image to a/an _____.

5. A Windows 2000 installation can be automated with the use of a/an _____.

LAB WRAP-UP

Did you feel as if you were making a career out of the first lab? There is a lot of detail to remember about Setup Manager and Sysprep. However, for the exam, Microsoft only expects you to remember when and why you would use these tools. These labs may have given you more experience with these tools than required for the exam, but we also hope to equip you for using them on the job. However, automated installations are very, very complex, and if you truly are part of a team planning to use these tools, you will want to go beyond the techniques in these labs. Check out resources such as the README.TXT and UNATTEND.DOC files that were copied to your Deptool folder, as well as the Windows 2000 Resource Kit, Microsoft online help, and their web sites such as www.microsoft.com/windows2000/en/professional/help/.

LAB SOLUTIONS FOR CHAPTER 3

Lab Solution 3.01

Step 1   The seven files copied into the DEPTOOL folder when you extract the contents of the DEPLOY.CAB folder are: DEPTOOL.CHM, README.TXT, SETUPCL.EXE, SETUPMGR.EXE, SETUPMGX.DLL, SYSPREP.EXE, and UNATTEND.DOC.

Steps 2 through 4.   No additional instructions are required for these steps.

Step 5.   The Platform page gives you the choice between Windows 2000 Professional or Windows 2000 Server. For this lab, select Windows 2000 Professional.

lab
Hint   *If you want to create a script for installing Windows 2000 Server, there are additional settings that must be included, such as Client Access License (CAL) mode.*

Step 6.   Your selection is for a fully automated installation, but in reality it will not be fully automated, because it will require you to provide the 25-character product key when you later install using this script. You may have noticed that Exercise 3-12 in the *MCSE Windows 2000 Professional Study Guide* showed separate pages for choosing user interaction and accepting the license agreement. This is one of the differences you see when you use Setup Manager to create a Sysprep install (as you've done here), versus an unattended installation (as was done in Exercise 3-12). The Unattended Installation also offers several choices in user interaction.

Step 7.   Remember that you will only be using Sysprep images if your organization has a volume license. Therefore, in the name box, you might enter the name of the department or division that owns the licenses, while in the organization box you may enter the company name (or government agency or other organization that owns the licenses).

Step 8. The best practice is to keep your computer names as simple as possible, 15 characters or less, using only lower or upper case alpha characters and number symbols (0-9).

Step 9. The Administrator password is a piece of information that is stripped out by Sysprep. Therefore, you must provide a password to be stored in the local computer's security database (SAM) as the password for the Administrator account. Because this is just a practice lab, you can keep the password simple. But when you're on the job, be sure to comply with the password security standards of your organization. Also, this password is stored in clear text in the script file, so you will want to change it on each computer that receives an image and uses this script.

Step 10. Even the most elementary user soon learns how to modify Display settings. In a security-conscious operating system such as Windows 2000, an ordinary user cannot modify the settings you see on this page. Therefore, you will want to do this for an automated setup. Once the operating system is installed, ordinary users can make other modifications through the Display applet—modifications that are saved with each user's profile, such as Background, Screen Saver, and Appearance.

Step 11. If you select Typical Settings, TCP/IP will be installed, the computer will be configured as a DHCP client, and the Client for Microsoft Networks will be installed. Ask your instructor if this is appropriate for your lab network.

Step 12. If you keep the default at this point, your computer will be a member of the workgroup name Workgroup. If the lab computers have access to a domain, or use a different workgroup name, your instructor will provide you with that information.

Step 13. Pay close attention when you select your time zone. It is easy to be careless on this screen and select the wrong time zone, especially when trying to select the Central Time zone for the US and Canada, which is at GMT –6:00 (but so are three others).

Step 14. Up to this point you have created a very basic answer script for Mini-Setup. We will not have you do anything fancy with these additional settings, except to notice the variety of things you can add to this script.

Step 15.　The default settings for the Telephony page include Do Not Specify This Setting in the first and fourth boxes, and blanks in the second and third boxes.

Step 16.　Regional Settings include the language in which menus and messages display, as well as the formatting of numbers, time, currency, and dates. The default settings for the Regional Settings page specify the default Regional settings for the version of Windows you are installing.

Step 17.　The Languages page allows you to add support for one or more additional languages.

Step 18.　Adding a printer during this lab is optional. Only do this if your instructor can provide you with the share name of a printer on the lab network.

Step 19.　The Run Once page allows you to provide one or more commands that are run the first time a user logs on. Although you may have situations in which you wish to use this, you are less likely to need it for an imaged installation like this one.

Step 20.　The Sysprep folder will be created on the computer so that it will be part of the image. The script you are creating will be saved in this folder, and you would also place in the Sysprep folder any additional files that were not part of the installation of Windows 2000 on this computer, but which may be needed on the computers that will receive the images. This can include device drivers (copy them to SYSPREP\I386\OEM) and language support files (copy them to SYSPREP\I386\LANG), depending on the script and the differences between the template computer and the receiving computers. This folder will be deleted at the end of Setup.

Step 21.　Unlike Run Once, commands listed in Additional Commands do not depend on a user logging on. They are simply run at the end of Setup.

Step 22.　The OEM Branding page allows you to display a bitmap on the upper right portion of the screen or as background during the GUI portion of Setup.

Step 23. The computer you use as your template computer does not have to be absolutely identical to the target computers, but it must have the same Hardware Abstraction Layer (HAL) and the same drive controllers. Beyond that, Mini-Setup performs Plug and Play detection, and can install Plug and Play drivers for detected devices. However, if the drivers for the Plug and Play devices on the target computers are not among those included with the Windows 2000 source files, you can use the Additional Files or Folder page to provide these driver files. (They will be copied into the appropriate folders under the Sysprep folder.) If you select either of the two yellow folders on this page, it will not allow you to proceed until you provide the additional driver or install files. If you have inadvertently done this, reselect the top folder (User Supplied Files), and then click Next. If you have not yet provided the location of the Sysprep.exe file, you will have to do so now. If you have done so already, the Wizard will proceed to the next page.

Step 24. The OEM Duplicator String allows you to save identifying information in the registry of the target computer so that you can identify the Sysprep image used for that installation.

Step 25. No additional instructions are needed.

Lab Solution 3.02

Step 1. The three files that have been added to the DEPTOOL directory are SYSPREP.BAT, SYSPREP.INF, and SYSPREP.UDF.

SYSPREP.INF is the actual answer file. SYSPREP.UDF is a uniqueness database file that can be used to assign unique information, such as computer name, to each computer. SYSPREP.BAT is a batch file that is created to show you the correct syntax for working with these files.

If the SYSPREP folder does not exist, you may have skipped step 20. To fix that oversight create a folder at the root of C: named SYSPREP, and copy the following files from the DEPTOOL folder: SYSPREP.INF, SETUPCL.EXE, and SYSPREP.EXE. If you must manually create the SYSPREP folder, you do not have to create the other folders, unless you are supplying Plug and Play drivers and Language support files.

Step 2. Browse to the SYSPREP folder and double-click on the SYSPREP.EXE file.

Step 3. Do not restart your computer until Lab Exercise 3.03, because it will run the Mini-Setup at startup.

Lab Solution 3.03

Steps 1 through 3. No additional instructions are required.

Step 4. We have found that when we run SYSPREP (if it is invoked from the SYSPREP folder), we get a message after the reboot on our images saying that the folder SYSPREP is not available. That is why in lab 3.02 you were instructed to run Sysprep from the DEPTOOL folder. If you get that message at this point, this is the reason, and you would not get it if you ran the program from a directory that would not be removed.

Step 5.

a. No. The Mini-Setup program removed the SYSPREP folder.

b. Yes. The C:\DEPTOOL folder was not removed, because Mini-Setup only removed the SYSPREP folder and subfolders.

ANSWERS TO LAB ANALYSIS TEST

1. A script does not have to accompany a Sysprep image. The Sysprep image is a very fast way to install an operating system, application software, and settings in many computers that require a similar configuration. All that the script does for you is to answer questions that are asked by the Mini-Setup program that runs the first time this image boots up. Someone can manually answer these questions—even an end user. It does not take a great deal of time.

2. You can back up as far as you wish (as long as you do not cancel) and Setup Manager will save your intervening answers, allowing you to edit the ones you wish to change. Setup Manager is simply a specialized script editor (that also creates folders and copies files). It does not write to the script file until you actually click the Finish button.

3. To check on the presence of the Sysprep script file, look for the SYSPREP folder and the file SYSPREP.INF. If it is not here, look in the folder containing the Setup Manager program. Then you can use any text editor or the Setup Manager program to open this file and look at its settings. If you want this file used by the Mini-Setup, it must either be in the SYSPREP folder or on a diskette that you place in drive A: when Mini-Setup is run.

4. No, you cannot simply boot up a computer that has had Sysprep run on it and be back to "life as it was before Sysprep." That computer has lost its identity! If you reboot it, you must be prepared to answer the Mini-Setup Wizard's questions to give the computer an identity. Sysprep was intended to allow you to place a standard configuration on many computers that receive their unique identity (computer name, workgroup/domain, etc.) when the Mini-Setup program runs at restart.

5. Sysprep is not an option when you want to upgrade to Windows 2000, because placing a Sysprep image on a hard drive wipes out the contents of the drive. When you do an upgrade you are actually installing on top of another operating system with the objective of saving the settings, software, data, and preferences already on that computer. A better option for automating an upgrade is an automated setup using an answer file. Lab 3-12 in the *MCSE Windows 2000 Professional Study Guide* has you create such a script.

ANSWERS TO KEY TERM QUIZ

1. Setup Manager
2. SYSPREP.INF
3. UNATTEND.TXT
4. network share
5. script

MICROSOFT CERTIFIED SYSTEMS ENGINEER

4

Implementing and Conducting Administration of Resources

LAB EXERCISES

By now you have installed Windows 2000 (at least once) and you have applied a service pack. It is time to look more closely at the features of Windows 2000. This post-installation exploration began in Chapter 4 of the *MCSE Windows 2000 Professional Study Guide* in which you learned about administering access to files and folders. The major player in this area is the newest version of the NT File System, NTFS version 5, which we will simply call NTFS5 when we wish to distinguish it from the previous versions. Most often, however, we will continue to refer to this file system as NTFS.

You began with the file compression capabilities of NTFS5 (a capability that was included in NTFS for NT 4.0), which you practiced in Exercise 4-1 in the *MCSE Windows 2000 Professional Study Guide*. Then you moved on to NTFS permissions, exploring the basics of file and folder permissions. The *MCSE Windows 2000 Professional Study Guide* provides two tables (Table 4-2 and Table 4-3) on these two sets of permissions, and rules for calculating effective permissions when, through group membership, a user has been granted permissions more than once.

Your first lab exercise in this chapter of the lab manual gives you practice in implementing an NTFS permissions plan, assigning permissions for users based on combined permissions applied to them individually and/or through multiple group membership.

In the second lab exercise you practice several tasks related to working with shares. First, you will create a share, then assign permissions, configure caching of the share to clients, and finally you will test client access to the share.

In the third and final lab exercise you will practice connecting to an FTP server. That's it. Just three lab exercises. Three *very* busy lab exercises.

LAB EXERCISE 4.01

Using NTFS Permissions to Control Access to Files and Folders

90 Minutes

You have created a plan for permissions on a shared Windows 2000 Professional computer in a small regional sales office in your company. Because this computer is not a member of a domain, you will be working strictly with local accounts. After talking with the sales manager, Laura Pederson, you have determined the folder structure they need on this computer, the local users and groups you need to create, and the permissions you need to assign to these folders. You are now implementing this plan on a test computer.

lab
Hint

In this lab you are working with local user accounts and local group accounts. These are accounts that only exist in a computer's local security (SAM) database. But on the job, if the Windows 2000 Professional computer is a member of a domain, you generally do not create local users and groups (beyond the default). Instead, you create and use accounts in the domain. When the computer joins the domain, the group Domain Users becomes a member of the local Users group, and the group Domain Admins becomes a member of the local Administrators group. Because of these memberships (and the local rights set in Group Policy), the user logs on to the domain but can access resources on the local computer. Note: You'll be studying Group Policy in Chapters 9, 10, and 12.

So, you may be wondering why you want to work with local users and groups. These skills are useful in a small office/home office (SOHO) setting, in which you have a peer-to-peer network or Windows computers in a workgroup. Networking them together with shared folders and printers is quite common. Many computer-savvy people fail to think of this simple solution to their home computing problems.

Learning Objectives

After completing the lab, you will be able to perform the tasks needed to implement an NTFS permissions plan, including the following skills:

- Create local user and group accounts
- Assign NTFS folder and file permissions to users and groups

Lab Materials and Set-Up

In this lab, you'll need the following tools and components:

- An Intel-based PC with Windows 2000 Professional installed and configured

cross
Reference

*To best prepare for this lab, read about NTFS permissions in "Certification Objective 4.01" in Chapter 4 of the **MCSE Windows 2000 Professional Study Guide**.*

Getting Down to Business

In the following steps you create the user and group accounts, and add the correct users to groups. Then you create the folder structure you plan to use, and you assign permissions to the appropriate users and groups to accomplish the level of security desired. Finally, you test the security by logging on as each of the users you created and attempting to perform various actions on the folders and their contents.

lab
ⓗint

In order to work with permissions, you will be creating user and group accounts. User and group accounts are examined more closely in Chapters 9 and 12 of the **MCSE Windows 2000 Professional Study Guide.** *You may want to read ahead in these two chapters, or see how you do using the Windows 2000 Help, as suggested in the lab.*

Step I. Log onto your computer as the local Administrator, and then create the users and groups listed in the planning form shown in Table 4-1. By default, all local users are members of the built-in Users group. Therefore, you will not have to add the users to that group. The Users group is included here for planning purposes. Notice that Sandra Fisher is a member of only this one group. She is a temporary employee and only needs limited access to one folder. As you create the accounts, use a blank password for each user, but be sure to leave a check in the box for User Must Change Password at next logon.

lab
ⓗint

If you need help creating accounts, open Computer Management and click on the Help button (the question mark icon). In the Contents pane, select Local Users and Groups then find the topics on creating new user and group accounts.

TABLE 4-1	User name	Full name	Group(s)
User and Group Accounts Planning Form	lpederson	Laura D. Pederson	Managers, Sales, Staff, Users
	mfrost	Marvin B. Frost	Sales, Users
	nrjones	Nancy R. Jones	Sales, Users
	sfisher	Sandra H. Fisher	Users
	njones	Norman A. Jones	Sales, Users
	jsmith	John I. Smith	Sales, Staff, Users
	jfrank	Jill K. Frank	Administrators, Sales, Staff, Users

lab
ⓗint

When planning for users and groups, you should have a naming convention that allows for duplicate user names. Notice the Norman Jones and Nancy Jones user names.

When you have created all the users, the Users folder in Computer Management should resemble Figure 4-1. Note the accounts that were upgraded on our lab computer when we upgraded the operating system from Windows 98.

When you have created all the groups, the Groups folder in Computer Management should resemble Figure 4-2. You can see the three groups created for this lab, plus the six built-in groups. We added an optional description to the groups we created. The descriptions of the built-in groups will help you to understand their functions.

lab
ⓗint

Check out the definition of built-in groups in the Glossary section of Windows 2000 Professional Help.

Step 2. Create the following folders on your hard drive. If you need help with this task, look in the Windows 2000 Help under the topic "Create a new folder."
C:\SALES\DATABASE
C:\SALES\EXCELDOCS
C:\SALES\PROMOS
C:\SALES\WORDDOCS

FIGURE 4-1

Computer
Management
with a list of
Local Users

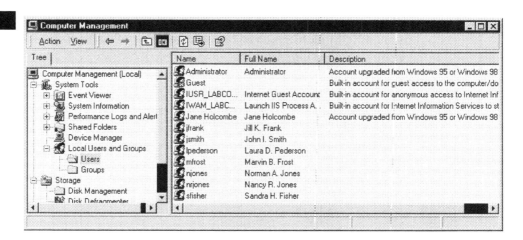

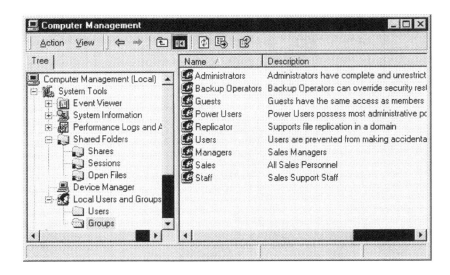

FIGURE 4-2

Computer
Management with
a list of Local
Groups

Step 3. Your plan includes giving the built-in Administrators group Full Control permissions for all folders and files in the SALES folder and blocking inheritance to the SALES folder from the parent folder. You will also remove all permissions for the Everyone group from the SALES folder and all folders and files below. Members of the Users group should only have permission to list folder contents on the Sales folder hierarchy, and read and execute on the WORDDOCS folder. All members of the Sales group must have read and execute and write access to the WORDDOCS folder. All members of the Sales group should be able to read and execute documents in the EXCELDOCS folders, but only members of the Staff group can create and modify these documents. All members of the Sales groups should be able to read documents in the database folder, but only members of the Managers group may modify the contents of this folder. The database folder contains a product DATABASE that is updated once a month from a master file by the manager, who makes final decisions about pricing data in this file before making it available to the rest of the Sales department. All members of the Sales group should be permitted to modify the contents of the PROMOS folder. You have created the planning form shown in Table 4-2 as a worksheet to use when testing in the lab. You will revise this worksheet, if necessary, and then use it to assign permissions on the workstations in the sales office.

Using Table 4-2, assign permissions to the folders you created earlier.

TABLE 4-2	Path	User/Group Assignment	NTFS Permissions	Block Inheritance? Yes/No
Permissions Planning Form	SALES	Administrators	Full Control	Yes
		Users	List Folder Contents	
	SALES\ DATABASE	Administrators	Full Control (inherited)	No
		Sales	Read and Execute; List Folder Contents; Read;	
		Users	List Folder Contents (inherited)	
	SALES\ EXCELDOCS	Administrators	Full Control (inherited)	No
		Sales	Read and Execute, List Folder Contents, Read	
		Staff	Modify, Read and Execute, List Folder Contents, Read, and Write	
		Users	List Folder Contents (inherited)	
		Managaers	Modify, Read and Execute, List Folder Contents, and Read	
	SALES\ PROMOS	Sales	Modify, Read and Execute, List Folder Contents, Read, and Write	No
		Users	List Folder Contents (inherited)	
		sfisher	Modify, Read and Execute, List Folder Contents, Read, and Write	
	SALES\ WORDDOCS	Administrators	Full Control (inherited)	No
		Sales	Read and Execute, List Folder Contents, Read and Write	
		Users	Read and Execute, List Folder Content (inherited), Read	

lab
ⓘint

If you need help assigning permissions, open Windows 2000 Help and search for the topic "Set, view, change or remove file and folder permissions." Remember that you are working with local accounts, and if you are logged onto a domain in your class lab, you will have to choose the local computer from the Look in box.

Step 4. Test the permissions assigned in Step 3. For each user you will log on with the user name and perform the action or actions described on the folder or folders listed. The Desired Result column in Table 4-3 shows the desired results. If you have any other results, you will need to verify that you have set your user group memberships and permissions per the planning sheets in Table 4-1 and 4-2. If you have done this correctly, and still do not get the desired results, you will have to alter the permissions or group memberships.

In order to save time in the lab, this is a limited test of the permissions design. In reality, using every user account, you would do a more extensive test to attempt several types of actions in each folder.

TABLE 4-3	User	Folder(s)	Action	Desired Result
Testing Permissions	Administrator	All	Copy or create one or more files in each folder.	Success
	lpederson	SALES\DATABASE	Create a text file named lpederson.txt.	Success
	njones	SALES\DATABASE	Create a text file named njones.txt.	Failure
			Read lpederson.txt.	Success
	jfrank	SALES	Create a text file named jfrank.txt	Success
	nrjones	SALES\PROMOS	Create a text file named nrjones.txt.	Success
	mfrost	SALES	Read the file jfrank.txt	Failure
	njones	SALES	Create a file named njones.txt.	Failure
			Open a file in SALES\PROMOS	Success

LAB EXERCISE 4.02

Managing Shares

45 Minutes

You will now build on the scenario described in Lab Exercise 4.01, in which you created user accounts and implemented a permissions plan for allowing users in a very small office to access the files and folders on a shared Windows 2000 Professional computer. In Lab Exercise 4.01, because there was no provision for sharing the folders with users accessing the computer over the network, you only provided for interactive access. This means that each user would have to be sitting at that computer when accessing the files and folders. In this lab, you will share the SALES folder and set appropriate share level permissions to allow the sales department users to access the files over the LAN. The assumption is that this computer is not a member of a domain, but is a member of a workgroup. In this case, you will have to create local accounts on each computer. For instance, on Laura Pederson's computer, you will create an account identical to the one you create on the shared computer. Laura will log on locally to her computer, but when she tries to access a share on the shared computer, her logon credentials will be presented to the shared computer. If the credentials match, she will have access to the shares (and files and folders within them) to which she has permissions.

In Chapter 4 of the *MCSE Windows 2000 Professional Study Guide* you learned that multiple permissions for a single user (applied to the user and group accounts) are combined at the NTFS level. This is also true at the share level. However, when a user accesses an NTFS file or folder through a share, the share and NTFS permissions are not combined. The result is that the most restrictive will apply.

lab
Hint   *On the job, even a small regional office is likely to have a WAN connection to the corporate network, and the Windows 2000/NT/XP computers will have accounts in the domain, as will the users in the office. This is a much more secure environment, with a more rigorous authentication process.*

Learning Objectives

By the end of this lab, you'll be able to

- Create shares
- Assign permissions to shares

■ Control caching of shares

■ Test the effect of combining share and NTFS permissions.

Lab Materials and Setup

The materials you need for this lab are:

■ A PC with Windows 2000 installed

■ A lab partner with a similarly configured computer

■ Computers should be networked together properly

cross
Reference

For an overview of working with shared folders, read the section titled "Certification Objective 4.02" in Chapter 4 of the **MCSE Windows 2000 Professional Study Guide***.*

Getting Down to Business

This lab depends on the successful completion of Lab Exercise 4.01. In the following steps, you will share the Sales folder, set share permissions, configure caching, and then test the ability to connect to this share from the computer of a lab partner.

lab
Hint

If you need help with any of the following steps search the Windows 2000 Help.

Step 1.   Share the SALES folder as SalesData and set the permissions so that the only permissions set on this share assign Full Control to the Authenticated Users group.

Step 2.   Modify the Caching setting for this share so that documents will be automatically cached.

Step 3.   When you and your lab partner have completed the first two steps, each of you can attempt to connect to the share on the other's computer, using the accounts you created in the previous lab exercise. Using Table 4-3, log on as each user in turn and connect to the SalesData share. Once connected to the share, you should be able to perform the same tasks you performed in Lab 4.01 to test the permissions as outlined in Table 4-3. If you encounter any problems, verify that you have created the correct users and groups, and placed the correct users in each group.

lab
⏱int *If you are not familiar with connecting to a share, see the section titled "Connecting to a Windows Shared Folder" in the* **MCSE Windows 2000 Professional Study Guide.** *There are three methods described there. Take your pick.*

Once you complete the test with the same results shown in Table 4-3, the lab is complete.

LAB EXERCISE 4.03

Installing IIS and Connecting to an FTP Server

45 Minutes

People working on a computer today (using any operating system) expect to be able to effortlessly connect to various Internet resources, including, but not limited to, web pages and FTP servers. Once again, imagine you are a desktop support analyst getting to know the features of Windows 2000 before your organization actually rolls it out to the user desktops. Right now you wish to try out the client-side of FTP—in other words, how to connect to an FTP server. In a test environment, you will need an FTP server on your network to which you will connect. In this lab, you are given instructions to create and configure the FTP server on your own computer, then connect to it as a client. Thus your Windows 2000 Professional computer will play the roles of both FTP server and FTP client.

lab
⏱int *Alternatively, your instructor may point you to another FTP server—perhaps one on the Internet or one created separately in the classroom lab.*

Learning Objectives

By the end of this lab, you'll be able to

- Install Internet Information Services (IIS)
- Use the IIS Management Console
- Add a file to an FTP server
- Connect to an FTP server
- Copy files from an FTP server.

Lab Materials and Setup

The materials you need for this lab are:

- A PC with Windows 2000 installed

cross
Reference

To get the most out of this lab exercise, read the sections titled "Connecting to an FTP Server" and "IIS" in Chapter 4 of the MCSE Windows 2000 Professional Study Guide.

Getting Down to Business

In Steps 1 through 4 you will install and test Internet Information Services on your Windows 2000 Professional lab computer. This will give you both a web server and FTP server to which you may connect from that same machine or from other computers on the lab network. Then in Step 5, you will connect to the FTP server you created on your own computer. Alternatively, you may skip the first four steps and connect to another FTP server as directed by your instructor.

lab
Warning

In this lab you will be installing IIS in order to use its FTP server. IIS has security problems and should only be used in a real-world situation under the management of an experienced administrator who can plug the security holes. Installing IIS on any computer will make it very easy for someone else to access that computer from the Web. If IIS is to be installed at home, the user should install a firewall that allows them to disconnect IIS from talking to the Web. ZoneAlarm (www.zonelabs.com) is one decent (and free) product that can protect a home computer.

Step 1. Logon as Administrator, then follow the instructions for installing IIS in the Windows 2000 Professional Help in the topic, "IIS, installing, upgrading."

Step 2. Test your installation of IIS by opening Internet Explorer (IE) and entering the following URL in the address box: http://localhost. The result should be two IE windows: one containing the localstart page (Figure 4-3) and another containing the IIS 5.0 Documentation (Figure 4-4). The localstart page contains overview information about IIS 5.0 and a link to the Online Documentation, while the IIS 5.0 Documentation window contains the full set of IIS 5.0 Online Documentation.

FIGURE 4-3

IIS Local
start page

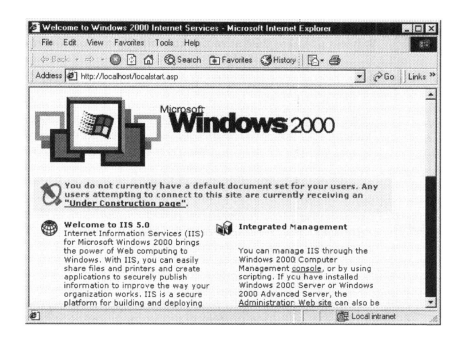

Step 3.   To open the management tool for IIS, right-click on My Computer and select Manage. This starts the Computer Management console. Select Services and Applications | Internet Information Services. Figure 4-5 shows the Computer Management console with the Internet Information Services snap-in.

FIGURE 4-4

IIS 5.0
Documentation

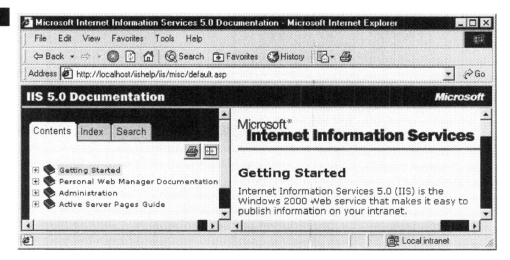

lab
ⓗint
Alternatively, you can run MMC.EXE and add the Internet Information Services snap-in, then save the console file on your Start Menu or desktop.

Step 4. At present, the IIS services are not configured. The FTP server has no files for users to copy, and the web site has no home page. You will now add files to the FTP server so that you can connect to it and test the client side of FTP. Right-click on Default FTP Site and select Explore. This will open Windows Explorer focused on the FTPROOT folder, as shown in Figure 4-6. Notice that the folder is empty. FTP servers are usually established to allow users to connect and copy files to and from the site. Create or copy a file into this folder.

lab
ⓗint
You can also place shortcuts in the FTP folder. When an FTP client accesses a shortcut, Internet Explorer will ask if you want to save or run the program. Running it will, of course, follow the link.

FIGURE 4-5

Computer
Management
Console Including
Internet
Information
Services

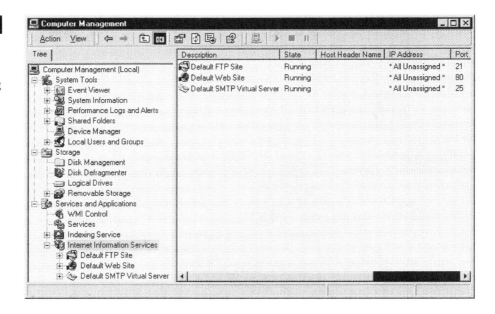

FIGURE 4-6

The FTPROOT folder

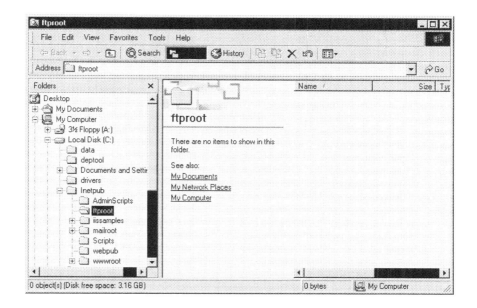

Step 5. Now test your ability to connect to the FTP server. Open Internet Explorer. In the address box, enter the following URL: ftp://*computername* (where *computername* is the name of your computer), and click Go. (Your instructor may give you a different URL). Figure 4-7 shows Internet Explorer connected as an FTP client to the FTP server on the computer named labcomputer1. A single file, labmanual.txt can be seen in the contents windows. An FTP server can hold files and folders, and you can control access to the files and folders through permissions. If you have succeeded in connecting to your FTP server, close all open windows.

FIGURE 4-7

Internet Explorer connected to an FTP server

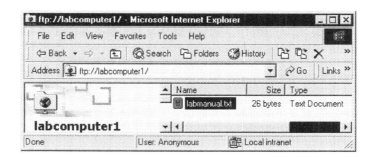

lab

①int

In this lab, you use your graphical Internet browser (Internet Explorer) to access an FTP server. Veteran Internet users know that you can also access FTP servers from the command prompt, using the FTP command and a cryptic set of subcommands or via a third-party FTP client, like WS-FTP or CuteFTP. You can learn more about these excellent products at www.ipswitch.com (WS-FTP) and at www.cuteftp.com (CuteFTP).

LAB ANALYSIS TEST

1. What are the standard NTFS file, folder and share permissions in Windows 2000?

2. In Lab Exercise 4.01 the user, Sandra Fisher (sfisher), is able to view the contents of the SALES folder and all the child folders. She cannot create a file in SALES\PROMOS, but she can open a file in that folder. Explain why this is possible.

3. In Lab Exercise 4.01 jfrank is able to create a file in the SALES folder, but njones cannot perform this same task. Explain why two members of the Sales group cannot open a file in this directory.

4. In Lab Exercise 4.02, the group Authenticated Users is given the Full Control share permission. However, when accessing the folder through this share as different users, using Table 4-3, you had the same results you had when you accessed them directly. Considering that the share provided you Full Control, why were your effective permissions less?

5. Years ago, you experienced connecting to an FTP site using a command line interface. It was not a pleasant experience. What alternatives do users have now?

KEY TERM QUIZ

Use the following vocabulary terms to complete the sentences below. Not all the terms will be used.

> Administrators
>
> caching
>
> FTP
>
> IIS
>
> Internet Explorer
>
> local group account
>
> local user account
>
> permissions
>
> offline files
>
> share

1. To control user access you can set _____ on files and folders.

2. To provide network access to a folder, you create a/an _____ for that folder.

3. A/an _____ and _____ only exist in a computer's local accounts database.

4. The _____ setting on a share allows an administrator to control the server side of offline files, a feature that allows Windows 2000 clients to make shared network files available when they are not on the network.

5. _____ is a service that allows users to connect to a server for the purpose of downloading files to the local computer.

LAB WRAP-UP

Did you find it challenging to work with all the permission assignments in Lab Exercises 1 and 2? Imagine how much more complex it is to design and implement files and folder assignments on hundreds of folders! In most organizations, users must save their data files on network servers, and administrators of those servers plan, manage, and maintain the permissions on files, folders, and shares. In these labs you worked with a Windows 2000 Professional computer, which gave you a small taste of this part of the job as a desktop support analyst, or, in the case of shares on a server, an administrator. The planning and implementation are the same. The scale is different.

In the last lab exercise, you installed Internet Information Services to make your computer an FTP server. You may have skipped this first part at your instructor's direction. Then you connected to the FTP server using Internet Explorer.

LAB SOLUTIONS FOR CHAPTER 4

In this section, you'll find solutions to the lab exercises, Lab Analysis Test, and Key Term Quiz.

Lab Solution 4.01

Step 1. To open the Computer Management console, right-click on My Computer and select Manage. Within the tree pane, browse to System Tools | Local Users and Groups | Users. Right-click on Users and select New User. For each user, enter the User name, the full name, leave the password blank, and ensure that there is a check by User Must Change Password At Next Logon. Click Create. This creates the new user and clears the fields in the box so that you can create a new user. Continue in this manner until all users are created, then click Close.

To create groups, return to the Computer Management console and browse to System Tools | Local Users and Groups | Groups. Right-click on Groups and select New Group. This opens the New Group dialog box in which you can create several groups. For each group, enter a Group name and (optionally) a Description, then click the Add button and add each user for that group, as shown in Table 4-1.

lab
Hint   *When you click the Add button in the New Group dialog box, the Select Users or Groups dialog box appears. It can be frustrating finding users and groups in this list because they are not sorted alphabetically. Click the Name bar to sort them.*

When you have added all the correct users to a group, click the OK button in the Select Users or Groups dialog, which will bring you back to the New Group dialog. To create another group, click Create, which will create this group and clear the dialog box so that you can create a new group. When you have finished creating the groups, click Close.

Step 2. No additional explanation is required to complete this step.

Step 3. Begin by accessing the properties dialog box for the SALES folder, click on the Security tab, and click the Add button. Be sure that the Look In drop-down box contains the name of your computer. If you logged onto a domain, this box will show the name of the domain. Use the arrow button on the right of the drop-down box to select your computer. The list of user and group accounts in the box below will appear in an unsorted order. You should get into the habit of sorting these names by clicking on the Name bar, then select the Administrators group account and click the Add button. Then click OK. Back in the Sales Properties dialog box you will see both Administrators and Everyone in the Name box. Notice that the Administrators group was only given the default permissions of Read & Execute, List Folder Contents, and Read. Select Full Control so that the Administrator has the highest level of permissions. *Do not* close this box, yet.

Click on Everyone. Notice that the permissions for Everyone are greyed out. This means that these permissions were inherited from the folder above (the root of the drive). You cannot administer these permissions from this level. You wish to remove the Everyone group, and since you do not want inheritance of permissions to modify the security you wish to have on this folder hierarchy, you will block inheritance. Therefore, click to remove the check from the box labeled Allow Inheritable Permissions From Parent To Propagate To This Object. As soon as you do this, the Security message box shown in Figure 4-8 appears.

Click the Remove button, because you want to remove the permissions that were inherited. The Sales Properties Security page should only show the Administrators group with Full Control. Click OK.

Continue through the subfolders below Sales, using Table 4-2, Permissions Planning. Only the Sales folder should have inheritance blocked. Leave the default setting of Allow Inheritable Permissions On Each Of The Child Folders.

Step 4. You may choose the files you copy into the SALES folder and its child folders. Logged on as Administrator, we used the Start | Find command to find files ending with TXT, then copied several of them into each folder.

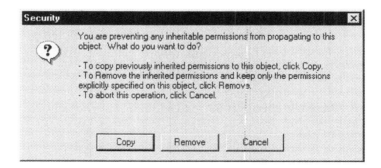

FIGURE 4-8

Security Message Box

Lab Solution 4.02

Step 1.   Right-click on the SALES folder, and select Sharing. Select Share This Folder. In the Share name box type **SalesData**, then click the Permissions button. Notice that the default permissions for a new share are Everyone Full Control. Click the Add button and add Authenticated Users. Click OK. Notice that the default permission for an added account is Read. Change this to Full Control for the Authenticated Users group, then remove the Everyone group. Click OK to close the Permissions dialog box. Leave the Sales Properties dialog box open.

Step 2.   Click the Caching button. This is the "server" side of offline files, allowing you to control the clients' caching of this share. Notice that, by default, caching of files from a share is enabled, and the default setting is Manual Caching For Documents. This means that the users would have to initiate the caching of documents to their local computer. Use the button in this box to select Automatic Caching For Documents. Then any user connecting from a Windows 2000 or newer version of Windows will automatically cache files from this share. Finally, click OK on the Caching Settings dialog box and again on the Sales Properties dialog box.

Step 3.   No additional instructions are required for this step.

Lab Solution 4.03

Step 1.   From the Start Menu select Help. In the Help program click on the Index tab and enter the keyword **IIS**, then double-click the subtopic Installing, Upgrading. A Topics Found box opens with two topics listed. Double-click on IIS installation. The IIS Installation topic will appear in the contents windows on the right. Follow the numbered steps to install IIS version 5.0. When you follow these instructions, the Windows Components Wizard will install IIS 5.0 on your computer. At the conclusion, click Finish on the final page of the Windows Components Wizard.

Steps 2 through 5.   No additional instructions are required for these steps.

ANSWERS TO LAB ANALYSIS TEST

1. The standard file permissions are Full Control, Read & Execute, Modify, Read, and Write. The standard folder permissions are Full Control, Modify, Read & Execute, List Folder Contents, Read, and Write. The standard share permissions are Full Control, Change, and Read.

2. Sandra Fisher is a member of only one group: Users. By default every local user account is a member of the local Users group. As a member of this group she is granted the permission List Folder Contents to the Apps Folder. Through inheritance, she has this permission to all the folders and can simply look at the list of files and folders in each directory. This does not allow her to open files in any folder. However, she has been directly granted (as sfisher) Read & Execute, List Folder Contents, and Read permissions to the PROMOS folder. Therefore, she can open a file in this folder, but not in any other folder.

3. In Lab Exercise 4.01 jfrank is able to create a file in the SALES folder, because she is a member of the Administrators group, the only group with sufficient permissions to create a file in this folder. Users can have multiple group memberships. When a user is a member of one or more groups, their NTFS folder and file permissions applied through groups, and/or directly to their user account, are combined. The exceptions to this rule are the Deny permissions which override Allow for the same permission level. For instance, if a user has the Allow permission set for Modify, Read & Execute, List Folder Contents, Read, and Write via their membership in one group, but the Deny permission set on Write, this user will not be permitted to write to any file or folder in that folder.

4. When connecting to files and folders through a share (assuming the files and folder are on an NTFS volume), you are actually going through two doors. First, the share door is where your effective permissions are calculated based on combining all the permissions at that level and then they are applied to your user and member group accounts; then, at the NTFS door where your NTFS permissions are similarly combined. The result of these calculations at both doors is not combined to give you the most access. Rather, whichever of the two, share or NTFS, is most restrictive, will be the one that is used.

   One strategy to use when you have numerous users accessing files and folders through the same share is to set the permissions at the share level to be at the least restrictive level you need for any user or group. Then you do your fine-tuning of restrictions at the NTFS level. If you do it the other way around, users may not make it through the first door.

5. Users can now use Internet Explorer to connect to many FTP sites. To do this, they must know the URL and be sure the protocol portion of the URL includes the FTP.

ANSWERS TO KEY TERM QUIZ

1. permissions

2. share

3. local user account, local group account

4. caching

5. FTP

5

Implementing Printing and File Systems

I n the first three chapters of this lab manual you worked through various tasks required of a desktop support analyst during the planning and testing phase of the Windows 2000 Professional rollout to the desktop computers of an organization. In Chapter 4 you practiced skills required of desktop support analysts and/or administrators. You focused on implementing the management of file and folder resources, including NTFS permissions at the file and folder level, applying security at the share level, and working with both levels of permissions when a network user accesses an NTFS file or folder through a shared folder. There are, of course, resources other than files, folders, and shares. In this chapter you will work first with shared printers, then practice some of the skills required to configure and manage file systems.

Continuing in your role as a desktop support analyst, imagine that you are planning to set up a new printer for the remote sales office you worked with in the previous chapter. Like many support analysts and administrators, you have learned that, as part of good management, you must document everything. Therefore, in Chapter 4, you used planning forms (Tables 4-1 and 4-2) to document the proposed, and eventually implemented, user and group accounts. You created the users and groups, and set the permissions based on these forms. Then you used a testing form (Table 4-3) to document the testing procedure you followed to test your implementation of users, groups, and permissions.

Similarly, in this chapter you will work with a New Printer form to document the required settings for each printer. You will find that well-managed organizations use such forms. As busy as it gets in Information Technology work, it is always worth taking the time to document your plans, testing, and implementation. These forms can be filled out and then serve as an audit trail, a template for the future, and documentation to be used as part of a disaster recovery plan. *You can't put things back together if you don't have a map of how they once were.*

LAB EXERCISE 5.01

Installing and Sharing a Local Printer

30 Minutes

You are preparing to install a printer at the remote sales office you worked with in Chapter 4. This printer will be connected to the computer on which the SALES folder hierarchy resides, and the printer is to be shared by everyone in the Sales office.

Learning Objectives

By the end of this lab, you'll be able to

- Install a local printer
- Share a local printer
- Pause a printer.

Lab Materials and Setup

The materials you need for this lab are:

- A PC with Windows 2000 installed
- This lab depends on the successful completions of Lab Exercise 4.01

cross Reference *To best prepare for this lab exercise, read the section titled "Connecting to Local and Network Print Devices" in Chapter 5 of the* **MCSE Windows 2000 Professional Study Guide.**

Getting Down to Business

In the following steps you will first use the Add Printer Wizard to create a new printer, using the information supplied in the New Printer form. Then you will verify the creation of the printer. Note that an actual printing device is not needed to complete this lab.

Step 1.   Log on as Administrator or as jfrank (a member of the Administrators group).

You have created a table for each printer you must configure similar to Table 5-1. The Page column indicates the Page of the Add Printer Wizard. The Field column indicates the individual field (with a radio button, check box, text box, or list). The Settings column indicates the setting for the field; where Select means to click on the radio button or check box, or highlight an item in a list, whichever is used in that field, and Clear indicates that a radio button or check box must not be selected. Any other string in the Settings column must be selected from a list or entered into a text box.

TABLE 5-1	Page	Field	Settings
New Printer form for Add Printer Wizard	Local or Network Printer	Local printer	Select
		Automatically detect...	Clear
		Network Printer	Clear
	Select the Printer Port	Use the following port	Select
		List of ports	LPT1
		Create a new port	Clear
	Manufacturer and Model	Manufacturer	HP
		Printers	HP LaserJet5si
	Name Your Printer	Printer Name	HP LaserJet 5si
		Do you want... default printer?	Select Yes
	Printer Sharing	Do not share this printer	Clear
		Share as	Select and enter: SalesLJ01
	Location and Comment	Location	Sales Support Desk
		Comment	Printer Manager: John Smith
	Print Test Page	Do you want to print a test page?	No
	Completing	*Verify settings.*	Click Finish

Step 2. Verify the printer installation by viewing the new printer in the Printers folder. It should look like Figure 5-1. Leave the Printers folder open.

FIGURE 5-1

Printers Folder with New Printer

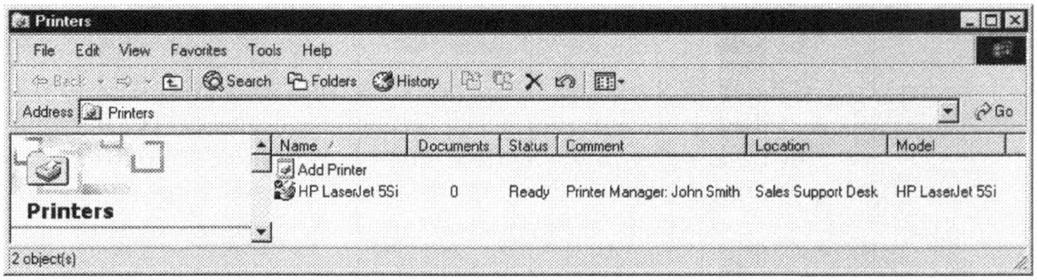

Step 3. Although you have installed the software components for the printer to communicate with and manage the print device and print jobs, you do not actually have a physical print device. The remaining print labs depend on pausing the printer. Pause the printer, and then leave the Printers folder open.

LAB EXERCISE 5.02

Managing Permissions for a Printer

30 Minutes

Among the information on the Add Printer form you used in Lab Exercise 5.01 is that John Smith is the printer manager. You entered this information as a comment. This makes it clear who the person is on-site doing the day-to-day management of the printer. In your company, this person's duties include keeping the printer filled with paper, taking care of paper jams, managing all documents in the printer queue, pausing and resuming the printer through the GUI, and being the one who calls service if there is a problem with the printer. By default anyone in the built-in Administrators local group on that computer can manage the printer. This means that Jill Frank, who is a member of this group, has permission to manage the printer. Because John Smith is the staff member who works closest to the computer, he has been trained and designated to take care of the printer.

In this lab you will make this permission effective by making John Smith a member of the Power Users group, which has the Manage Printer permission. This permission does not give him as much overall power as he would have as a member of the Administrators group, and that is exactly the point. We are delegating this one job to him. While he can manage printers that retain this default security setting for Power Users, he cannot do some of the system-wide tasks of a member of the Administrators group. You will learn more about Power Users in this lab exercise.

Learning Objectives

By the end of this lab, you'll be able to

- Define printer permissions
- Assign permissions to a printer

■ Understand capabilities of the Power Users group

■ Understand the capabilities of the Administrators group.

Lab Materials and Setup

The materials you need for this lab are:

■ A PC with Windows 2000 installed

■ This lab depends on the successful completion of Lab Exercise 5.01

cross
Reference

For an overview of printer permissions, read the section titled "Using Permissions to Control Access to Printers" in Chapter 5 of the **MCSE Windows 2000 Professional Study Guide.**

Getting Down to Business

In the following steps you will log on as Jill Frank, examine the security settings for the HP LaserJet 5si and research the capabilities of the printer permissions. You will then use the Computer Management console to add John Smith to the Power Users group, after which you will research the capabilities of the Power Users group and the Administrators group. Finally, you will remove the Everyone group from the permissions list, and replace it with the Authenticated Users group because the Everyone group includes all network users, both authenticated and unauthenticated, while Authenticated Users only includes users who were successfully authenticated.

Step 1. Log on as Administrator or as jfrank (a member of the Administrators group). Open the Properties dialog box for the printer you added in the previous lab exercise and look at the Security settings. Answer the following questions (you may have to use Windows 2000 Help).

1. What users or groups have Print permission?

2. What users or groups have Manage Printers and Manage Documents permissions?

3. Define Print permission.

4. Define Manage Printer permission.

5. Define Manage Documents permission.

lab

Hint **Step 2.** Add the user jsmith to the Power Users group and close all open windows.

On the job, you would go back to your user and group accounts planning sheet (Table 4-1) and update it with this new group membership!

Step 3. Use the Windows 2000 Help to answer the following questions:

1. What are the default capabilities of the built-in Power Users group?

2. What specifically can a Power User not do?

3. What are the default capabilities of the built-in Administrators group?

lab

Hint *Use the MCSE Windows 2000 Professional Study Guide or the Windows 2000 Professional Help, if necessary.*

Step 4. In the Security settings for the HP LaserJet 5si, add the group Authenticated Users and remove the group Everyone. Close all open windows.

lab
Hint   *You are removing the Everyone group, because it is a good practice to remove this group from objects that you are administering. Anyone who has access to your network is a member of this group (unauthenticated users as well as authenticated users), so if you give this group permissions, people who do not have individual accounts or are not somehow members of local groups will have access to this resource. Perhaps this is not important to you for a simple shared printer, but there are instances when you want to control access to a printer, and it is always a good practice to replace the Everyone group with a more restrictive group.*

LAB EXERCISE 5.03

Testing Printer Permissions

30 Minutes

Now that you have set permissions on the printer and added a user to the Power Users group, you need to test this implementation. Once again, it is common to document all such administrative implementations, as well as the procedures you use to test the implementations. As with the NTFS and Share permissions, you have a form to guide you through this test.

Learning Objectives

By the end of this lab, you'll be able to

- Test the effects of the permissions on a printer
- Manage a print queue through Windows 2000
- Manage a print device through Windows 2000.

Lab Materials and Setup

The materials you need for this lab are:

- A PC with Windows 2000 installed
- The Windows 2000 Professional CD (or a local or network location containing the contents of the I386 directory)

lab
ⓗint
For an overview of printer permissions, read the section titled "Using Permissions to Control Access to Printers" in Chapter 5 of the MCSE Windows 2000 Professional Study Guide.

Getting Down to Business

In this lab exercise you will test the effect of the permissions you set in the previous lab, using a test form as a guide.

Step I. Using the following test form as a guide (see Table 5-2), log on as each user in turn and perform the suggested actions. The result column shows the expected result. We tested each of these in our own test lab, and got these results. If you do not have the same outcomes, revisit Lab Exercise 5.02 and make sure you have your group memberships and permissions set correctly.

lab
ⓗint
On the job you would do more extensive testing.

TABLE 5-2	User name	Action	Result
Printer Permissions Test Form for Sales	lpederson	Print two documents	Success
		Pause one document	Success
		Resume document	Success
		Cancel one document	Success
		Resume the printer	Failure
	mfrost	Print one document	Success
		Pause, Resume, Restart, or Cancel lpederson's document	Failure
	jsmith	Print one document.	Success
		Pause, Resume, Restart or Cancel lpederson's or mfrost's documents	Success
		Cancel all documents in the queue	Success
		Assign the Deny Print, Deny Manage Printers and Deny Manage Documents permissions to sfisher.	Success
	sfisher	Print one document.	Failure

LAB EXERCISE 5.04

Creating a Volume and Converting from FAT to NTFS

60 Minutes

In Chapter 4 you worked with NTFS permissions, implementing the permissions designed for the Sales office. Now you are going to look beneath the file system and create a partition on a drive. Once partitioned, you will format the new partition as FAT or FAT32. At this point it is referred to as a volume (See New Volume (G:) in Figure 5-6 in the *MCSE Windows 2000 Professional Study Guide*). You will copy some files onto the new volume, and then you will use the command line tool, CONVERT, to do a non-destructive conversion of the FAT volume to NTFS. Finally, you will verify that your files survived the conversion.

To best prepare for this lab, read the entire section titled "Certification Objective 5.02" in Chapter 5 of the MCSE Windows 2000 Professional Study Guide, paying close attention to Table 5-1 and the "From the Classroom" sidebar discussion on Terminology. If you can, try Exercise 5-5, in which you use the Disk Management tool in the Computer Management console to convert a FAT volume to NTFS. Keep in mind, that this is a destructive operation, destroying any data on the disk you are converting.

Learning Objectives

By the end of this lab, you'll be able to

- Use the Disk Management tool to create a new volume
- Use Disk Management to format a new volume
- Convert a volume from FAT to NTFS.

Lab Materials and Setup

The materials you need for this lab are:

- A PC with Windows 2000 installed
- Unpartitioned disk space beyond the volume hosting the operating system

Getting Down to Business

In the following steps you will use the Disk Management tool in the Computer Management console to create a new volume in the unpartitioned disk space on your lab computer, formatting it as FAT32. Remember that FAT32 is more efficient than FAT16, but does not have the security and other advanced features of NTFS. Once you have completed this procedure you will have a new logical drive with a drive letter automatically assigned to it. This done, you will switch from the Computer Management console to Windows Explorer and copy some folders and files into the new drive. You will then open a command prompt and run the CONVERT command to convert the drive from FAT to NTFS. Finally you will verify that the drive is now NTFS and that your files are still there after the conversion.

Step 1. Log on to your lab computer as the Administrator, or as a member of the Administrators group. Open the Disk Management tool and locate unallocated space. Figure 5-2 shows partitions on a disk that may be more complicated than your lab computer. You can see the unallocated space that we eventually chose to become a new partition. We do not recommend converting such a small volume to NTFS, because the file system takes up too much disk space in overhead (Master Table, etc.) for such a small volume, but this is simply practice.

Step 2. Leaving at least 1MB unallocated, use Disk Management to convert unallocated space on your disk to a volume. *Be sure to leave the 1MB unallocated, because you will need this space for a lab you will do in Chapter 6.* When prompted for a volume label, you may leave it blank. If you do give it a volume label, which is just a name for the volume, be sure to remember it. You will need it a few steps further on. Format the new volume with FAT32, allowing Disk Management to assign a drive letter. Figure 5-3 shows Disk Management with the newly created volume, formatted and assigned drive letter E:. Write down the new drive letter that was created on your computer and the volume label (if one was created).

lab
Ⓗint

The 1MB of unallocated free space is so that you can later (in a lab in Chapter 6) convert the disk from basic to dynamic. This space is only required if Windows 2000 did not create all (including the first) partitions on your hard drive. If you created the first partition during Windows 2000 Setup you do not have to leave free space on your drive to be able to later convert it to dynamic. What is a dynamic disk? Read ahead in Chapter 6 of the **MCSE** Windows 2000 **Professional Study Guide.**

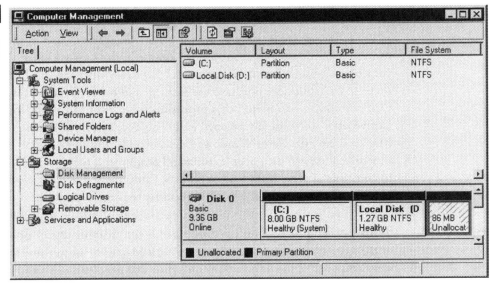

FIGURE 5-2

Disk Management *before* creation of the new volume

Step 3. Switch out of Computer Management and, using My Computer or Windows Explorer, copy some files and folders from another drive to the new drive. After you have done this, close all open windows and any other applications that appear on the Task Bar.

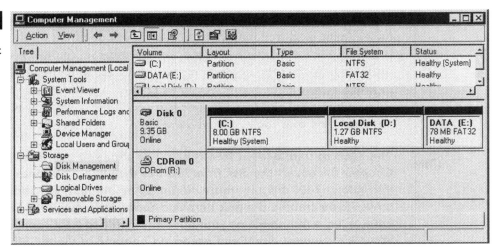

FIGURE 5-3

Disk Management *after* creation of the new volume

Step 4. Open a command prompt. At the command prompt enter:

```
CONVERT d: /FS:NTFS /V
```

where *d:* is the drive letter. The /FS:NTFS parameter requests the NTFS file system, and the /V parameter requests verbose mode, which will display the most information on your screen.

Figure 5-4 shows the convert command and the resulting output to the screen. In this case, the drive contained a folder, UTILITIES, with four folders below it, WINZIP, REALAUDIO, KEYAUDIT, and ADOBE. Within each folder there was only one file.

lab
ⓗint

Remember when we told you to close all open applications in Step 3? If you failed to do that, and any files were left open on the drive you are converting, convert will not run at this time. However, it will be scheduled to run on the next restart.

Step 5. Verify that the new drive is, indeed, now an NTFS volume, and that the files and folders are still on the new drive after the conversion.

FIGURE 5-4

Running the
CONVERT
command

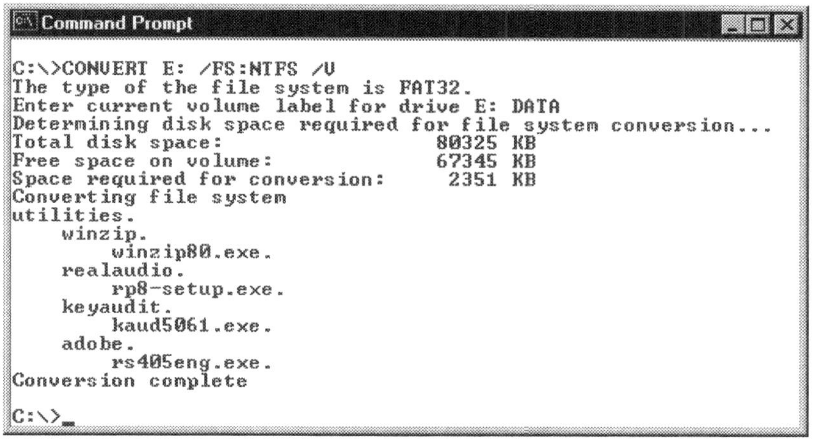

```
C:\>CONVERT E: /FS:NTFS /V
The type of the file system is FAT32.
Enter current volume label for drive E: DATA
Determining disk space required for file system conversion...
Total disk space:                80325 KB
Free space on volume:            67345 KB
Space required for conversion:    2351 KB
Converting file system
utilities.
    winzip.
        winzip80.exe.
    realaudio.
        rp8-setup.exe.
    keyaudit.
        kaud5061.exe.
    adobe.
        rs405eng.exe.
Conversion complete

C:\>_
```

LAB ANALYSIS TEST

1. You have received a call from Bruce Nelson, a manager in a small and remote customer service office. He has Windows 2000 on his desktop computer with a brand new printer connected to it and installed into Windows. He is able to print just fine from this computer. They have a small network in their office and had planned to allow other users on the network to connect and use the printer, but no one else can see his printer, even though they can find his computer in My Network Places. How can you help him?

2. Nancy Jones from the sales office called about the HP LaserJet 5si you set up for them. She wanted to pause the printer, but received the message, You Do Not Have Permission To Modify The Settings For This Printer. If You Need To Change The Settings, Contact Your Network Administrator. She had to walk over to the printer and use the button on its front panel to pause it. What can you tell her?

3. Why should you remove the group Everyone from a shared resource that you are administering?

4. Bruce Nelson has your number now! You helped him with his printer problem, so now when he calls Desktop Support, he asks for you by name. The drive C: on his computer was configured with NTFS. He would like to know why this was done, since he thought the FAT32 file system he used with Windows 98 was just fine. What will you tell Bruce?

5. You are preparing to install Windows 2000 on your home computer. You presently have Windows 98, and you would like to be able to dual boot between the two operating systems. What will your choices be for file systems?

KEY TERM QUIZ

Use the following vocabulary terms to complete the sentences below. Not all the terms will be used.

Add Printer Wizard

Local printer

Network printer

NTFS

FAT32

Power Users

Printer Port

Print queue

Printers folder

Volume

1. _____ is a group that only exists in the local SAM database of a Windows 2000 computer.

2. When you send a document to a printer, it waits in the _____ while earlier print jobs are printed.

3. If you use My Computer or Windows Explorer to look at your hard drive, the icon labeled C: is a disk _____.

4. In Windows 2000 you use the _____ when you want to install a printer.

5. _____ is an advanced file system supported by Windows 2000, Windows NT, and Windows XP, but not by Windows 95 or Windows 98.

LAB WRAP-UP

In this chapter you worked on two areas of Windows 2000 Professional operation—connecting to print devices, and configuring and managing file systems. You installed and shared a local printer. Sharing the printer granted a standard set of permissions which you will most often accept. However, in preparation for both the 70-210 exam and the situation in which you need to customize printer permissions, you granted a specified set of permissions for your shared printer. Then you tested the ability of various users to print to a printer and to manage printer and print jobs. Finally, shifting gears to file systems, you created a volume, formatted it with FAT or FAT32, copied files to the new partition, then did a non-destructive conversion from FAT or FAT32 to NTFS.

LAB SOLUTIONS FOR CHAPTER 5

Lab Solution 5.01

Step 1. Log on locally to your computer as an administrator, select the Start button, point to Settings, and then click Printers. The Printers window will open. Double-click the Add Printer icon. The Add Printer Wizard prompts you to click Next and then prompts you for the location of your printer. Make sure that the local printer button is selected, clear the Automatically Detect And Install My Plug And Play Printer checkbox since there is no printer connected that will be installed, and then click Next. Make sure that the Use The Following Port radio button is selected, and then under Use The Following Port, select LPT1. Click Next. The wizard will prompt you for the printer manufacturer and model. Choose the printer's manufacturer and model number as follows: In the Manufacturers list box, select HP for Hewlett Packard; in the Printers list box, select HP LaserJet 5si; and then click Next. To accept the default printer name, and to use this printer as the default printer for all Windows-based programs, click Next. The Printer Sharing page appears, prompting you for printer-sharing information.

lab
⊕int *In this lab exercise, we assume that you do not actually have a printer physically attached to your computer's parallel port. If you do, when the LTP1 port is select, the computer will pause for a few seconds, then display the current printer model so you will not need to select it, as you do in this lab.*

On the Printer Sharing page, select the Share As radio button. In the Share As text box, enter **SalesLJ01** and then click Next. The Location and Comment page appears. In the Location text box, enter **Sales Support Desk**, and click Next. In the Comment Field enter: **Printer Manager: John Smith**, then click Next. You are then prompted to print a test page. Select the No radio button since there is no printer to actually test, and then click Next. The Completing The Add Printer Wizard page appears and provides a summary of your installation choices, as seen in Figure 5-5. Confirm the choices. If you need to change anything, simply click the Back button until you reach the page where you need to make a change. Once everything is in order, return to the Completing page and click Finish. Windows 2000 Professional will copy files and complete the installation and configuration. Windows 2000 Professional copies the printer files, creates the shared printer, and creates an icon for the HP LaserJet 5si in the printer folder. Return to the Printer folder and verify that the icon is there. Close all applications and log off.

Completing the
Add Printer
Wizard

Step 2. Select Start | Settings | Printers and compare the results with Figure 5-1.

Step 3. Right-click on the printer and select Pause Printing. Leave the Printers folder open.

Lab Solution 5.02

Step 1. Open the Printers folder and right-click on the printer you created in the previous lab exercise. Click the Security tab.

1. Administrators, Everyone, and Power Users have Print permission.

2. Administrators and Power Users have the Manage Printers and Manage Documents permission.

3. Print permission allows a user or group to print to this printer. Users with Print permission may also manage their own documents in the print queue, but not the documents of other users.

4. Manage Printer permission allows a user or group to access the Printer Preferences for this printer, pause and restart the printer, change spooler settings, share a printer, adjust printer permissions, and change printer properties.

5. Manage Documents permission allows a user or group to pause, resume, or cancel *any* document in the print queue. You access a printer's print queue by opening a printer object in the Printers folder.

lab
(i)int
In Windows 2000 Help you will find information about these permissions in the topic "Printing security permission." You will learn more about print queues in the coming lab.

Step 2.   Right-click on My Computer and select Manage. Browse to System Tools | Local Users and Groups | Groups. Double-click Power Users. In the Power Users Properties dialog box, click Add. Select jsmith from the Name list, and click Add. Click OK.

Step 3.   We found the following definitions in Chapter 5 of the *MCSE Windows 2000 Professional Study Guide* and/or in the Windows 2000 Professional Help (see the topic "Default security settings" in Help).

1. The default capabilities of the built-in Power Users group includes:

   ■ Run applications non-certified for Windows 2000

   ■ Install programs if the installation does not modify operating system files or install system services

   ■ Customize system-wide resources (printers, data/time, power options, and others)

   ■ Create and administer local accounts

   ■ Stop and start system services

2. Power Users do not have many of the capabilities of the Administrators group, and they cannot do the following:

   ■ Although they can create and administer local users and groups, they cannot administer the Administrators group (e.g. add themselves to this group)

   ■ They cannot access the data of other users on an NTFS volume, unless granted permission

3. The default capabilities of the built-in Administrators group include:

■ Install the OS and components

■ Install Service Packs and Windows Packs

■ Upgrade and repair the operating system

■ Configure critical operating system parameters

■ Take ownership of files

■ Manage security and audit logs

■ Back up and restore the operating system

Step 4. Open the Properties dialog box of the HP LaserJet 5si, select the Security tab, and click Add. In the Select Users, Computers, or Group box, select Authenticated Users, click Add, and OK. Authenticated Users will only have the Print permission. Remain at the Security page.

On the Security page select Everyone, then click Remove. Your Security settings page should look like Figure 5-6.

FIGURE 5-6

Security Settings
for the
HP LaserJet 5si

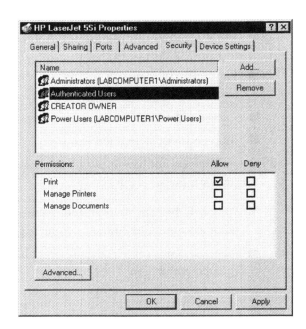

Lab Solution 5.03

Step 1.

1. Log on as lpederson. Open WordPad and create two documents; print each to the HP LaserJet 5si.

2. Open the Printers folder, then double-click on the HP LaserJet 5si to open the print queue in which you see the list of documents waiting to be printed. In Figure 5-7, you can see two documents owned by lpederson: prtperm1 and prtperm2. In the title bar the printer is shown as paused, because we did that back in Lab Exercise 5.01.

3. Still logged on as lpederson, right-click on one of the documents and select Pause. Notice that the status changes to Paused. Right-click on the same document and select Resume. This will resume printing the document at the point at which it was paused. If you select Restart, the document will resume printing from the beginning.

4. As lpederson, right-click on the same document and select Cancel (you can also select it and press the Delete key). This will leave just one document for lpederson in the queue.

5. Still as lpederson, click Printer on the menu bar. Notice that Pause Printing is selected (it has a check in front of it), but it is greyed out, so you cannot resume printing for the printer.

6. Log off lpederson and log on as mfrost.

7. As mfrost open WordPad, create one document, and print it to the HP LaserJet 5si.

8. Open the Printers folder, then double-click on the HP LaserJet 5si to open the print queue in which you see the list of documents waiting to be printed.

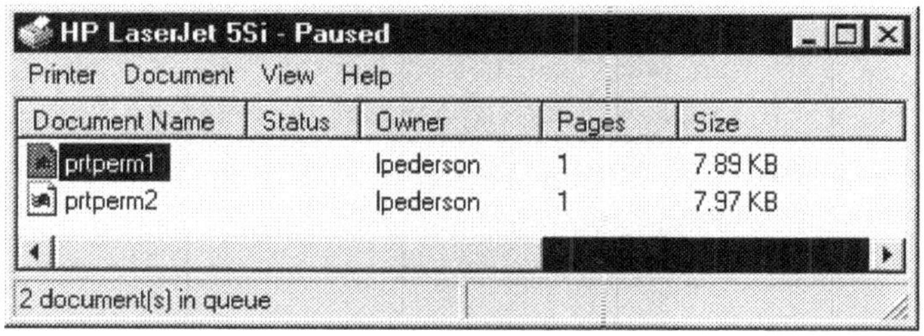

FIGURE 5-7

The HP LaserJet 5si print queue with lpederson's documents pending

You can see two documents—one owned by lpederson, and one owned by mfrost. Right-click on lpederson's document and select Pause. The result is subtle—the Status field does not change for this document, and you see the message Access Denied in the status bar at the bottom of the Printer queue window.

9. Select Resume, Restart, and Cancel in turn, and notice the same result.

10. Log off as mfrost and log on as jsmith.

11. As jsmith open WordPad, create one document, and print it to the HP LaserJet 5si.

12. Open the Printers folder, then double-click on the HP LaserJet 5si to open the print queue in which you see the list of documents waiting to be printed. You can see three documents—one owned by lpederson, one owned by mfrost, and one owned by jsmith.

13. Right-click on lpederson's document and select Pause. The Status field for this document will change to Paused.

14. Right-click on lpederson's document and select Resume. The Status field for this document will now be cleared.

15. Right-click on lpederson's document and select Restart. The Status field for this document will change to Restarting.

16. Right-click on lpederson's document and select Cancel. The document will be removed from the queue.

17. Click on the Printer item in the menu bar and notice that all the choices are available to you (none are grayed out), as was true for lpederson. Cancel all documents. This will empty the print queue for this printer.

18. Click on the Printer item in the menu bar, and select Properties. In the Properties dialog box for the HP Laserjet 5si, select the Security tab. In the Security sheet, click Add, then select sfisher from the Name list in the Select Users, Computers, or Groups dialog box , and click Add and OK. On the Security tab, select Sandra Fisher in the Name list, and then modify her permissions to Deny the Print, Manage Printers, and Manage Documents permissions.

19. Click OK on the Security tab of the Properties box. If a message box appears warning you that the Deny permission is drastic, close the message box.

lab
Hint   *There are usually several ways to do any task in the Windows GUI, and we will not attempt to tell you about all of them (because we do not know them all!), but sometimes we just can't resist telling you another one. From the Printers folder, you can simply right-click on the printer object, and select Properties to open the Properties dialog box of a printer.*

Lab Solution 5.04

Step 1.   Right-click on My Computer and select Manage. In the Computer Management console, select the Disk Management folder. If you have any unallocated space, you will see a rectangle in the contents pane labeled Unallocated. (If do not have such an item but do have one labeled Free Space, choose Create Logical Drive, and skip item 1 in Step 2).

Step2.

1. Right-click on the rectangle labeled Unallocated and select Create Partition. This will bring up the Create Partition Wizard. Click Next.

2. On the Select Partition Type page, select Primary partition and click the Next button.

3. On the Specify Partition Size select an amount of disk space that will leave at least 10MB Unallocated on the disk, and click Next.

4. On the Assign Drive Letter or Path page, leave Assign A Drive Letter selected with an automatically calculated drive letter and click Next.

5. On the Format Partition page, be sure that Format This Partition With The Following Settings is selected, change the file system to use FAT32 with the allocation unit size at Default, and give the volume a label of your choice. Then click Next.

6. On the Completing page, verify the information, checking to see that you selected a size that will leave 10MB free, and that you selected the FAT32 file system. Then click Finish.

7. After some delay, the new drive will appear in Disk Management. If the size after formatting was not exactly what you had designated, do not be concerned. We selected 76MB, but it formatted to 78MB. This is because a volume size

is defined, in part, by the geometry of the physical disk (which includes both sides of one or more platters). A partition boundary will always fall on a cylinder boundary. In our case, the nearest such boundary that would give us 76MB was at 78MB.

Step 3. The actual steps you take depend on your preferences.

Right-click on My Computer and select Explore. Open the icon for any drive and select one or two folders (preferably *not* the folder in which the OS is installed). Right-click on the selected folder(s) and select Copy. Then browse to the new drive, right click on the drive icon in the Folders pane (or right-click in the contents pane), and select Paste. After the files have been copied, verify that they are indeed on the new drive. Remember the new drive letter for the next step. Close Windows Explorer and all other applications.

Step 4. No additional instructions are required.

Step 5. Use any method you prefer to ensure that the drive is now NTFS and that the files are on the drive. Since we already had the command prompt open, we simply did a directory of the new drive within the command prompt, which showed that the files and folders were still there. Then we reran the convert command, as in Step 4 and received the message Drive E: Is Already NTFS. This is a quicker method for someone comfortable with the command prompt. There is certainly no shame in using Windows Explorer or My Computer to view the files and to look at the properties of the drive. The General tab of the Properties dialog box will show that the file system is NTFS.

ANSWERS TO LAB ANALYSIS TEST

1. It sounds like everything is set up correctly, except that the printer is not configured for sharing. If he or someone else in the office can log onto his computer as a member of the Administrators or Power Users group, you can direct them to configure the printer to share, as you did on your lab computer in Lab Exercise 5.01.

2. What she is trying to do requires the Manage Printer permission. If the permissions are in place as you configured them for this printer, and if the group memberships have not been changed since you created the group memberships on this computer, she must ask either Jill Frank or John

Smith to pause the printer from the Printers folder. By default, the Manage Printer permission is assigned to members of the Administrators and Power Users groups. Jill Frank is a member of the Administrators group and John Smith is a member of the Power Users group on the shared computer.

3. You should remove the group Everyone from a shared resource because the Everyone group includes people on the network who have not been authenticated. Therefore, anyone who gets access to your network and is able to see your computer's shares can access a resource that gives permissions to the Everyone group.

4. You don't mind educating an interested user, since sometimes you feel like you are only two steps ahead of some of them. You can explain to Bruce that the FAT file system saves files more efficiently because it uses smaller cluster sizes, but FAT32 does not have the advanced features of NTFS, including the security of file and folder permissions and the ability to compress files. The latest version introduced with Windows 2000, NTFS5, includes new features such as encryption and indexing at the file system level. These are just a few of the features supported by the NTFS file system.

5. Whenever you are setting up a computer for dual-booting between Windows 2000 and Windows 98, you must consider the file systems that they both support. Windows 2000 supports FAT16, FAT32, and NTFS. While Windows 98 supports the two versions of FAT, it does not support NTFS. You will probably want to leave the file system as is. The computer most likely is using the FAT32 file system, and it is unlikely that it has any unallocated disk space on which you can partition and create a new volume formatted as NTFS. If there are multiple volumes in this computer and you format or convert one to NTFS, you must remember that Windows 98 will not be able to see that drive. It is, essentially, non-existent when you are running Windows 98.

ANSWERS TO KEY TERM QUIZ

1. Power Users

2. Print queue

3. Volume

4. Add Printer Wizard

5. NTFS

6

Implementing, Managing, and Troubleshooting Disks and Displays

I n several of the previous chapters, the labs required you to perform tasks involving disks, drives, files, folders, and file systems. Before you could install Windows 2000, you needed to ensure that you had enough disk space. If you were doing an installation—whether a clean installation or an upgrade—you had to decide what file system to use. In Chapter 4 you practiced skills necessary to work with share permissions and with NTFS file and folder permissions. In Chapter 5, in order to convert a FAT volume to NTFS, you first had to use Disk Management to partition and format it, which are actually skills taught in Chapter 6 of the *MCSE Windows 2000 Professional Study Guide*. Now, in this chapter, you will review disk terminology and spend more time with the Disk Management snap-in, the principal GUI tool for managing disks.

LAB EXERCISE 6.01

Using and Understanding Disk Management

60 Minutes

Imagine yourself, once again, as a help desk support analyst involved in rolling out and supporting Windows 2000. Today, you and your fellow team members are considering the disk management capabilities of Windows 2000 Professional. You have decided to begin with a review of the basic concepts of disk partitioning, then you will review how Windows NT handles disk partitioning, and finally you will look at the new features for disk partitioning and disk management that exist in Windows 2000.

In this lab you will read some information about Disk Management, then compare information in a screen print of Disk Management on a test computer to the information on your lab computer.

Because there is so much confusion about disk partitioning, you should review the following summary of the rules of disk partitioning:

- Before it can be formatted for use by any file system, a disk must be divided into one or more areas called partitions. Each partition must then be formatted by the operating system that will use it.

- Partitioning information is written to the partition table, which resides in the master boot record (MBR). There is only one MBR (and therefore only one partition table) per hard disk.

■ The partition table can hold information for four partitions, *but* only advanced operating systems such as Windows NT, Windows 2000, and Windows XP can create or access more than two partitions.

■ Each of the four partitions defined in a partition table can be one of two different types: primary, and extended, but only one of the four may be extended.

■ DOS and Windows 9x get around their partition limits with the use of a special partition type called an extended partition. These operating systems can create (using FDISK) one primary partition and one extended partition. Within an extended partition you may define multiple logical drives.

■ Although there can be up to four partitions per disk (created by Windows NT, Windows 2000, or Windows XP), DOS and Windows 9x operating systems can only see one primary partition and one extended partition per disk.

■ Advanced operating systems can create four partitions in the following combinations: up to four primary partitions, or up to three primary partitions, and one extended partition.

■ Each primary partition has a single drive letter assigned to it, beginning with C:. Then each logical drive within the extended partition is assigned a drive letter.

■ The partition from which the operating system boots is the primary partition that is marked as Active on the first hard disk. This is done with partitioning software. DOS and Windows 9x use their respective versions of *FDISK*, Windows NT uses its setup program or *Disk Administrator* and Windows 2000 and Windows XP use its setup program or *Disk Management*, which is a tool in the Computer Management console.

■ Only one primary partition per hard disk can be marked as active.

■ Once formatted with FAT16, FAT32, NTFS4, or NTFS5, each partition has a Boot Sector, sometimes also called a Boot Record—which must never be confused (Ha!) with the one and only Master Boot Record on the disk. The Master Boot Record is the first sector on the entire hard disk, while the Boot Sector or Boot Record is the first sector within *each* formatted partition. The Boot Sector contains the bootstrap code and information on the format of the partition.

Have you digested that information? We hope so, because there is more.

What you have just read describes how partitions are defined, based on the industry standard of using the partition table on all computers defined as PCs (the descendents of the original IBM PC), and complies with the standards that grew from it. Although the partition table represents a limit in disk configuration, in Windows NT Microsoft introduced one method of going beyond the limits of the partition table, but in Windows 2000 they abandoned the NT method and introduced a new method.

In Windows NT, when you go beyond the limits of the partition table, the configuration information for this fancy partitioning is kept in the local registry. What constitutes going beyond the limits of the partition table? Using the operating system (rather than a RAID controller) to configure your disks to use stripe sets, stripe sets with parity, mirror sets, or volume sets. If these terms are new to you, check out the Glossary section of the *MCSE Windows 2000 Professional Study Guide*, or search at one of the Internet-based computer dictionary/encyclopedia sites, such as www.webopedia.com.

Beginning with Windows 2000, Microsoft introduced a new way to go beyond the limits of the partition table using what they call a new *storage type* and storing the advanced disk partitioning information on an area of disk outside the limits of normal partitions. This new storage type is called *dynamic storage*. The old storage type, which only used the partition table to store partitioning information, is now called *basic storage*. Each physical hard disk system can only be one storage type. On a basic storage disk, referred to as a basic disk, Windows 2000 only uses the partition table to define the partitioning of the disk. That's it! Nothing fancy, just a maximum of four partitions, limited to the two types—primary or extended, and only one of the partitions can be an extended partition. Just as before, each primary partition can have only one logical drive letter assigned, while an extended partition can have many logical drives, each with its own drive letter. Windows 2000 cannot do anything fancy with basic disks. That means no striping, mirroring, or volume sets. The only way that Windows 2000 can be involved with any of these methods on basic disks is if you upgrade a computer from NT that already had striping, mirroring, or volume sets. The operating system can be upgraded, and Windows 2000 can handle the fancy stuff, storing the configuration information for these disks in its registry the way NT does, but it cannot create any of these on basic disks.

Now, here is a subtle difference: when referring to the areas of disk that are defined in the partition table on basic disks, Microsoft uses the word *partition*. In an extended partition you can create one or more logical drives, which are then referred to as volumes. When referring to the individual areas of disk that are defined on dynamic disks, Microsoft uses the word *volume*. This is congruent with the use of this word for logical drives on an extended partition, because a volume is a portion of the disk seen as a single logical drive. You can, and usually do, assign a drive letter to a volume. On a dynamic disk, the old four-partition limit is gone. You can have many volumes—you are not even limited by drive letters—since you can create a volume without assigning a drive letter.

When you install Windows 2000 on a hard disk system, it is a basic disk. If you add a brand new, additional, disk system to a Windows 2000 computer it will also be a basic disk. The only way Windows 2000 can create one of the fancy volumes (spanned, mirrored, striped, or RAID-5) is on disks that have been converted to dynamic. Additionally, some of this fancy stuff cannot be done on Windows 2000 Professional, but only on a computer running one of the Windows Server products beginning with Windows 2000. Windows 2000 Professional can only create simple volumes, spanned volumes, or striped volumes. The Windows 2000 Server products can create all these types of volumes, plus mirrored volumes, and RAID-5 volumes. These last two provide fault tolerance, and only the server products have the necessary support for fault tolerance.

One last point: once a disk is converted to dynamic, only Windows 2000 or newer versions of Windows can use that disk. If you do this on a computer that previously dual-booted between Windows 2000 and Windows 98, you will no longer be able to boot up into Windows 98.

You may be wondering why you would care to create more than one partition on a hard disk. Why not simply keep the entire disk in one partition? Here are just a few scenarios:

- On a desktop computer, use the first partition (C:\) for the operating system, and create a second data partition on the hard disk. This will allow a reinstall of the OS without losing data.

- On a file and print server, again, use the first partition for the operating system, and create a second partition for the shared user folders. In addition, move the print spooler (an advanced task documented at www.microsoft.com/technet) to that second partition. This can prevent the server from crashing if the users fill their drives or the print spooler stalls (maybe).

- On a dual-booted computer each OS tends to be happiest when occupying its own partition. The rule to remember here is that the first partition must be formatted in a file system that all installed operating systems can use, because they will all have their initial boot-up from this partition.

Learning Objectives

By the end of this lab, you'll be able to use Disk Management to identify the following

- Type of storage
- Type of partition
- Type of volume
- Unallocated disk space
- Free space on an extended partition.

Lab Materials and Setup

The materials you need for this lab are:

- A PC with Windows 2000 installed

**cross
Reference**   *To best prepare for this lab exercise, read the section titled "Implementing, Managing, and Troubleshooting Disk Devices" in Chapter 6 of the* **MCSE Windows 2000 Professional Study Guide.**

Getting Down to Business

After reading the prior review information on partitioning, go through the following steps in which you first match a set of disk management terms with a screen shot of Disk Management. Next, you will be referred to a figure in an earlier chapter and you will answer some questions regarding the disk information shown in that figure. Finally, you will open Disk Management on your lab computer and answer a set of questions about it.

Step 1.   Study Figure 6-1 and the following list of terms. For each item in the list, identify it by writing its number on the figure in the appropriate place.

1. basic disk
2. primary partition
3. extended partition

4. logical drive in an extended partition

5. free space in an extended partition

6. a volume with the FAT file system

7. a volume with the NTFS file system

Step 2. Refer to Figure 5-2 in Chapter 5 and answer the following questions:

1. How many physical hard drives are shown?

_____

2. What storage type is shown?

_____

3. How many partitions are shown?

_____

4. Describe the type(s) of partitions shown.

_____

5. Can another partition be created on this disk? If so, what type can it be?

_____

FIGURE 6-1

Example of Disk
Management

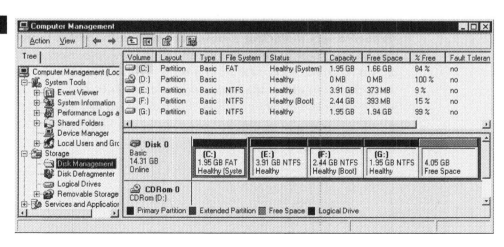

Step 3. Open the Disk Management snap-in on your lab computer and answer the following questions:

1. How many physical hard drives are shown?

   _____

2. What storage type is shown?

   _____

3. How many partitions are shown?

   _____

4. Describe the type(s) of partitions shown.

   _____

5. Can another partition be created on this disk? If so, what type can it be?

   _____

lab
ⓗint

There is no good reason for using extended partitions on a computer with only Windows 2000 (or Windows NT) installed. You only need to use an extended partition if you need more than one partition on a computer that is dual booting between one of these advanced operating system and an older operating system such as Windows 95, Windows 98, or DOS. Think of extended partitions as a clumsy solution to an old problem. A logical drive in an extended partition, especially a logical drive after the first one on that partition, is accessed through a very inefficient process. For more information search for and read the article, "Disk Management Basics" at www.microsoft.com/technet. This article (actually a chapter from a book) gives the whole disk management story. To learn about the inefficiencies of extended partitions, check out the information in the section titled "Logical Drives and Extended Partitions."

LAB EXERCISE 6.02

Managing CD-ROM Drives

30 Minutes

Today you have time in the test lab, and you want to test something you learned about CD-ROM drives. You normally install Windows 2000 on drive C:. If there are no other logical drives, the CD-ROM drive is automatically allocated the letter D. If you then add another logical drive to this computer by partitioning unallocated space on the first hard drive, or by adding and partitioning another hard drive, the next letter available will be E:. In the lab today, you want to practice allocating a different drive letter to the CD-ROM drive. This is a task you will want to do for the desktop computers you manage. You know it is best to do this before you create new hard disk partitions and install applications that will either reside on the new partition or depend on the drive letters for their data paths.

After you finish reassigning the CD-ROM drive, and in keeping with the CD-ROM theme, you will study a standard you have heard about relating to CD-ROMs called El Torito. You will see what you can find out about it on the Internet.

Learning Objectives

By the end of this lab, you'll be able to

■ Change a drive letter for a CD-ROM drive
■ Define the El Torito standard.

Lab Materials and Setup

The materials you need for this lab are:

■ A PC with a CD-ROM drive and with Windows 2000 installed
■ Access to the Internet

cross
Reference

To best prepare for this lab exercise, read the section titled "Implementing, Managing, and Troubleshooting Disk Devices" in Chapter 6 of the **MCSE Windows 2000 Professional Study Guide.**

Getting Down to Business

In the following steps, you will first change the drive letter on a CD-ROM drive from D: to R:, just to practice this ability to reassign drive letters. Then you will research the El Torito standard.

lab
Hint

We have made it our standard practice to always assign the drive letter "R" to a CD-ROM drive so we always know what letter the CD-ROM uses. Then we can create partitions and otherwise mess with the hard drive(s) without having to worry about needing to do other reassignments.

Step 1. Log on as Administrator (or a member of the Administrators group) and use the Disk Management snap-in to give the drive letter "R" to your CD-ROM drive. Figure 6-2 shows the context menu command you use to do this in Disk Management. When you have made this change, close Computer Management and use another tool (My Computer, Windows Explorer, or the command prompt) to verify that R has indeed been assigned to the CD-ROM drive.

lab
Warning

If you change the drive letter of your CD-ROM drive, and you have software that depends on the use of the CD-ROM drive, you may need to reconfigure the software to use the new drive letter. Also, if a mapped drive is already using this drive letter, you will have to select another letter.

FIGURE 6-2

Disk Management snap-in with the Change Drive Letter command

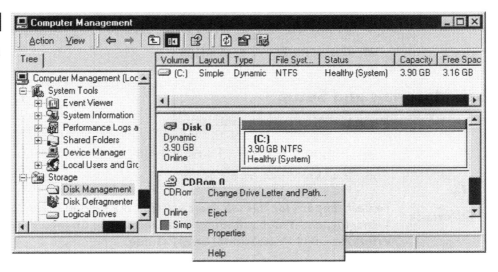

Step 2. The *MCSE Windows 2000 Professional Study Guide* makes a reference to the El Torito standard in the second paragraph under the title "CD-ROM" in the section named "Installing, Configuring, and Managing Devices." Using Internet resources, research this standard and write a short paragraph in which you define the purpose of the standard, the sponsors, and what it entails.

LAB EXERCISE 6.03

Using Disk Cleanup

30 Minutes

One issue many Windows 2000 desktop support people have faced with earlier versions of Windows is the proliferation of junk files that accumulate on the users' hard drives. These include temporary Internet files, programs downloaded from the Internet while browsing, a buildup in the Recycle Bin, other temporary files, and Windows components and other programs that the users install and then never use. You have heard of the Disk Cleanup tool, and today you plan to test its use on your lab computers.

Learning Objectives

By the end of this lab, you'll be able to

- Run the Windows 2000 Disk Cleanup Utility
- Confirm the selection of files to be deleted by Disk Cleanup
- Understand that a disk cleanup should be followed by a disk defragmentation.

Lab Materials and Setup

The materials you need for this lab are:

■ A PC with Windows 2000 installed

Getting Down to Business

In the following steps you will run the Disk Cleanup utility to rid your lab computer of files that are no longer needed or useful to you, and to free up disk space. After you do this, you should run the Disk Defragmenter, following the instructions in Exercise 6-5 in the *MCSE Windows 2000 Professional Study Guide.*

Step 1. Log on as Administrator (or a member of the Administrators group). Select Start | Run, then type **CLEANMGR** and click OK. The Select Drive dialog box will appear:

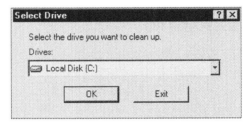

lab
Hint   *You can also start this utility by clicking the Disk Cleanup button on the General page of a volume's Properties.*

Select the drive you wish to clean, then click OK. The Disk Cleanup box will appear with a progress bar as it calculates the space it can free up on the drive you select. This may take several minutes on a large drive with many files.

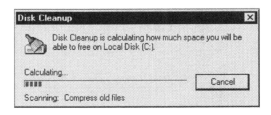

Step 2. When Disk Cleanup completes the calculations, a dialog box (Figure 6-3) will appear with the results of the calculations. You may select which files you wish to clean. Your lab computers may not have a great number of files to be cleaned, but we ran this on a Windows 2000 computer we have used for over a year without doing a cleanup, and you can see the difference it can make. The View Files button will open an appropriate folder for the category of files selected so that you can see the files that will be deleted if you keep this selection. Do *not* click OK yet.

Step 3. Click on the More Options tab, to select Windows Components And Other Installed Programs For Removal. Click on each of the Clean up buttons and see if there are components or programs that you are willing to remove. After you have selected all the files, components, and programs you want Disk Cleanup to remove, click OK. You will see the Disk Cleanup box with a progress bar, this time announcing that it is cleaning up the drive.

When Disk Cleanup is finished, close all open windows.

Normally, you would run Disk Defragmenter after deleting many files. Run it now. If you need instructions to run it, see Exercise 6-5 in the *MCSE Windows 2000 Professional Study Guide.*

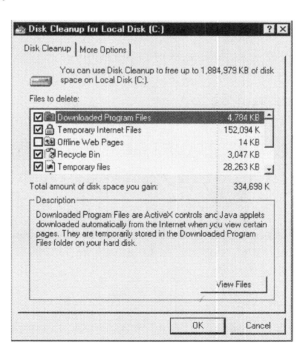

FIGURE 6-3

Disk Cleanup
Calculation
Results

LAB EXERCISE 6.04

Troubleshooting Disks: Removing a Boot Sector Virus

25 Minutes

The built-in security of Windows 2000 makes it less likely that your computer will be infected with a boot sector virus, but there are no absolutes in this world. A boot sector virus is difficult to eradicate, because you cannot remove it while Windows is running. The most common method supported by Microsoft for removing a boot sector virus is to boot up with a DOS or DOS-like operating system and run anti-virus software designed to remove a boot sector virus. One comes with Windows 2000, AVBoot from Computer Associates. You decide to test this anti-virus software on a test lab computer.

Learning Objectives

By the end of this lab, you'll be able to

- Install anti-virus software
- Fix a Master Boot record virus.

Lab Materials and Setup

The materials you need for this lab are:

- A PC with Windows 2000 Professional installed
- The Windows 2000 Professional CD-ROM
- A blank diskette

cross
Reference

*To best prepare for this lab exercise, read the section titled "Troubleshooting Disks and Volumes" in Chapter 6 of the **MCSE** Windows 2000 Professional Study Guide.*

Getting Down to Business

In the following steps you will first create the anti-virus boot diskette, then you will boot from this diskette and run the anti-virus software.

Step 1. Label a blank, formatted diskette **AV Boot Disk** and insert in drive A:. Insert the Windows 2000 Professional CD-ROM in the CD drive. Open a command prompt and type the following command:

```
d:\VALUEADD\3RDPARTY\CA_ANTIV\MAKEDISK
```

where *d:* is the drive letter of your CD ROM drive. You will see the message shown in Figure 6-4.

Press any key to continue. It will take a few minutes (floppy drives are slow) while MAKEDISK creates a DOS boot diskette.

lab ʘint *You can also run the MAKEDISK batch file by clicking on it in Windows Explorer or My Computer. However, when you run a batch file from the GUI, the Command Prompt window will close at the completion of the batch file, and you will not be able to see any error messages. In our tests (on several computers), we received the error message shown in Figure 6-5. However, after verifying that the disk was not write-protected, and doing a directory of the disk and finding that files were placed on the disk, we proceeded, and the disk worked. We have not investigated, but it is probably a simple error in the batch file MAKEDISK.BAT. We used two different Windows 2000 Professional CDs. Both were the Not for Resale version, which should be functionally identical to the retail version. We did not try this with the Evaluation version (120-Day).*

FIGURE 6-4

The MAKEDISK message

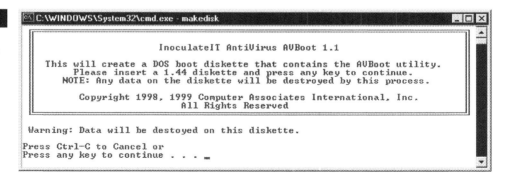

FIGURE 6-5

MAKEDISK Error
Message

```
C:\WINDOWS\System32\cmd.exe                                    _ □ ×

          Copyright 1998, 1999 Computer Associates International, Inc.
                           All Rights Reserved

Warning: Data will be destoyed on this diskette.

Press Ctrl-C to Cancel or
Press any key to continue . . .
Copyright Microsoft Corporation 1996 v1.1
FD144.EXE: copy disk image file to 3.5" 1.44MB floppy disk A or B
Detected 3.5" 1.44MB floppy disk
Disk error or disk is write-protected
You must have a formatted 1.44MB 3.5" diskette in drive A
Insert diskette and try again

R:\VALUEADD\3RDPARTY\CA_ANTIV>
```

Step 2. Verify that the contents of the diskette match the list of files in
Figure 6-6. You can use My Computer or Windows Explorer to view the disk,
but you will only see all the files if you have the View settings set to Show Hidden
Files. In a command prompt, you can see all files on the diskette (regardless of
the attributes) by using the command DIR A: /A, as we did. Leave the diskette
in drive A: and reboot your computer.

Step 3. After the reboot, you will see a message from AVBoot and a small menu
of choices. Press **1** to have AVBoot scan for boot viruses. A message will display while
AVBoot is loading (see Figure 6-7). Notice the message about the age of the virus
signature being used. It is quite old, since it was placed on the Windows 2000

FIGURE 6-6

The Contents of
the AVBoot Disk

```
C:\WINDOWS\System32\cmd.exe                                    _ □ ×

R:\VALUEADD\3RDPARTY\CA_ANTIV>dir a: /a
 Volume in drive A has no label.
 Volume Serial Number is 3373-18F9

 Directory of A:\

08/24/1996  11:11a            214,836 IO.SYS
08/24/1996  11:11a             65,271 DRVSPACE.BIN
02/17/1999  05:43p                  6 MSDOS.SYS
08/24/1996  11:11a             93,812 COMMAND.COM
08/24/1996  11:11a              5,175 CHOICE.COM
09/20/1998  06:09p                 20 CONFIG.SYS
08/24/1996  11:11a             33,191 HIMEM.SYS
08/24/1996  11:11a             10,471 MORE.COM
11/02/1999  10:16a            333,106 AVBOOT.EXE
10/28/1999  06:47p            130,479 VIRBOOT.DAT
02/18/1999  11:33a              2,083 AUTOEXEC.BAT
06/21/1999  06:30p              1,931 README.TXT
              12 File(s)        890,381 bytes
               0 Dir(s)         563,712 bytes free

R:\VALUEADD\3RDPARTY\CA_ANTIV>
```

FIGURE 6-7

AVBoot message
during scan

```
InoculateIT AntiVirus Avboot V1.1
Copyright 1997-99 Computer Associates International, Inc.
 and/or its subsidiaries. All Rights Reserved.

*WARNING:  The virus signature which identifies recent boot sector viruses
in the wild is 851 days old.  Please visit the web site
 http://www.cai.com
to update this floppy diskette with a new virus signature.

Engine version: 5.12 10/28/1999
Data version:   5.25 10/28/1999

No Viruses Were Detected In Workstation Memory


Boot Sector Summary:

Floppy Drive A... No Boot Sector Viruses Detected
Floppy Drive B... Not Installed
Hard Disk 1...... No Boot Sector Viruses Detected
Hard Disk 2...... Not Installed

Press any key to continue . . .
```

Professional CD during production in 1999. A web site is provided where you can
obtain a newer virus signature for future use. For now, allow the program to continue
with the search for boot sector viruses, checking the boot sector of all disks it can find.
When it is complete, press any key to continue. When the menu appears, select 3
to quit, remove the diskette from the drive, and reboot your computer.

LAB EXERCISE 6.05

Troubleshooting Video: Starting Up in VGA Mode

20 Minutes

Your next task is to test a procedure for working with video problems. If you install
the wrong video driver or make a configuration change to an existing video driver,
there is a chance that the display will be blank or out of control the next time you
start Windows 2000. As with Windows NT, as long as you have not logged on before
things deteriorated, there is a method that lets you select the last known good
configuration. However, if this does not work, or is not an option (Last Known Good
is not an option if you have more than one hardware profile), then you have a VGA
mode, similar to that of Windows NT, now accessed during startup through the F8
Advanced Options menu.

Learning Objectives

By the end of this lab, you'll be able to

- Start up Windows 2000 in VGA Mode.

Lab Materials and Setup

The materials you need for this lab are:

- A PC with Windows 2000 installed

cross Reference

To best prepare for this lab exercise, read the section "Implementing, Managing, and Troubleshooting Display Devices" in Chapter 6 of the **MCSE Windows 2000 Professional Study Guide.**

Getting Down to Business

In the following steps you will first examine the current display settings, then practice starting up your Windows 2000 lab computer in a special mode that disables the currently installed video driver and uses a basic VGA driver. To do this, you will select this option from the Advanced Options menu. Then you will explore the settings in Display Properties that you would use to correct a configuration or driver problem.

Step 1. Log on as Administrator (or a member of the Administrators group) and look at the Settings tab in the Display Properties dialog box and click the Advanced button to see further settings. Record each of the following settings:

- Screen area (Resolution, shown as 800 by 600, 1024 by 768, etc.)

_____

- Color (color density)

_____

■ Font Size

■ Adapter Type

Verify that the adapter is working properly, then close out of Display Properties.

Step 2. Restart your computer, watching closely for the Starting Windows message. As soon as you see it, immediately press the F8 key. The Windows 2000 Advanced Options menu will appear, as shown in Figure 6-8.

Step 3. Use the down arrow to select Enable VGA Mode, then press Enter.

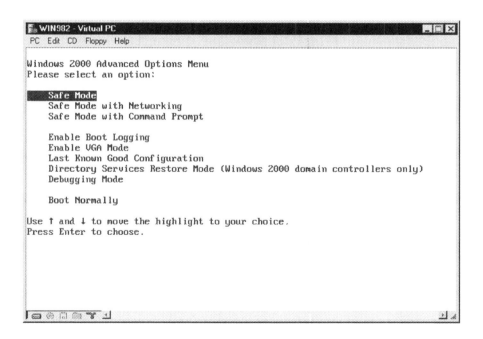

FIGURE 6-8

Windows 2000
Advanced
Options Menu

Step 4. After Windows starts up, log on as Administrator (or as a member of the Administrators group). Do you see any differences in the desktop in VGA mode from how it appears normally? Write down your observations of any changes you notice.

_____

_____

Step 5. Open the Display Properties dialog box, and look at the Advanced Settings. Notice that they do not refer to the basic video driver currently running while you are in VGA mode, but still show all the settings of your installed driver. This is where you can make any necessary settings, even removing or updating the driver. Alternatively, you can use Device Manager to remove or update the video driver.

When you are done, reboot, allowing Windows 2000 to boot normally.

lab
ⓗint

You will revisit Device Manager in Chapters 7, 8, and 11.

LAB ANALYSIS TEST

1. Herman, another help desk support analyst has asked you how to configure a new computer with Windows 2000 for a client who wants a multi-GB hard disk configured with the first partition being 2GB in size and holding the operating system. The other partitions will have equally-divided portions of the remaining space. What are his options?

_____

_____

2. Your co-worker, Sally, installed Windows 2000 on a new 20GB hard drive and created a 4GB partition for the operating system and several application programs. Then she used Disk Management to create a single partition for the remaining 16GB, accepting the default drive letter for this new partition. She configured each application to save its data files on the new partition. Afterward she noticed that the CD-ROM drive was D: and the new partition was E:. Everything works, but it upsets her sense of order to see the CD-ROM drive with a letter that falls between two hard drive volumes. What can she do?

_____

_____

3. An inventory control clerk in your company installed Windows 2000 on his office computer. Although company policy not to support dual-boot configurations, this user configured his computer to dual-boot. An old inventory analysis and reporting application that he uses daily is installed in Windows 98 because it is not compatible with Windows 2000. Yesterday he was logged on as Administrator in Windows 2000 and he decided to convert his basic disk to dynamic. Now he can't boot up into Windows 98. Can you help?

_____

_____

4. You attempt to install Windows 2000 on a computer by booting it from the CD-ROM, but when the computer boots up, it only attempts to boot from the hard disk. What will you do?

_____

_____

5. While experimenting in the test lab one day, you somehow completely messed up the video settings. You can't even see the screen well enough to log on. What are your options?

_____

_____

KEY TERM QUIZ

Use the following vocabulary terms to complete the sentences below. Not all the terms will be used.

> basic storage
>
> Disk Management
>
> dynamic storage
>
> extended partition
>
> free space
>
> logical drive
>
> mirror set
>
> partition
>
> VGA Mode
>
> volume

1. The MMC snap-in that you use to create and manage partitions and volumes in Windows 2000 is _____.

2. Before you can add disk space from another physical disk to a simple volume, making it a spanned volume, both physical disks must be using _____.

3. On a basic storage disk you may have a maximum of four _____(s).

4. A portion of a disk that is seen as a logical drive is a/an _____.

5. If you install a new video driver or make changes to your video adapter's configuration that causes the screen to be unusable, restart your computer in _____ and use Device Manager or Display Properties to undo the damage that you did.

LAB WRAP-UP

In this chapter you spent time reviewing both old and new methods of disk partitioning. You used the Disk Management snap-in to identify the configuration of disks. Then you changed the drive assignment for a CD-ROM drive and researched El Torito, a CD-ROM standard for booting a computer from CD-ROM. You practiced removing a boot sector virus with anti-virus software. Finally, you booted your computer up into VGA mode to explore your options for troubleshooting video problems.

LAB SOLUTIONS FOR CHAPTER 6

In this section, you'll find solutions to the lab exercises, Lab Analysis Test, and Key Term Quiz.

Lab Solution 6.01

Step 1. Figure 6-9 shows the solution for this step. To keep the graphic simple, we did not draw arrows to every object that matched an item. Therefore, your answer may vary in the following ways: E:, F: and G: are all logical drives in the extended partition, therefore, you may have indicated any or all of these for that item. Likewise, E:, F:, and G:, all are volumes with the NTFS file system. These should be the only variations in your answers.

FIGURE 6-9

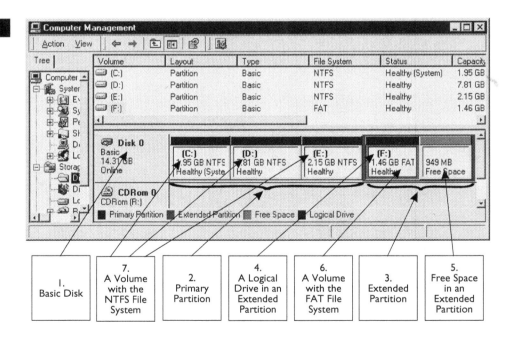

Step 2.

1. A single physical hard disk (0) is shown.

2. The disk is basic storage type.

3. Two partitions are shown.

4. The two partitions are the same type: primary.

5. Yes, another partition can be created on this disk because there is unallocated disk space. This new partition can be either primary or extended.

Step 3. Answers will vary. After answering the questions discuss them with your instructor or compare your answers with those of other students, and discuss and resolve any differences between you.

Lab Solution 6.02

Step 1. Right-click on the CD-ROM object in the Disk Management snap-in. Select Change Drive Letter And Path. In the Change Drive Letter and Path for (*d:*) dialog box click Edit. In the Edit Drive Letter or Path dialog box use the spin control (down arrow) to select R: and click OK. Click Yes to close the Confirm message box.

Open My Computer or Windows Explorer and browse to the CD-ROM drive, and confirm that it now has the drive letter R:.

lab
Hint
If the drive letter R: is not in the list of available drive letters, it may already be in use as a network (mapped) drive. In that case, select a different drive letter.

Step 2. Using the Google (www.google.com) search engine, we found a paper defining the El Torito Bootable CD-ROM Format Specification Version 1.0, dated January 25, 1995. The purpose of the standard is in the title of the paper: bootable CD-ROM format. The paper shows that Phoenix and IBM were the sponsors. It entails modifications to the system BIOS and modification of the system header on a CD-ROM disk. You enable a computer to boot from a CD-ROM by modifying the BIOS settings. Where formerly, BIOS gave us the following choices:

- A: then C:
- C: then A:
- C: only

A computer that complies with the El Torito standard will have additional choices that will include some, if not all of the following:

- A: then CD-ROM then C:
- CD-ROM then A: then C:
- CD-ROM then C: then A:
- C: then A: then CD-ROM
- CD-ROM only

Lab Solution 6.03

Steps 1 through 3. No further instructions are needed for these steps.

Lab Solution 6.04

Step 1. No additional instructions are needed.

Step 2. Use the directory command (DIR A: /AH) to view the contents of the diskette.

Step 3. No additional instructions are needed.

Lab Solution 6.05

Step 1. In the Display Properties dialog box you will find the screen area and the Colors settings on the Settings tab. When you click the Advanced button, an entirely new dialog box opens with several tab pages. You will find Font Size on the General page, and the Adapter Type on the Adapter page. You can verify that the adapter is working properly by clicking the Properties button on the Adapter page and looking in the box labeled Device status.

Steps 2 & 3. No additional instructions are needed.

Step 4. Answers will vary. You will see your normal preferences (background, etc.) and desktop objects. You may see a difference in the resolution, because the standard VGA driver may not support the resolution that your video driver supported. This is why you were asked to notice some of the settings. On some test machines, the VGA driver could support the screen area and color settings that were used previously, but on several test machines, we noticed that the VGA driver had to fall back to 640 by 480 pixels.

Step 5. The settings that you most likely will want to modify if you have a video problem will be on the Settings tab of the Display Properties dialog box. If you want to modify adapter settings or update the driver, click the Advanced button, select Adapter, then click the Properties button. This opens the Properties page of your video adapter. If you click on the Driver tab, you will see the buttons to view driver details, uninstall the driver, or update the driver, as shown in Figure 6-10.

The video adapter Properties page can also be accessed in Device Manager. Right-click on My Computer, select Properties, select the Hardware tab, and then click on the Device Manager button. In Device Manager, expand the Display Adapters node and double click the name of the adapter. This is the same page you accessed through Display Properties above.

FIGURE 6-10

Video Adapter
Properties with
Driver page

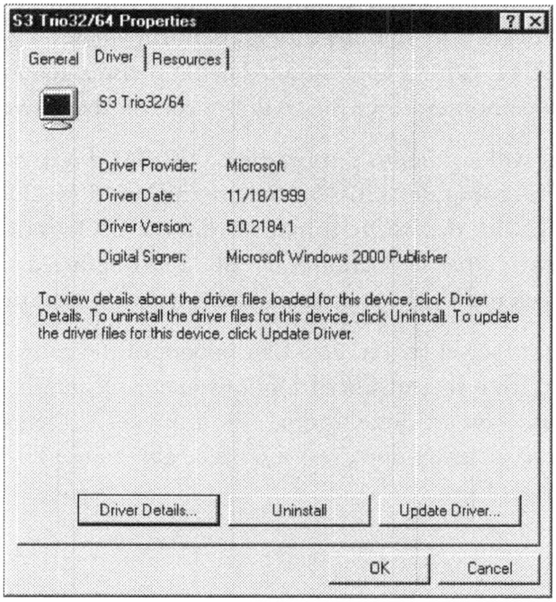

ANSWERS TO LAB ANALYSIS TEST

1. In order to have five logical drives on a single physical disk you can leave the disk as a basic disk (the default when you install Windows 2000) and add an extended partition in which you create four additional logical drives. But there are performance down-sides to this. A better strategy is to install Windows 2000, creating only the first partition in which you install the operating system. After the installation, use Disk Management to convert the storage type of the disk to dynamic. Dynamic storage supports more than four volumes, so after the reboot required by this conversion, you can create the four additional logical drives that are needed.

2. Sally can either leave it this way or change it. It is not a big deal, even though many of us also suffer from this same sense of order. If she cannot live with it, she can use Disk Management to change the drive letter assignment then reconfigure all the applications that depend on the old drive letter in the paths to their data files. This is a bigger problem if she actually installed software onto the new volumes before reassigning the drive letters. In that case we recommend that she not mess with it.

3. Maybe. Once you convert a disk from basic to dynamic, no operating system older than Windows 2000 can use that disk. You cannot convert it back. It is a one way street. You could do a little research on his special application and see if there is a newer version compatible with Windows 2000, or perhaps you can find a patch or script that can be run that will allow the version he is using to run in Windows 2000. If you can find such a solution, then you can install the software into Windows 2000, perform whatever procedure is required, and he can return to working with his application. Then it is also a good idea to remove all the Windows 98 files from the computer, since they will not run on that drive again.

4. If a computer will not boot up from the CD-ROM drive, the problem is with the CD-ROM disc or with the computer's BIOS. Because the Windows 2000 distribution CDs are bootable, the problem is with the BIOS. It may be that the BIOS is not El Torito compatible, or that it is compatible with that standard but the BIOS settings need to be adjusted. Boot into the BIOS setup and check out the boot order. Change it to one that puts the CD ahead of the hard disk.

5. If you have not logged on yet, do a hard reboot of the computer, press F8, then select Last Known Good from the Advanced Options menu. When the computer reboots, if the display works correctly, you are done. If not, restart, press F8, then select VGA Mode. When Windows 2000 starts up now, you should be able to use Display Properties or Device Manager to correct the problem.

ANSWERS TO KEY TERM QUIZ

1. Disk Management

2. dynamic storage

3. partition

4. volume

5. VGA Mode

7

Implementing, Managing, and Troubleshooting Hardware Devices and Drives

LAB EXERCISES

Y ou are now at the halfway point in your preparation for taking Microsoft MCSE Exam 70-210 and for working with Windows 2000 Professional. In Chapter 6 you studied the implementation, management, and troubleshooting of disks and displays. In this chapter you will perform similar tasks with other hardware devices. You will practice selecting power management options for mobile computers, look at the client side of offline files, use Device Manager to troubleshoot hardware problems, and install a USB device.

LAB EXERCISE 7.01

30 Minutes

Configuring Power Management for Mobile Computers

Among the standards for hardware support included with Windows 2000 are standards for power management. These include the older Advanced Power Management (APM) standard, and the newer Advanced Configuration and Power Interface (ACPI). ACPI improves on APM by adding stability and integrating power management into systems management. In addition to supporting clean power-down of components when they are not needed, this standard allows for components to again power-up in response to pre-configured network or modem activity.

The technology available on a computer depends on the BIOS support. If the BIOS only supports APM, then you are limited to the power management capabilities of that standard. If it supports ACPI, then all hardware that is also fully ACPI-compliant can be configured with appropriate power-down and power-up settings. You will need to identify the power management support available on a system. Finally, you will need to ensure that the supported power management standard is actually "turned on" in the BIOS. Now it is time to return to the lab and examine the power management capabilities of your lab computer.

Learning Objectives

By the end of this lab, you'll be able to

- Determine the power management standard being supported
- Determine appropriate power management settings based on usage
- View power management settings in BIOS setup.

Lab Materials and Setup

The materials you need for this lab are:

- A PC with Windows 2000 installed (preferably, but not necessarily, a laptop)
- The owner's manual for your computer

To best prepare for this lab exercise, read the introductory section as well as the section titled "Configuring Power Management" in Chapter 7 of the **MCSE Windows 2000 Professional Study Guide.**

Getting Down to Business

In the following steps, you will view the Power Options applet in order to identify the power management support on your lab computer. You will also review the Power Schemes and select the appropriate power options settings for various mobile computer scenarios.

Step 1. Open the Power Options applet in Control Panel and look for a tab identifying the power management support on your computer. Figure 7-1 shows the APM tab sheet in the Power Options Properties dialog box on a computer that has APM support. APM is an older power management standard. Your computer may support the newer standard, ACPI. If support for one of these power management standards is detected when Windows 2000 is installed, it will add the appropriate tab in Power Options Properties. You can enable or disable the support through that tab. If you find that power management is supported but disabled, enable it. This will require a reboot, after which you should open Power Options Properties for the next step.

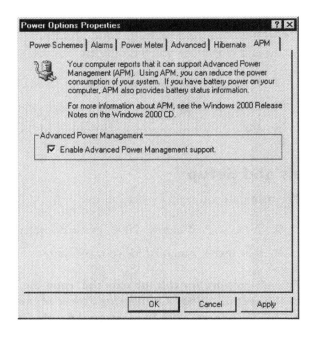

FIGURE 7-1

Power Options
Properties
showing APM
settings

Step 2. Open the Power Options applet in Control Panel and examine the power schemes and their settings. Figure 7-2 shows the Power Schemes on a laptop computer.

FIGURE 7-2

Power Options
Properties
showing Power
Schemes

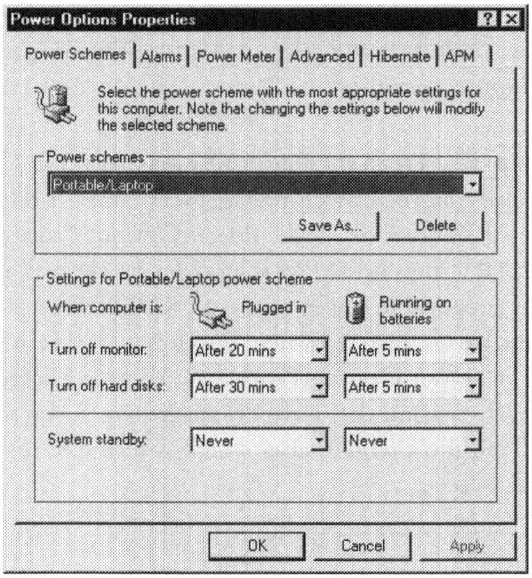

Leave the Power Options dialog box open and answer the following questions:

1. You are giving a 60-minute talk on Windows 2000 skills for end users during which your computer will be connected to a projector to display a PowerPoint slide show. It will also be plugged into AC power. Which power scheme will you use?

2. You have a two-hour layover in Detroit and plan to use the time to revise an article you are writing for the company newsletter. Which power scheme will you use?

3. You will be at a series of short meetings off-site and will have your laptop with you to take notes. Each meeting will be in a different room. Which Power Scheme will you use? Are there any other Power Options you should use?

Step 3.   Reboot your computer and access the BIOS setup program (also called the System Setup program). If necessary, consult your owner's guide for instructions on accessing and working with the BIOS setup. In the BIOS setup program, look through the menu pages and answer the following questions:

1. Identify the manufacturer and version of your BIOS.

2. Did you find information in the setup program indicating the power management standard supported by your computer's BIOS?

3. Was power management turned on or off in BIOS?

4. If permitted by your instructor, experiment with changing the BIOS power management options and record your results here.

lab
Warning   *Always record the current settings when you access BIOS setup. You can do this manually, by writing down each setting, or if there is a printer directly connected to your computer, simply press the Print Screen key on each page of the setup menu. You may have to manually advance the pages from the printer console, but we find we can usually fit two BIOS menu pages on each letter size page.*

Step 4.   Open Device Manager and expand the Computer object. If your computer supports ACPI, it will be listed, as shown in Figure 7-3.

LAB EXERCISE 7.02

Locating the Offline Cache Files

30 Minutes

You have recently studied the use of offline files in Windows 2000. You have been told that the offline files are files (usually data files) from a server share that are saved locally in a hidden folder named CSC in the system root (often shown in the notation %SYSTEMROOT%), which is the folder in which Windows is installed. You are concerned about the security of the files in this cache and, because this folder can grow, you plan to move it out of the folder in which Windows 2000 system files are installed to another partition on those computers that have a second partition. Microsoft provides a utility, Cache Mover, for this purpose in the Windows 2000 Resource Kit. You do not presently have the Resource Kit, but you will use your lab time to explore these client-side cache files.

FIGURE 7-3

Device Manager
showing support
for ACPI

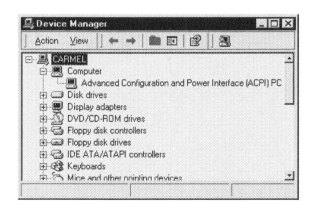

Learning Objectives

By the end of this lab, you'll be able to

- Locate %SYSTEMROOT%
- Locate the client-side cache folder used for offline files.

Lab Materials and Setup

The materials you need for this lab are:

- A PC with Windows 2000 installed and with more than one NTFS partition

To best prepare for this lab exercise, read the section titled "Managing and Troubleshooting the Use and Synchronization of Offline Files" and complete Exercise 7-2 in Chapter 7 of the **MCSE Windows 2000 Professional Study Guide.**

Getting Down to Business

In the following steps, you will first find the location of %SYSTEMROOT%, then view the location of the client-side cache folder on your lab computer and determine if you can access these files directly.

Step 1. Not sure about the system root location? As stated earlier, this is the folder in which the Windows system files are installed. If you are working on a test computer with more than one installation of Windows, this location may not be too obvious. Here is one of many ways to verify this location.

Open a command prompt and type the following command:

```
ECHO %SYSTEMROOT%
```

The result (on the line immediately following this command) is the path to the system root. As shown in Figure 7-4, the system root on this computer is C:\WINNT.

Close the Command prompt window.

Step 2. Use My Computer or Windows Explorer to locate the folder CSC in the system root of your lab computer.

FIGURE 7-4

Locating
%systemroot%

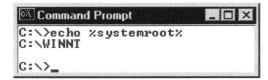

lab
(i)int *CSC is a hidden folder and is only visible if you set your view options to Show Hidden Files And Folders and deselect Hide Protected Operating System Files in Folder Options.*

You should see the client-side cache CSC folder under the system root, as shown in Figure 7-5.

Step 3. When you use offline files, you access your files using the same method whether you are online or offline. That can be through a mapped drive letter, a shortcut on the desktop, or any method you normally use to connect to the shared files. You never directly access the CSC folder. Open the CSC folder and answer the following questions.

FIGURE 7-5

CSC folder in system root

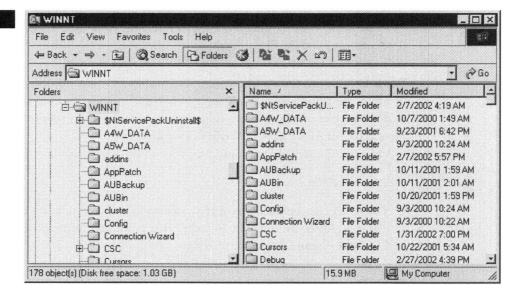

1. Can you identify the data in the CSC folder and subfolders?

_____

2. Considering your answer to question 1, do you see this as secure? Why?

_____

LAB EXERCISE 7.03

Troubleshooting a Network Card with Device Manager

45 Minutes

Device Manager is a tool that allows you to view and change device properties, update device drivers, and disable or enable devices. If you have worked with Device Manager in the past, you know it as a valuable tool. You reviewed the basics of Device Manager in Lab Exercise 1.03. Now you will learn to modify the viewing properties so that you can see hidden and non-present devices.

Hidden devices are devices, such as Non-PnP drivers that you do not normally change once they are configured properly. A non-present device is one for which there is a driver installed, but the physical device is no longer present. We have experienced situations in which we had error messages for a device that was no longer physically present, but found we could not remove the device driver because it was not visible in Device Manager. Simply using the View Hidden Devices menu option did not make this device visible. We learned of another setting that could only be made as an environment variable. In this lab you will work with the Show Hidden Devices setting, as well as the Show Non-Present Devices setting.

cross
Reference

To best prepare for this lab, read the two sections "Implementing, Managing, and Troubleshooting Input and Output (I/O) Devices" and "Installing, Configuring, and Troubleshooting Network Adapters" and complete Lab Exercise 7-3 in Chapter 7 of the MCSE Windows 2000 Professional Study Guide.

Learning Objectives

By the end of this lab, you'll be able to

- Turn on the View Hidden option in Device Manager
- Enable non-present devices to display in Device Manager
- Troubleshoot a non-present network card.

Lab Materials and Setup

The materials you need for this lab are:

- A PC with Windows 2000 installed

Getting Down to Business

In the following steps you will practice the procedures necessary to make both hidden and non-present devices visible in Device Manager, which you would need to do in order to remove a driver for a device that is no longer present.

Step 1. Open Device Manager and verify that the Show Hidden Devices setting on the View menu is not selected. Look at the contents in Device Manager, noticing the nodes that are displayed. Figure 7-6 is an example of Device Manager with Show Hidden Devices turned off.

Step 2. Turn on the Show Hidden Devices setting then record the differences you notice in Device Manager. Close Device Manager.

Step 3. Next, you will make non-present devices visible in Device Manager. To set this up, we will show you several Device Manager screen shots. The first one, Figure 7-7, shows one of our test computers in which we had two network cards. (The duplication is due to some special software, which creates a virtual Ethernet switch for each physical network card.)

FIGURE 7-6

Device Manager
with Show
Hidden Devices
turned off

We physically removed the Realtek network card, and then we tried to assign the static IP address that had previously been assigned to the Realtek network card

FIGURE 7-7

Device Manager
showing two
network cards

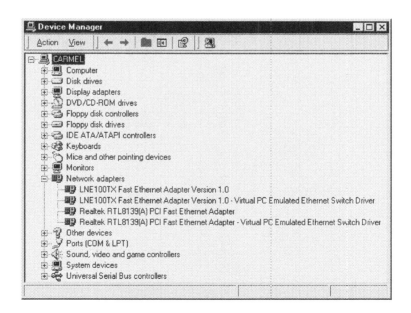

to the Linksys card. Because the Realtek card was no longer present, we received the following message.

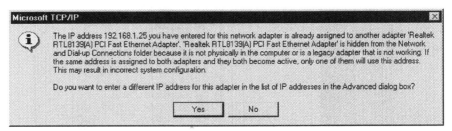

If Yes is selected and a different address is given to the card, this message will not appear again. But if No is selected and the existing card is given the IP address of the non-present device, this message will occur every time you click OK on the Internet Protocol (TCP/IP) Properties dialog box as long as the driver for the non-present device exists. Figure 7-8, shows that we cannot see the non-present device. It must be visible before we can remove the driver. We could not even see the non-present device with Show Hidden turned on.

To make non-present devices visible in Device Manager, you must use an environment variable. On your lab computer, add a new user environment variable in which the Variable name is devmgr_show_nonpresent_devices and the Variable

Device Manager
after removing
the Realtek
network card

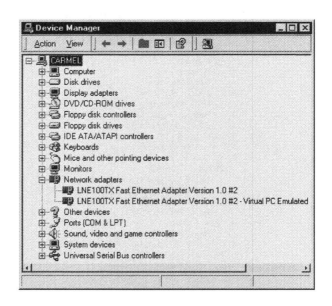

value is 1 (the number one). If you are not familiar with environment variables, use Windows 2000 Help to learn more about them and for directions for adding this value. The resulting Environment setting should look like Figure 7-9.

Step 4. Open Device Manager and observe the changes in the view. There will probably not be any difference unless you had such a non-present device. Figure 7-10 shows Device Manager on our test computer after turning on both Show Non-Present Devices and Show Hidden Devices. Notice that the icon in front of a non-present device is greyed out.

Now that the non-present devices are visible in Device Manager, they can be selected and deleted.

Close all open windows.

FIGURE 7-9

User
Environment
Settings

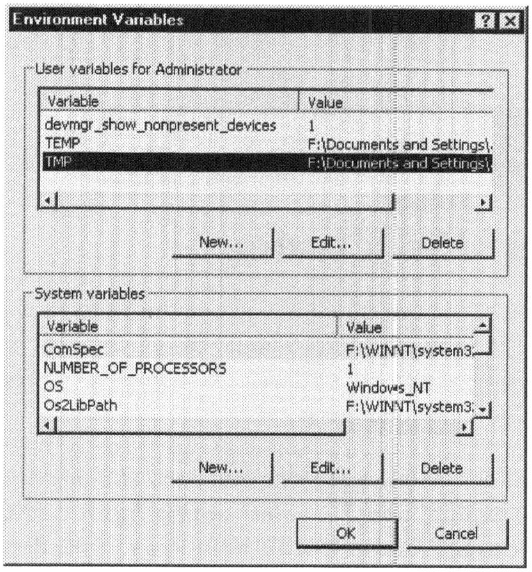

FIGURE 7-10

Device Manager
with Show
Hidden and Show
Non-Present
Devices turned on

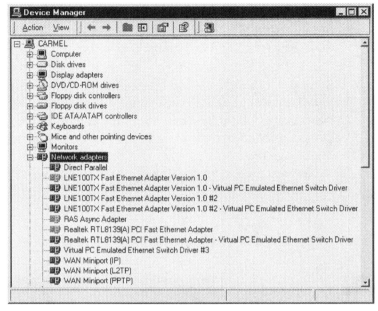

LAB EXERCISE 7.04

Installing a USB Device

30 Minutes

You have been called to the operations department to install a USB mouse on a Windows 2000 Professional computer. This is just the kind of simple task that users are timid about doing for themselves. It also can be done incorrectly, so you are going to practice it.

To best prepare for this lab, read the entire section titled "Implementing, Managing, and Troubleshooting Input and Output (I/O) Devices" in Chapter 7 of the MCSE Windows 2000 Professional Study Guide.

Learning Objectives

After you've completed this lab you will be able to:

■ Identify specific steps to take when installing USB devices

■ Identify specific steps to take when configuring USB devices

Lab Materials and Setup

The materials you need for this lab are:

■ One fully PnP desktop computer with an available USB port

■ Windows 2000 Professional installed on the computer

■ One USB mouse

■ The user manual for the USB mouse

■ The user manual for the computer

Getting Down to Business

The following steps were appropriate for the USB mouse that we installed in our test lab. We have included a cautionary Step 1 because a different USB mouse or other USB device may not have the same installation procedures.

Step 1. As with all new peripherals (or any hardware, for that matter), read all documentation that came with the USB mouse. Remove the mouse from its packaging, remove any packing material from within it, or taped or otherwise attached to it, and perform any assembly or other steps that are described in the documentation.

Step 2. Power up the computer and log on. After the desktop appears, plug the USB mouse into a USB port. The mouse should automatically be recognized without the need for additional software unless the mouse driver is not available with your operating system. Record your observations below, as well as any action you were required to take after installing the mouse.

lab **Warning**

Once again, read the instructions for your device! If it requires you to install software before installing the USB device, make sure you do it. Then make sure the system is running before plugging in a USB device for the first time. If it is not running when the device is plugged in for the first time, the system cannot recognize that it has been connected, and you will spend considerable time trying to figure out why an easy-to-install PnP device doesn't work. Sometimes, depending upon the device, it may take considerable effort to try getting back to square one if you didn't install software first.

Step 3.   Unplug the USB mouse and describe what appears on your monitor as a result of this action.

_____

_____

Step 4.   Plug the USB mouse back into the computer and record your observations below.

_____

_____

LAB ANALYSIS TEST

1. You are setting up a laptop for a traveling auditor who spends one week each month at a different regional office. During his stay in each office, he works at a station where his laptop is plugged in all day. Because of the nature of his work, he only uses the laptop in an office situation, never using it when he is in transit. What power scheme would be appropriate for the auditor?

   _____

   _____

2. Your company is rolling out Windows 2000 Professional to the desktop, but keeping Windows NT 4.0 on all the servers for another six months. One of your team members has questioned whether the Windows 2000 Professional computers will be able to enable offline files if the servers hosting the shared folders are not Windows 2000 servers. While this issue may not have been directly addressed in the lab exercises in this chapter of the lab manual, it was addressed in the *MCSE Windows 2000 Professional Study Guide.* Is it possible to enable and use offline files in this situation?

   _____

   _____

3. While working in the test lab with offline files, one of your co-workers could not find the client-side cache. Can you help him?

   _____

   _____

4. You want to move the client-side cache for offline files from %SYSTEMROOT% to another hard drive partition. Should you simply copy the CSC folder?

   _____

   _____

5. A sales person in your company has brought his laptop to you to remove a PS/2 mouse and add a new USB mouse. Windows 2000 was already installed on the laptop. You plugged in the USB mouse and booted up the computer, but the mouse was not recognized. What will you do next?

   _____

   _____

KEY TERM QUIZ

Use the following vocabulary terms to complete the sentences below. Not all of the terms will be used.

ACPI

APM

client-side cache

Device Manager

environment

Hibernate mode

hidden devices

non-present devices

offline files

USB

1. If a device needs a driver upgrade, you can use _____ to locate the device and initiate the upgrade.

2. You can add settings (variables) to the _____ through the System applet in Control Panel.

3. _____ will save the entire contents of memory on disk so that when you resume, you are back in the application in which you were working before initiating this mode.

4. Previously we used Explorer Briefcase, but now there is a better option called _____ for people who find they need to work with the same files whether they are on or off the network.

5. Windows 2000 supports two power management standards including the latest one, _____, which improves on the previous standard.

LAB WRAP-UP

In this chapter you worked with configuration, management, and troubleshooting tasks. You explored power management options for laptop computers, examined offline cache files, made view changes in Device Manager to enhance your troubleshooting capabilities, and installed a USB device. In the next chapter you will shift gears and work with tools that let you maintain stability, monitor and optimize system performance.

LAB SOLUTIONS FOR CHAPTER 7

In this section, you'll find solutions to the lab exercises, Lab Analysis Test, and Key Term Quiz.

Lab Solution 7.01

Step 1. Here are two methods for opening Power Options Properties:

1. Right-click on an empty area of the Desktop and select Properties. In the Properties dialog box, select the Screen Saver tab. On the Screen Saver page, click the Power button.

2. From the Start menu, select Settings | Control Panel. In Control Panel, double-click on Power Options.

Step 2.

1. The best power scheme to use during a slide presentation, especially if you do not have to run the laptop from battery, is Presentation.

2. We will assume that you will not have AC power available during this layover, unless you are a member of a gold card frequent flyer program. Therefore, you should select the Portable/Laptop power scheme.

3. This is another opportunity to use the Portable/Laptop scheme. You should also consider checking out the Alarms settings so that you get plenty of warning before running out of battery power. Additionally, if you have sufficient disk space, consider using the Hibernate option. Then, when you have to leave one meeting room, everything you had in memory will be stored on disk. When you bring it out of hibernation in the next meeting, it will be right where you left it. This is especially useful if you are working in the same document in all of the meetings.

Step 3. Answers will vary, depending on the version of BIOS in the lab computer. Below is a set of answers we generated on our lab computers.

1. Our two-year old test laptop has the SystemSoft MobilePRO BIOS version 1.01.

2. We did not find information in the BIOS setup indicating the power management standard supported, only in the Power Options menu in Control Panel, which identified it as APM.

3. There was a set of power settings under Enable Power Saving or Disable Power Saving. Power management was turned off in BIOS.

4. We found the power management capabilities within Windows 2000 were the same whether we turned this on or off in BIOS. However, we have experienced problems on some computers when we changed the BIOS setting for power management after Windows 2000 was installed.

Step 4.   No additional instructions are required.

Lab Solution 7.02

Steps 1 *and 2.*   No additional instructions are required for these steps.

Step 3.

1. I cannot identify the data in the CSC folder and subfolders.

2. I consider the CSC folder to be secure because it stores the files in a special format, and cannot be interpreted by my user applications.

Lab Solution 7.03

Step 1.   No additional instructions are required.

Step 2.   With Show Hidden Devices turned on, the Non-Plug and Play Drivers and Storage Volumes nodes display, as shown in Figure 7-11. These would be used for advanced troubleshooting. Close Device Manager when you have observed the differences.

Step 3.   To modify the user environment variable, right-click on My Computer and click Properties. In the System Properties dialog box click the Advanced tab,

Device Manager
with Show
Hidden Device
turned on

then click the Environment Variables button. Click the New button below the User Variables box. In the Variable Name box type: **devmgr_show_nonpresent_devices**. In the Variable Value box type: **1**.

Step 4. No additional instructions are required.

Lab Solution 7.04

Step 1. Reading the documentation is an important step, because with some devices you may actually be required to install software before connecting the device. This is true of some of the USB cameras we have tested.

Step 2. Answers will vary. When we installed a Microsoft Optical Wheel Mouse on a computer running Windows 2000 the message box titled Found New Hardware displayed with the following message: USB Human Interface Device. No additional steps were required.

Step 3. Answers will vary, but in general, this is a non-event, with no message appearing. If there is no other mouse on the computer, you will lose the mouse cursor.

Step 4. Observations will vary, but this is, once again, a non-event. In Windows 2000, the message described in Step 2 only occurs the first time that the mouse is installed. If this is your only mouse, you will regain the mouse cursor.

ANSWERS TO LAB ANALYSIS TEST

1. The most appropriate power scheme is Home/Office Desk because he does not plan to use the computer when it is not plugged in to power. Therefore he does not need one of the settings that preserves battery power.

2. Yes, it is possible to turn on and use offline files on a Windows 2000 Professional computer for a shared folder hosted on a Windows NT 4.0 server. The only requirement is that the share be a Microsoft share—that is, one using Microsoft's file and print sharing protocol. Offline files is a client-side service. However, if the share is hosted on a Windows 2000 computer (Professional or Server), you have additional server-side control, as shown in Lab Exercise 4.02 in Chapter 4 of this lab manual.

3. The client-side cache is saved in a hidden folder in the %SYSTEMROOT% location. First ask if he is looking in that location, then ask him to look in the Folder Options applet in Control Panel and make sure that his view options are set so that Show Hidden Files and Folders is selected and Hide Protected Operating System Files is deselected.

4. No, you should not simply copy the CSC folder to move the client-side cache. The method Microsoft recommends for moving this folder is to use the Cache Mover utility, found with the Windows 2000 Resource Kit utilities.

5. Remove the USB mouse and restart the computer. After the restart, log on and then plug in the USB mouse.

ANSWERS TO KEY TERM QUIZ

1. Device Manager

2. environment

3. Hibernate mode

4. offline files

5. ACPI

8

Monitoring and Optimizing System Performance and Reliability

I n this chapter of the lab manual, your first lab exercise is one without a direct relationship to the labs in the book. It is simply a lab for customizing the Start Menu that we felt should be included in this lab manual. This lab is followed by labs to supplement and complement the content and exercises of Chapter 8 of the *MCSE Windows 2000 Professional Study Guide* in which you study six certification objectives pertaining to monitoring and optimizing system performance and reliability.

You will explore tools and utilities that are part of *Windows File Protection* (WFP). This feature can guarantee the stability of Windows 2000 by preventing Windows system files from being replaced by altered versions during software and driver installations, which has been a major cause of instability of Windows in the past. In Exercise 8-1 in the *MCSE Windows 2000 Professional Study Guide*, you used the *File Signature Verification* tool to verify that all driver files were digitally signed. Then you looked at the *Driver Signing Options* settings on your computer. These settings control the level of enforcement of file signature verification. In the second lab in this Lab Manual chapter you will consider what action you should take when unsigned files are discovered. You will also use the *System File Checker* (SFC) utility, another WFP component, to maintain the integrity of protected files and the DLL cache on your computer, which is a folder containing a copy of protected files.

In Chapter 8 of the *MCSE Windows 2000 Professional Study Guide* you studied Performance Logs and Alerts, and determined the objects and counters to use to detect possible bottlenecks. In the third lab exercise in this chapter of the lab manual you will learn how to set alerts to warn you when certain thresholds for disk and network performance are exceeded.

And in the last lab exercise in this chapter you will explore the three Safe Mode options for starting up Windows 2000 when it will not start up normally. Once in Safe Mode you can troubleshoot and correct the cause of many startup problems.

LAB EXERCISE 8.01

Configuring the Start Menu

30 Minutes

On a Windows 2000 Professional computer, the default settings for the Start Menu do not include the Administrative Tools. By default, this folder is accessed through the Control Panel. In this lab manual we have instructed you to use various tools through Control Panel or through other default locations. As a computer support person, you will need to know the default locations of these tools as you work with various desktop computers. In this first lab we will explore just a few of the many ways that you can customize the Start Menu to make tools available directly from the Start Menu.

You will use the Advanced Properties of the Taskbar to first configure it to display the Administrative Tools from the Programs menu. Then you will use other settings in Advanced Properties to change the result of selecting the Start Menu items for Control Panel, Network and Dial-up Connections, and Printers. By default when you select one of these items from the Start Menu, a new folder window opens with a set of icons, and you can select the icon you wish to use. By modifying the settings for certain folders in the Advanced Start Menu Properties for Control Panel, each can be configured so that, rather than open a new folder when you select, say, Control Panel, another menu appears with the icons for the Control Panel applets that would normally be displayed in the Control Panel folder. You can then select the applet you wish to open without opening the Control Panel folder window. The same, of course, is true of several other folders.

Learning Objectives

By the end of this lab, you'll be able to

- Configure the Start Menu to display Administrative Tools
- Configure the Start Menu to expand Control Panel
- Configure the Start Menu to expand Network and Dial-up Connections
- Configure the Start Menu to expand Printers.

Lab Materials and Setup

The materials you need for this lab are:

- A PC with Windows 2000 installed

Getting Down to Business

In the steps below you will first add the Administrative Tools to the Programs menu, then change the Start Menu properties for Control Panel, Printers, and Network and Dial-up Connections.

Step 1. Verify that the Administrative Tools are not displayed on the Start Menu by opening the Programs menu. The default Programs menu should look like Figure 8-1.

Step 2. Use the Taskbar and Start Menu Properties to enable the display of the Administrative Tools on the Start Menu, as shown in Figure 8-2.

Step 3. Verify that the Administrative Tools are now on the Start Menu, as shown in Figure 8-3.

Step 4. Verify that selecting Control Panel from the Start Menu | Settings menu causes a new folder window to open, as shown in Figure 8-4.

FIGURE 8-1

The default
Programs menu

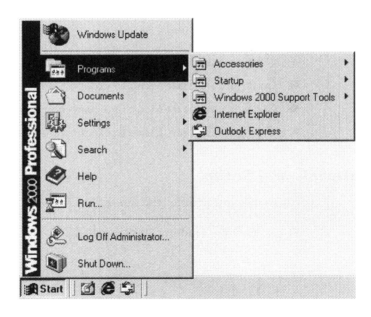

FIGURE 8-2

Taskbar and Start
Menu Properties
Advanced settings

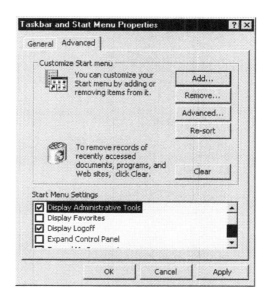

FIGURE 8-3

Start Menu with
Administrative
Tools

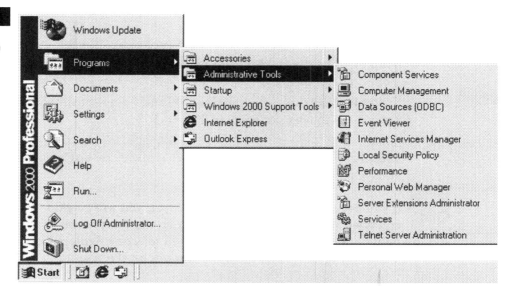

FIGURE 8-4

Control Panel
folder window

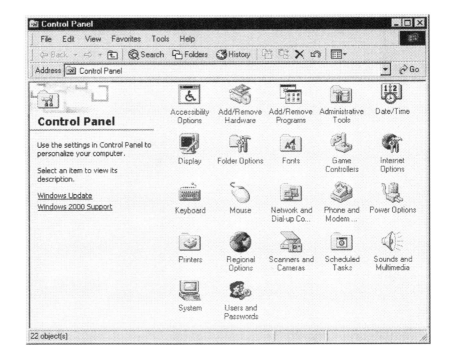

Step 5. Use the Taskbar Properties to enable the Expand Control Panel option.

Step 6. Verify that selecting Control Panel from the Start | Settings menu causes a new menu to open, as shown in figure 8-5.

Step 7. Repeat steps 4, 5, and 6 for Network and Dial-up Connections and for Printers.

lab

ⓗint

If you haven't already discovered this yet, you will be glad to know that you can open Windows Explorer focused on the Start Menu folders by simply right-clicking on the Start button, then selecting Explore from the context menu. Try it, as well as the other options on this menu.

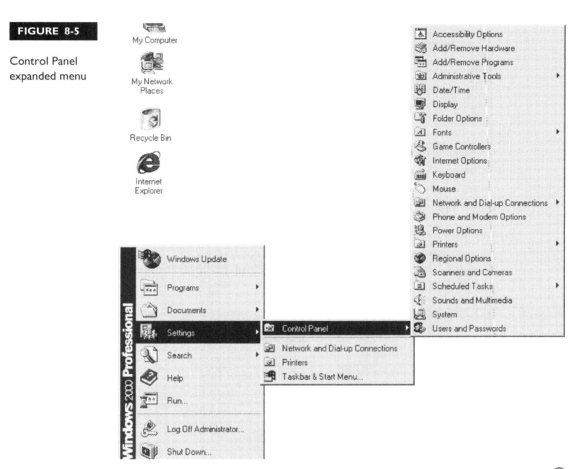

FIGURE 8-5

Control Panel
expanded menu

LAB EXERCISE 8.02

Managing and Troubleshooting Driver Signing

30 Minutes

You are now ready to explore the management and troubleshooting of driver signing. You learned in Chapter 8 of the *MCSE Windows 2000 Professional Study Guide* that by default Windows 2000 has file signature verification set to *Warn*. This means that when an Administrator is running an installation program, if the program attempts to install a driver file that has not been signed, he will receive a warning, and can choose whether or not to have the application proceed with the installation. This is how unsigned driver files get installed. Unless your organization has very rigid standards and tight controls on software installation you may find such files when you run the File Signature Verification Tool. If there are strong organizational controls in place, the default Driver Signing Options should be set to Block, which prevents the installation of unsigned files. In this lab you will examine the log file created when you run the File Signature Verification Tool and you will determine the next step to take if unsigned files are found. Then you will run the System File Checker (SFC), a component of WFP which verifies that protected files are valid and replaces problem files. In addition SFC checks the DLL cache (%SYTEMROOT% \SYSTEM32\DLLCACHE) and ensures that all required files are in this cache.

cross ꓤeference

To best prepare for this lab exercise, read the section titled "Managing and Troubleshooting Driver Signing" and complete Exercise 8-1, "Using Driver Signing," in Chapter 8 of the **MCSE Windows 2000 Professional Study Guide.**

Learning Objectives

By the end of this lab, you'll be able to

- Locate the files found by the File Signature Verification tool
- Determine the action to take when unsigned files are found
- Run System File Checker.

Lab Materials and Setup

The materials you need for this lab are:

- A PC with Windows 2000 installed
- The Windows 2000 Professional CD or access to a network share containing the source files
- Exercise 8-1 from the *MCSE Windows 2000 Professional Study Guide* completed

Getting Down to Business

This lab depends on the successful completion of Exercise 8-1 in the *MCSE Windows 2000 Professional Study Guide* in which you run the File System Verification tool (SIGVERIF.EXE). If you have not completed that exercise, do so now, (logged on as Administrator or a member of the Administrators group). Leave the Signature Verification Results window open on your desktop.

Step 1.   If the Signature Verification Results window is still open, record the files listed in the results window, being sure to note the folder location. If you have closed the results windows you can either run SIGVERIF again or use Notepad to open the SIGVERIF log file, SIGVERIF.TXT in %SYSTEMROOT%. If you are looking in the log file, search for "not signed." Record these files with their full paths below:

Step 2.   Decide whether these files should be removed. How do you determine if a file should be removed? Some organizations have such strict rules that there is no question; if the file is unsigned, it must be removed. Such a policy should also be backed up by a rigid standard defining exactly what software is authorized for each computer. If you are in such an organization, you will take steps to remove the unauthorized software. If not, you will investigate further to see if there are other reasons to remove the driver. Perhaps it will cause problems with other applications or with Windows. A good place to begin is by noting the path to the files as you did above, then using Windows Explorer to view the properties of the files. This will probably tell you what vendor installed this file, and usually what application is associated with this file. If this is an application that should not have been installed, consider removing the application through Add/Remove Programs or its own uninstall program.

lab
Hint

We have observed that organizations do indeed range from those with the very tightest controls over the end-user desktop to those that require their support people to support whatever the user wants to install on the desktop. The first extreme may seem draconian, but if you work in an organization that is at the opposite extreme, you will find yourself desiring stricter enforced standards because your job may be made much more difficult when you attempt to make software work. In reality, most organizations strike a balance that is somewhere between these two extremes.

If the files you have found are Windows 2000 system files that were altered by an application's installation, you should consider running System File Check (SFC) which will replace the altered file with the correct file from the DLL cache.

lab

Warning

After SFC replaces the modified driver file with one from the DLL cache, the application that installed the modified driver file may not work properly. However, leaving the modified file in place may cause Windows or other applications to work incorrectly. On the job, you will have to make a judgement call in situations like this, or just follow company procedure.

Step 3.   Close all applications before doing this step because SFC is very resource intensive, and it would affect the performance of the other applications. As practice for when you discover that Windows 2000 driver files were replaced, run the System File Checker now by opening a command prompt and entering the following command:

```
SFC /SCANNOW
```

There may be a delay, then you will see a message box with a progress bar that will display during the scan, as shown in Figure 8-6.

Insert your Windows 2000 Professional CD, if you see the following message:

After you insert the CD, the progress bar will reappear. When System File Checker is finished, any problem files will have been replaced, but SFC may not give you any feedback. Just close the progress bar message window.

FIGURE 8-6

Windows File
Protection
message with
progress bar

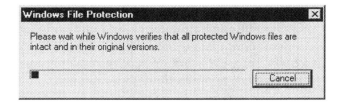

LAB EXERCISE 8.03

Monitoring Network and Disk Performance

30 Minutes

All administrators want to be proactive and avoid problems that could bring systems down and interrupt the day-to-day operations of the organization. Administrators of Windows 2000 Professional have some of the tools for proactive management of the desktop that are available to server administrators. One of these tools is the Event Viewer, which allows an administrator to view certain log files. Another tool is Performance Logs and Alerts through which you can also configure Alerts to watch for certain thresholds that can indicate a potential problem. You can combine these two tools by configuring an Alert to write to the Application Event Log when a certain threshold is crossed.

Learning Objectives

By the end of this lab, you'll be able to

- Determine thresholds for detecting a possible disk bottleneck
- Determine thresholds for detecting a possible network bottleneck
- Create and configure Alerts.

Lab Materials and Setup

The materials you need for this lab are:

- A PC with Windows 2000 installed

cross
Reference

To best prepare for this lab read the sections titled "Optimizing and Troubleshooting the Performance of the Windows 2000 Professional Desktop" and "Performance Logs and Alerts" in Chapter 8 of the MCSE Windows 2000 Professional Study Guide.

Getting Down to Business

In the following steps you will configure two alerts—one to be triggered when a certain disk counter value is exceeded; the second to be triggered when a certain network counter value is exceeded.

Step 1. Log on as Administrator (or a member of the Administrators group), open Computer Management, expand Performance Logs and Alerts, and set two alerts—one for disk performance and one for network performance. Use the Performance Alert Configuration Form shown in Table 8-1.

When you have completed this task, two new alert objects will appear under Alerts, as shown in Figure 8-7. At first the alert icons will be red, but once started, they will turn green.

lab
ⓗint

In this lab you set up alerts configured to write events to the application event log. On the job you would follow up on this by checking the Application Log on a regular basis—even daily—to watch for the alert event. Actually, such diligence is usually applied to servers, rather than desktop computers, in which case there is an entire set of daily, weekly, and monthly tasks most server administrators discipline themselves to perform in order to be proactive about system and network performance.

TABLE 8-1

Performance
Alert
Configuration
Form

Field	Disk Alert	Network Alert
Name	Disk Usage	Network Usage
Comment	Blank	Blank
Performance object	Physical disk	Network Interface
Counter	% Disk Time	Output queue length
Alert When Value is	Over	Over
Limit	80	2
Action	Log an entry in the application event log	Log an entry in the application event log
Start scan	At 10 minutes after current time	At 10 minutes after current time
Stop scan	After 1 day	After 1 day

FIGURE 8-7

Performance Logs
and Alert with
two New Alerts

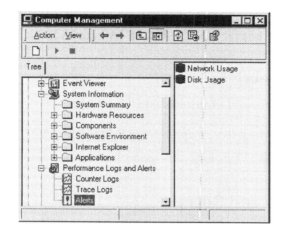

LAB EXERCISE 8.04

Exploring Safe Mode

45 Minutes

As you work with Windows 2000 Professional computers you may run into computers
that fail to start up normally. When this occurs immediately after installing a new
driver, but before you have logged on again, you may want to try the Last Known
Good option available from the F8 menu. However, we have found this to be
a rather fickle and limited tool. Also, it is not available on a computer with more
than one hardware profile. Therefore, you will more often find yourself using a
familiar, but improved Windows 9x-type Safe Mode option. Safe Mode starts up
without using some drivers and components that would normally be started. It loads
only very basic, non-vendor-specific drivers for mouse, VGA monitor, keyboard,
mass storage, and system services. Then you can work to locate and correct the source
of the problem. There are actually three Safe Mode variants available from the
Windows 2000 Advanced Options menu that you can access by pressing F8 during
bootup. They are Safe Mode, Safe Mode without Networking, and Safe Mode with
Command Prompt. If your computer will not start up in any form of Safe Mode,
you will need to try using the Emergency Repair Process (using the Emergency Repair
Disk) or the Recovery Console.

To best prepare for this lab, read the entire section titled "Safe Mode" in Chapter 8 of the **MCSE Windows 2000 Professional Study Guide.**

Learning Objectives

By the end of this lab, you'll be able to

■ Select an appropriate Safe Mode option

■ Define the differences between the Safe Mode options.

Lab Materials and Setup

The materials you need for this lab are:

■ A PC with Windows 2000 installed

Getting Down to Business

In the following steps you will explore the three Safe Mode variants available from the Windows 2000 Advanced Options menu.

Step 1.   Restart your computer. When you see the black text-mode screen with the Starting Windows message, press F8. The following text-mode menu will appear:

```
Windows 2000 Advanced Options Menu
Please select an option:

    Safe Mode
    Safe Mode with Networking
    Safe Mode with Command Prompt

    Enable Boot Logging
    Enable VGA Mode
    Last Known Good Configuration
    Directory Services Restore Mode (Windows 2000 domain controllers only)
    Debugging Mode

    Boot Normally

Use ↑ and ↓ to move the highlight to your choice.
Press Enter to choose.
```

lab
Hint *If your computer is configured to dual-boot, you will press F8 when you see the text-mode operating system selection screen. That screen does not display on a Windows 2000 computer that is not configured to dual-boot.*

Step 2. Select Safe Mode, and then press Enter. The following message will appear on a black text-mode background (with the build version at the top of the screen and Safe Mode in each corner of the background).

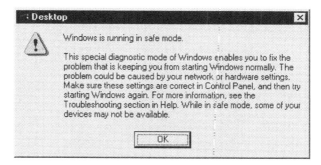

Press Enter. When prompted, log on as Administrator (or a member of the Administrators group). The desktop should resemble Figure 8-8.

FIGURE 8-8

Safe Mode GUI
desktop

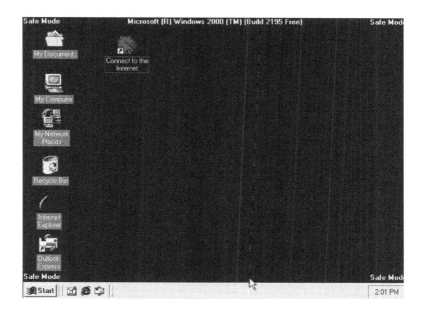

Step 3. Attempt to connect to a network share. Are you able to do so? Record your observations below:

_____

Step 4. Open Device Manager. This is the main tool you would use in Safe Mode. Notice that you can access the properties for all the devices. The status displayed for the device is the status for a normal startup. Even the network card will show as enabled. You can disable any suspect device or perform other tasks, such as removing or updating the driver.

Close Device Manager.

Step 5. Restart your computer in Safe Mode with Networking.

Step 6. Log on as an Administrator (or a member of the Administrators group) and attempt to connect to a network share. Were you able to connect?

_____

Step 7. Restart your computer in Safe Mode with Command Prompt. The same text-mode background will display while Windows 2000 completes the load process, then a small GUI box with the message Starting Windows 2000, followed by the Log On to Windows dialog box. Log on as you have done previously. After you log on, Windows 2000 would normally load your desktop, but this depends on the program EXPLORER.EXE, the GUI shell to Windows. In place of this GUI shell, Safe Mode with Command Prompt loads the command prompt (CMD.EXE) as the shell to the operating system, as seen in Figure 8-9. This is a handy option to remember if the desktop does not display at all, which, once you have eliminated video drivers, can be caused by the corruption of the EXPLORER.EXE program. From within the command prompt, you can delete the corrupted version of EXPLORER.EXE and copy an undamaged version. This requires knowledge of the command line commands for navigating the directory structure, as well as knowledge of the location of the file that you are replacing. Do not replace any files, but do take a few minutes to try out some of the command line commands like DIR and CD. Typing Help at the command line will give you a list of the commands, and typing a command name followed by "/?" (without quotes) will give you the syntax for that command. Have fun!

FIGURE 8-9

Safe Mode with
Command
Prompt

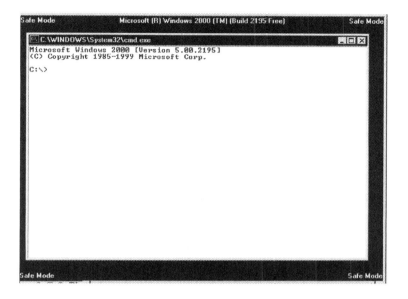

lab
ⓗint

Are you wondering where you would find an uncorrupted version of EXPLORER.EXE? You will find a compressed version of it in the I386 directory of the Windows 2000 CD. Open a command prompt and use the Expand command (it is installed with Windows 2000) to expand it. The syntax is:

    EXPAND *d:\I386\EXPLORER.EX_ PATH\EXPLORER.EXE*

In this command, the *d:* represents the drive letter of the CD-ROM drive and *PATH* represents the full path to the directory in which you want the file expanded.

Step 8.   To exit from Safe Mode with Command Prompt press CTRL-ALT-DEL, which will bring up the security menu. Select Shut Down from this menu.

Because you are required to log on in all three variants of Safe Mode, you can only access those resources to which you have rights or permissions.

LAB ANALYSIS TEST

1. One of your coworkers is confused by the many locations for various administrative tools and wants to configure his desktop so that he can quickly navigate to these tools from the Start Menu. Describe an option that you can tell him about.

   _____

   _____

2. The finance department is replacing 50 Windows 98 desktop computers with new Windows 2000 computers. They had a problem with previous versions of Windows that would occur after a new, third-party application was installed. One or more Windows shared system file(s) (usually a dynamic link library, or DLL file) would be overwritten with a new "improved" version, which often disabled some functionality for Windows or other applications. This usually happened when users installed unauthorized software themselves. The manager had the desktop support team clean out the rogue applications and instituted strict rules against his employees installing applications on their desktop. What can you tell this manager to assuage his concerns?

   _____

   _____

3. You have received an error message or seen a system event log message that the DLL cache is corrupt. What action can you take?

   _____

   _____

4. You are planning to configure Alerts on a few key desktop systems that must always perform as optimally as possible. You have selected several counters and corresponding thresholds, but you do not want to have to check log files in order to discover that a threshold has been exceeded. What option can you configure?

   _____

   _____

5. Another manager who presently has Windows 98 on 100 computers in her department is looking forward to the security provided by Windows 2000, but is concerned that Safe Mode will be a security hole because she heard that the system is not secure when in Safe Mode. How will you respond to this manager?

   _____

   _____

KEY TERM QUIZ

Use the following vocabulary terms to complete the sentences below. Not all of the terms will be used.

> Alerts
>
> counters
>
> Driver Signing Options
>
> File Signature Verification
>
> objects
>
> Safe Mode
>
> Safe Mode with Command Prompt
>
> Safe Mode with Networking
>
> System File Checker (SFC)
>
> Windows File Protection (WFP)

1. If you need to identify and locate unsigned files on your computer you can use the _____ tool, which you can start by using its executable name, SIGVERIF.

2. _____ detects attempts by other programs to replace or move protected files by checking the file's digital signature.

3. A command line utility, _____, can be used to scan and verify the versions of all protected system files, replacing overwritten protected files with saved versions from the %SYSTEMROOT%\SYSTEM32\DLLCACHE.

4. If the desktop will not display after startup, and you have eliminated the video driver as a problem, EXPLORER.EXE may be corrupted, and you should consider starting your computer in _____.

5. If you would like to proactively find potential bottlenecks before they become a problem, configure _____ with thresholds for critical counters of the objects you wish to monitor.

LAB WRAP-UP

In this chapter, you configured your Start Menu so that the Administrative Tools and Control Panel applets would be more readily available from the Start Menu. Then you worked with the File Signature Verification and System File Checker tools to troubleshoot problems with shared system files. You configured Alerts to monitor network and disk performance, and you experimented with the three Safe Mode startup options. In the next chapter you will work with user profiles, the desktop settings, and the accessibility services.

LAB SOLUTIONS FOR CHAPTER 8

In this section, you'll find solutions to the lab exercises, Lab Analysis Test, and Key Term Quiz.

Lab Solution 8.01

Step 1. Select Start Menu | Programs and verify that Administrative Tools is not listed. Then close the Start Menu.

Step 2.

1. Right-click on an empty area of the Taskbar to display the context menu for the Taskbar.
2. Click Properties on the context menu.
3. In the Taskbar and Start Menu Properties dialog box click on the Advanced tab.
4. In the Start Menu Setting at the bottom of the box, click to place a check in the selection box by Display Administrative Tools.
5. Close the Taskbar and Start Menu Properties dialog box.

Step 3. Verify that Administrative Tools have been added: click Start | Programs | Administrative Tools.

Step 4. Select Start Menu | Settings | Control Panel. Verify that the Control Panel folder window opens.

Step 5.

1. Right-click on an empty area of the Taskbar to display the context menu for the Taskbar.
2. Click Properties on the context menu.

3. In the Taskbar and Start Menu Properties dialog box click on the Advanced tab.

4. In the Start Menu Setting at the bottom of the box, click to place a check in the selection box by Expand Control Panel.

Step 6. Select Start | Settings | Control Panel.

Step 7. No additional instructions are required.

Lab Solution 8.02

Step 1. No additional instructions are required.

Step 2. On one of our test computers, File Signature Verification found two unsigned files, both with the INF file extension. We examined these files and discovered that they were installation scripts for software we had installed. Strictly speaking, these are not driver files, but instructions for installing drivers and other components. As such, they do not represent a problem unless they replaced the instruction files for another application. Obviously, if any other files were installed by this application into the protected folders, they were signed. We decided not to take any action on these files.

Step 3. No additional instructions are required.

Lab Solution 8.03

Step 1. To configure the Disk Usage Alert:

1. Right-click on My Computer and select Computer Management. In the Tree pane browse to System Tools | Performance Logs and Alerts. Right-click on Alerts and select New Alert Settings. In the New Alert Settings dialog box enter the name **Disk Usage**, then click OK. A new dialog box will open with the name of the new alert. In this box, on the General page, leave the Comment field blank. Click the Add button, which will bring up the Select Counters

dialog box. Select Use Local Computer Counters, then in the Performance object box select Physical Disk. Ensure that Select Counter From List is selected, then select %Disk Time, click the Add button, and then click the Close button. Back on the General Tab select Over in the box titled Alert When The Value Is. In the limit box enter **80**.

lab
(i)int

A %Disk Time value of 90 percent or higher is an indication of a possible hard disk bottleneck. We suggest using a lower threshold so that you can be more proactive in investigating a possible problem. If %Disk Time exceeds the threshold, investigate further. See the discussion under the topic "Disk Performance" in the **MCSE Windows 2000 Professional Study Guide** *to determine what you would do next.*

2. Click on the Action tab of the Disk Usage dialog box and select Log An Entry In The Application Event Log.

3. Click on the Schedule tab of the Disk Usage dialog box and configure the scan to start at 10 minutes after the current time and to stop after 1 day.

4. Click OK on the Disk Usage dialog box.

To configure the Network Usage Alert:

1. Right-click on My Computer and select Computer Management. In the Tree pane, browse to System Tools | Performance Logs And Alerts. Right-click on Alerts and select New Alert Settings. In the New Alert Settings dialog box enter the name **Network Usage**, then click OK. A new dialog box will open with the name of the new alert. In this box on the General page leave the Comment field blank. Click the Add button, which will bring up the Select Counters dialog box. Select Use Local Computer Counters, then in the Performance object box, select Network Interface. If there is more than one network interface listed in the instance box to the right, be sure to select the one you wish to monitor. Ensure that Select Counter From List is selected, then select Output Queue Length, click the Add button, then click the Close button. Back on the General Tab of the Network Usage dialog box select Over in the box titled Alert When The Value Is. In the limit box enter **2**.

lab
(i)int

An Output Queue Length of more than 2 is an indication of a possible network interface bottleneck.

2. Click on the Action tab of the Disk Usage dialog box and select Log An Entry In The Application Event Log.

3. Click on the Schedule tab of the Disk Usage dialog box and configure the scan to start at 10 minutes after the current time and to stop after 1 day.

4. Click OK on the Disk Usage dialog box.

5. Confirm that the new alerts appear in the Alerts detail pane under Performance Logs And Alerts. When you are done, close Computer Management.

lab
Hint

Notice that you can also configure Alerts to send a network message or run a program. Also, in this lab you are instructed to have the Alert stop after 1 day. This is only suggested so that Alert does not continue to run on your lab computer. You may choose another setting if you would like to continue monitoring your lab computer.

Lab Solution 8.04

Steps 1 and 2.   No additional instructions are required for these steps.

Step 3.   You are not able to connect to a network share because the network drivers have not been installed. You should get an error message that the network is not present or is not started.

Steps 4 and 5.   No additional instructions are required for these steps.

Step 6.   Yes, you are able to connect to a network share when using Safe Mode with Networking.

Steps 7 and 8.   No additional instructions are required for these steps.

ANSWERS TO LAB ANALYSIS TEST

1. You can tell your coworker about the Advanced Properties of the Taskbar where he can configure the Administrative Tools to appear in Start | Programs. He may also be interested in having the Control Panel, Printers, and other special folders expand from the menu. There are several Advanced options that allow you to do this.

2. You can tell the manager that you can control the installation of software on Windows 2000 computers by not allowing the users to be a member of a group with the right to install software on their own desktops. In addition, you can explain that Windows now has the capability to protect the shared system files that were overwritten in the past. Windows File Protection can be configured to prevent the replacement of protected files, and you have tools that will remove the unsigned files and restore the correct files from the DLL cache.

3. If you receive a message that the DLL cache is corrupt, you can run the System File Checker, which checks protected system files, and also verifies the integrity of the DLL cache. If it is damaged, it can be replaced by using either the Windows 2000 CD or the network share location from which Windows 2000 was installed.

4. In the properties for the Alert, you can configure the Action to Send A Network Message, then provide your user name, including the domain name, if you are logging on with a domain account, or the computername if you are logging on with a local computer account. If you are logged on as ssmith in the Houston domain, you would enter: **houston\ssmith** in the Send A Network Message To box. It would also be prudent to log an entry in the application event log so that you can refer to this after you have been notified.

5. You can assure this manager that a logon authentication is part of all three varieties of Safe Mode. Therefore, this is not a security hole.

ANSWERS TO KEY TERM QUIZ

1. File Signature Verification

2. Windows File Protection (WFP)

3. System File Checker (SFC)

4. Safe Mode with Command Prompt

5. Alerts

9

Configuring and Troubleshooting User Profiles and the Desktop Environment

I n this chapter of the lab manual, you will create a new default user profile—one that will be the beginning profile for every user who logs on to a Windows 2000 Professional computer using a local account. You will also learn more about the structure of a user profile and see how Windows 2000 reacts to a corrupt profile, after which, you will take steps to repair the profile. You will use local policy settings to control the desktop, add a program to the Quick Launch bar, and finally, you will experiment with some of the Accessibility Options and utilities available in Windows 2000.

LAB EXERCISE 9.01

Creating a Custom Default Profile

30 Minutes

Windows user profiles are similar, but not identical, in Windows 9x, Windows NT, Windows 2000, and Windows XP. We will not discuss the subtleties of the differences, but instead we'll talk about the basics of Windows 2000 user profiles in order to supplement the excellent discussion in the *MCSE Windows 2000 Professional Study Guide*. In addition to the folders and shortcuts discussed there, a very important file is part of each user profile. This file is NTUSER.DAT, and it contains the user's portion of the registry. Once a user logs on, the settings in this registry file are read into memory, applied to the user's desktop, and can be viewed in the registry editor under the HKEY_CURRENT_USER subtree. While the folders of a user profile contain files, folders, and shortcuts, this very important file in your profile contains your preferences—settings that are unique to you when you are logged on. These settings include the display background, screen saver, appearance, and other preferences. It also saves settings for many of your applications, such as the default directories in which you save your data, and other settings that are stored in the user's portion of the registry. Any changes you make to your preferences for the desktop and for many of your applications are also saved in this file. When you add shortcuts, files, and folders to the desktop, they are saved in the Desktop folder in your profile.

When a user first logs onto a computer, Windows creates a set of folders and files (including NTUSER.DAT) as their profile in a folder named with their username below the Documents and Settings folder. Where does this initial profile for a user come from? It is a copy of the Default User profile.

On several occasions we have encountered situations in which an organization wanted every user to start out with a default profile containing a certain set of drive mappings, special shortcuts on the desktop, and the corporate logo wallpaper. To do this on a large scale for the desktop computers in an organization with a Windows domain is beyond the scope of this book, but we will show you how to do this for a single computer. You might do this in a small organization with desktop computers in a workgroup.

Learning Objectives

By the end of this lab, you'll be able to

- Understand the role of NTUSER.DAT in a user profile
- Customize a profile
- Copy a profile
- Modify the Default User Profile.

Lab Materials and Setup

The materials you need for this lab are:

- A PC with Windows 2000 installed

cross
Reference   *To best prepare for this lab exercise, read the section titled "Configuring and Managing User Profiles" in Chapter 9 of the* **MCSE Windows 2000 Professional Study Guide.**

Getting Down to Business

In the following steps, you will create and customize a new user profile, then copy it to the Default User profile—actually replacing that profile. From that point on, any user logging onto your lab computer for the first time will start out with the new default profile.

Step 1.   Log on to your lab computer as Administrator (or a member of the local Administrators group). Open My Computer or Windows Explorer and browse to *%systemdrive%*\DOCUMENTS AND SETTINGS (where *%systemdrive%* is the drive in which the Windows system is installed). Notice the folders named with the user name for each user who has logged on to this computer, as well as for the Default User. Browse into some of the username folders and notice the NTUSER.DAT file. Do not alter, move, or delete this file. It is actually a registry *hive*, a file that contains a hierarchy of registry keys and values. You will also see a folder named All Users. This profile contains folders and shortcuts common to all users. When you install software that you wish to make available to all users of a computer, install the shortcuts for those programs into this folder.

lab
ⓗint

Default User will not be visible unless you have configured the view settings in Folder Options to Show Hidden Files And Folders.

When you have finished browsing through these folders, close My Computer or Windows Explorer.

Step 2. Create two new local user accounts using the planning form in Table 9-1. Each user should only be a member of the Users Group. Provide (and remember) a password for each user.

When you have created these users you can verify them by viewing the new accounts in Users and Passwords, as shown in Figure 9-1.

Step 3. Log off. Log back on as Newdefault. Notice the desktop. First of all, the Getting Started window will open because it is part of the Default User profile. Also notice the background appearance. This is also part of the default profile, saved in the NTUSER.DAT file of the Default User profile. Perform the following steps to modify the Newdefault profile:

■ Ensure that the Getting Started window does not open the next time this user logs on.

■ Modify the desktop using the Appearance tab of the Display Properties, being sure to make a change that makes it look very different from the default desktop with which it started.

TABLE 9-1	User name	Full name	Group(s)
User and Group Accounts Planning Form	newdefault	New Default	Users
	rholcombe	Rex Holcombe	Users

FIGURE 9-1

Users and
Password with
Newdefault user

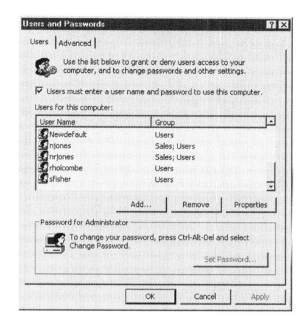

After you have made these changes to the desktop, log off.

Step 4.   Log on as Administrator (or a member of the local Administrators group). Open the System Applet in Control Panel and copy the Newdefault user profile to C:\DOCUMENTS AND SETTINGS\DEFAULT USER and when you are done, close out of System Properties.
Log off as Administrator.

Step 5.   Log on as rholcombe. If this is the first time you have logged on as this user, the desktop should reflect the changed profile you created and copied to Default User.

LAB EXERCISE 9.02

Troubleshooting a Corrupt Profile

30 Minutes

It is possible for a profile to become corrupted. This is more likely to happen in the case of a roaming profile, which is saved on a server and may become corrupted when a network connection fails while the profile is being saved. However, you may also see this occur to a locally saved profile. In either case, a corrupt profile is usually actual damage to NTUSER.DAT, and less often damage to the folders, shortcuts, and other files in the profile. Windows 2000 warns a user when their profile is corrupted, renames the folder holding their profile, and provides them with a temporary profile. It displays two message boxes: The first one informs the user that their user profile is corrupt and they must notify the administrator. The second one tells the user that because the profile is corrupt, Windows will give them a temporary profile, but any changes they make to this profile while logged on will not be saved. The user will receive these messages at every logon until an administrator corrects the problem. Windows renames the user's profile folder, adding a .BAK extension to the folder name. An administrator can log onto this computer, access this folder and fix the corrupted profile. In most cases, the problem is with the NTUSER.DAT file. However, as a practical matter, many administrators delete the entire profile when it is corrupted. This is the technique you will use in this lab. Then, when the user logs back on, a new profile will be generated from the Default User profile. The downside to this is that they will loose their data in My Documents. We suggest that you copy any data files out of My Documents before deleting the corrupted profile.

Learning Objectives

By the end of this lab, you'll be able to

- Troubleshoot a corrupt user profile
- Understand the process Windows uses when it encounters a corrupt user profile
- Repair a corrupt user profile (the easy method).

Lab Materials and Setup

The materials you need for this lab are:

- A PC with Windows 2000 installed

Getting Down to Business

In the following steps, you will first log on as a user and make several types of changes to the user's profile. Then, you will log off, log back on as an administrator, and deliberately damage the NTUSER.DAT file in that user's profile. When you log back on again as the user, you will see the messages Windows 2000 produces when it detects the damage and loads a temporary profile. You will then remove the damaged profile. The user will log back on and receive a new profile. Finally, you will observe and list what was lost versus what was not lost, between the damage and the repair process.

Step 1.   Log on to your computer as rholcombe and add a shortcut, a file, and a new folder to the desktop. Configure the Folder Options to Show Hidden Files And Folders. Arrange the icons on your desktop by name. Open up the Display Properties, select a different scheme then log off.

Step 2.   Log on to your lab computer as Administrator (or a member of the local Administrators group). Use My Computer or Windows Explorer to browse to \DOCUMENTS AND SETTINGS\RHOLCOMBE. Open the Properties for NTUSER.DAT and remove the Hidden file attribute. Close the Properties dialog, right-click on the file NTUSER.DAT, and select Open With. After you see the following message, click Open With again1.

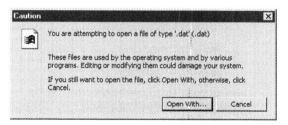

In the Open With dialog box, select WordPad and click OK. The file will load into WordPad, and look like garbage (a technical term), but it isn't garbage, yet. Not until you save it back onto itself. To corrupt the file, save it now, clicking Yes when you see the WordPad warning message. Figure 9-2 shows this message against the display of NTUSER.DAT in WordPad. After you have saved the file, exit WordPad.

Step 3.   Log off as Administrator. Log on as rholcombe. You will see the following message:

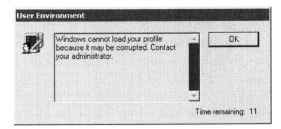

FIGURE 9-2

WordPad
warning message

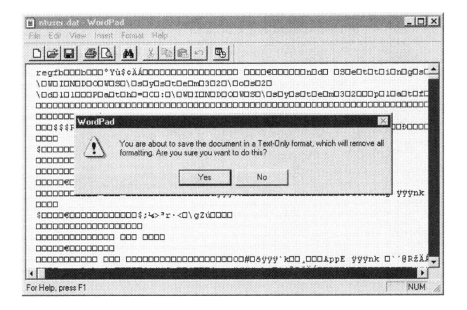

A user seeing this message should immediately call the administrator. The user will have a temporary profile loaded, so work is not interrupted, but they will not be able to save any changes they make to their profile, as the next message informs them:

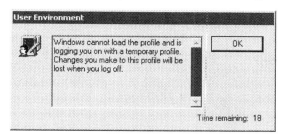

The user will continue to see these messages at every logon until an administrator corrects this problem. Inform the user to save all new data to a location outside of their profile folders (in other words, not on the Desktop or in My Documents).

1. Are the file, folder, and shortcut you created earlier on the desktop?

2. Are the folder view options set to show hidden files?

3. Is the desktop using the scheme you selected?

Step 4.   Create a new file on the desktop.
Create a new file in the My Documents folder.
Configure the Display properties to use another scheme.
Log off.

Step 5.   Log on as Administrator (or a member of the Administrators group) and use My Computer or Windows Explorer to browse to \DOCUMENTS AND SETTINGS. Notice that the RHOLCOMBE folder has been renamed RHOLCOMBE.BAK. Delete this folder and its contents. If there are any other folders in Documents and Settings with rholcombe in the filename portion of the folder, delete them as well.

lab
ⓗint

This is just one solution. For a "graduate level" solution, see the Microsoft document titled "HOW TO: Restore a User Profile in Windows 2000 (Q314045)," which you can find by doing a search on the Q number at www.microsoft.com/technet. To test this, you will need a test computer, a rainy Saturday, and lots of patience!

Step 6. Log on as rholcombe. Review the changes you made in Step 1 and determine which changes survived the corruption and repair process. Record your observations below, then log off.

LAB EXERCISE 9.03

Controlling the Desktop with Group Policy Settings

60 Minutes

As a desktop support analyst or administrator you may not need to learn a great deal about how group policies can control the desktop. This is because any organization with a Windows 2000 (or .NET) Active Directory domain can set group policy centrally. The specifics of how this is done at that level is far beyond the scope of this book. Suffice it to say that if your Windows 2000 Professional computers are in such a domain, the preferred and most powerful way to control the desktop is through group policies set centrally; in which case, most administrators and desktop support people will not be concerned with setting Local Policy. If you do set Local Policy on a computer in a domain, it will be overridden by any conflicting settings set at a higher level.

What follows is a very brief description of how policies are set. When a computer starts up, all computer Configuration policies for that computer are applied (from all sources). While the computer is running, these policies are also refreshed (meaning that new or changed policies will be applied) several times a day at a preconfigured interval.

When a user logs onto a Windows 2000 computer, all User Configuration policies that are enabled (from all sources) are applied to that user's profile. While the user is logged on, these User Configuration policies are refreshed at a preconfigured interval. Some user policy changes will be applied while the user is logged on, while others that might disrupt the user if applied while they are logged on will not take effect until the next time the user logs on.

Learning how to set Local Policies has value for several reasons. For one, it is a method for configuring and troubleshooting desktop settings, which is an exam objective. Another reason is that you may support computers that are not members of a domain, especially in a small organization, and this would be the only way to set policies. A third reason is that learning local policies is a step toward learning group policies in general. So, if you expect to go on to become a domain administrator, consider learning and working with local policies as training wheels for learning and working with Active Directory Group Policies. Just like using training wheels on your first two-wheeler, working on policies at the local level limits the damage you can do.

Learning Objectives

By the end of this lab, you'll be able to

- Use local policies to control the Desktop
- Test the effect of setting local policies.

Lab Materials and Setup

The materials you need for this lab are:

- A PC with Windows 2000 installed

 To best prepare for this lab exercise, read the section "Configuring and Troubleshooting Desktop Settings" and complete Exercise 9-5 in Chapter 9 of the **MCSE Windows 2000 Study Guide.**

Getting Down to Business

In the following steps you will control desktop settings on a Windows 2000 Professional computer through local policies, and then you will observe the effect on the currently logged-on user to see which policies took effect without logging off and on again. You will then log off and log on again to update any policies that did not take effect. All policies should take effect for any user who logs on to this machine. To test that, you will log on as another user and see if the policies also apply to that user.

Step 1. Log on as Administrator (or a member of the local Administrators group). Open the Local Computer Policy snap-in that you configured in Exercise 9-5 in the *MCSE Windows 2000 Professional Study Guide*. Alternatively, review the Help topic "Using MMC snap-ins," and create an MMC console, adding the Group Policy snap-in focused on the Local Group Policy Object. Name the console and save it on your desktop. We saved ours as Local Policy.

Step 2. Expand Local Computer Policy | User Configuration | Administrative Templates | Start Menu & Taskbar. You will enable each policy by double-clicking on it to open Properties, then selecting Enabled, as shown in Figure 9-3. Click OK. Enable the settings for the following policies:

- Remove Network & Dial-up Connections from Start Menu
- Disable personalized menus

FIGURE 9-3

An Enabled Policy

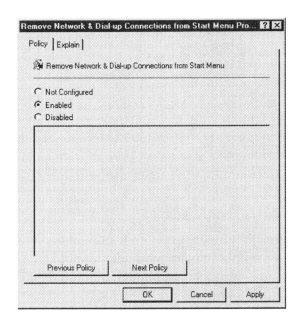

Step 3. Expand Local Computer Policy | User Configuration | Administrative Templates | Desktop. Enable the settings for the following policies:

- Hide My Network Places icon on desktop
- Prohibit user from changing My Documents path

lab
Hint *Curious about these settings? Each policy under Administrative Templates has an Explain tab that tells you about that policy. Sadly, this is not true of all policy settings, but fortunately, the Administrative Templates are the ones you are most likely to use.*

Step 4. Expand Local Computer Policy | User Configuration | Administrative Templates | Control Panel. Enable the settings for the following policy:

- Hide Specified Control Panel Applets: Display

lab
Hint *Hide Specified Control Panel Applets is different from many of the other settings. When you select Enabled, read the instructions in the box below to add Display. See Figure 9-4.*

FIGURE 9-4

Properties for
Hide Specified
Control Panel
Applets

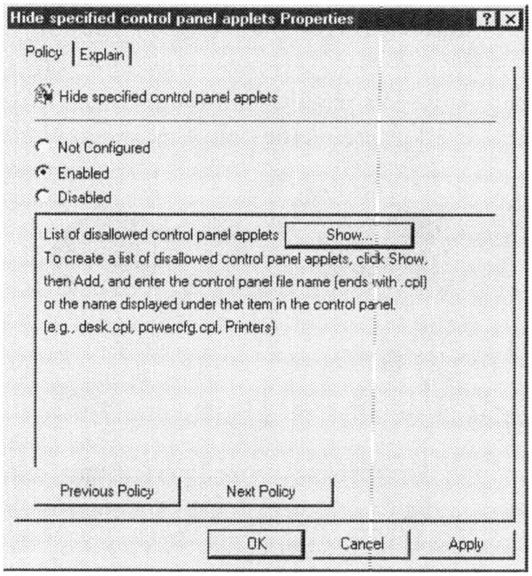

TABLE 9-2	Policy	Enabled? (Yes/No)
Policy Status Table	Remove Network & Dial-up Connections from Start Menu	
	Disable personalized menus	
	Hide My Network Places icon on desktop	
	Prohibit user from changing My Documents path	
	Hide Specified Control Panel Applets: Display	

Step 5. After you have completed setting these policies, close out of the console and see which settings have taken effect immediately for the logged on administrator. Record the results in Table 9-2.

Step 6. If any of the policies did not take effect, log off and log on again as the same user and recheck the policies that were not enabled before.

Step 7. Log off and log on as a different user and verify that the policies also affect this user. All local policies apply to all users who log on to this computer.

Step 8. When you have verified the policy settings, clean up your computer so that these settings do not interfere with the remaining lab exercises in this book. To do this, log off and log back on as Administrator (or a member of the Administrators group) and remove all the policy settings. This means selecting each one that was enabled and changing the policy setting to Not Configured.

LAB EXERCISE 9.04

20 Minutes

Adding a Program to the Quick Launch Bar

Windows 2000 reserves a small area of the Taskbar, just to the right of the Start button as the Quick Launch bar. An icon placed in the Quick Launch bar will start up when you simply point and click on it. By default, this bar contains three icons:

Show Desktop, Launch Internet Explorer Browser, and Launch Outlook Express. You don't want to get carried away adding icons to this bar, because it can get rather crowded and maybe confuse more than it helps. However, a user might have a favorite program that he launches frequently. This gives him yet another option for doing just that.

Once again, imagine that you are part of a team that is rolling out Windows 2000 Professional, and you will be responsible for ongoing support of the desktops. You will test adding an application to the Quick Launch bar so that you can offer this option to the users you support. Because this setting stays with a profile, you must be logged on as the user who will use this setting in order to configure it at the desktop. This could be a setting that you configure in a profile that you are creating as a default profile for a computer, as you did in Lab Exercise 9.01.

lab
Hint *To best prepare for this lab exercise, read the Windows 2000 Help topic "Add a program to the Quick Launch bar," which you will use as a guide.*

Learning Objectives

By the end of this lab, you'll be able to

■ Add a program to the Quick Launch bar

■ Test the use of the Quick Launch bar.

Lab Materials and Setup

The materials you need for this lab are:

■ A PC with Windows 2000 installed

Getting Down to Business

In the following steps you will use the Windows 2000 online Help as a guide to add a program to the Quick Launch bar.

Step I. Log on as a non-administrator user. Open Windows 2000 Help program and search on "quick launch" (include the quotes). Then, using the instructions under

Add a program to the Quick Launch bar, add the program file WORDPAD.EXE to the Quick Launch bar, as shown here.

Step 2.   Launch the WordPad program from the Quick Launch bar. Close WordPad when you are done.

LAB EXERCISE 9.05

Configuring Accessibility Options

45 Minutes

In this chapter you have looked at various ways to customize the desktop—sometimes for control, other times to make things more convenient for the user. It is important to make the computing experience of all users as comfortable as possible, because for many, the computer is a tool that they use their entire working day. In this last lab of this chapter you will try out some of the Accessibility options that you may want to apply to desktops when they help meet the individual needs of the user. These features will help you and your company to comply with the Americans with Disabilities Act (ADA).

cross
Reference

To best prepare for this lab, read the entire section titled "Configuring and Troubleshooting Accessibility Services" and complete Exercise 9-6 in Chapter 9 of the **MCSE Windows 2000 Professional Study Guide.**

Learning Objectives

By the end of this lab, you'll be able to

■   Enable Display options.

Lab Materials and Setup

The materials you need for this lab are:

■   A PC with Windows 2000 installed

■   A sound card and speakers are needed to do Step 3

Getting Down to Business

In the following steps you will test some of the options available from the Accessibility Options applet in Control Panel as well as those available from Start Menu | Programs | Accessories | Accessibility.

lab
ⓘint *To learn more about the Accessibility for Disabilities Act, check out www.usdoj.gov/crt/ada/adahom1.htm.*

Step 1.   Log on as a non-administrator user. Open Accessibility Options in Control Panel and turn on the High Contrast display option. Close Accessibility Options. Your desktop will be "transformed" into something like Figure 9-5. As you can see, it is definitely "contrasty." What is not clear in this gray-scale screen print is that, in addition to the black background and white letters, certain elements are brightly colored. The current window (Control Panel) has a bright yellow border, the Taskbar has a bright green border, and bright purple is used in the title bar of the active window as well as the currently selected object (Accessibility Options). You will want to work with this desktop until it suits the user by going back to Accessibility Options and trying another high-contrast color scheme. You can also enable the use of a shortcut key combination to switch between a normal desktop and the configured high contrast desktop. After you have experimented with other high-contrast color schemes, configure your desktop as you would like to normally work.

Step 2.   Rather than modify your entire desktop, you can use a portion of the desktop as a magnifying lens. To do this, run the Magnifier utility that can be found at Start | Programs | Accessories | Accessibility | Magnifier. When you first enable this program you will see the following message:

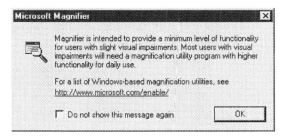

Click to select Do Not Show This Message Again, then click OK to close the message.

FIGURE 9-5

The High
Contrast
Desktop

The Magnifier Settings window allows you to modify the settings to suit your needs. The area around the mouse pointer is magnified in the magnifier lens at the top of the desktop as shown in Figure 9-6. Optionally, open WordPad and create or edit a document.

After experimenting with Magnifier return your desktop to the settings you prefer.

Step 3. Windows 2000 has a really cool program, Narrator, that uses a speech synthesizer to interpret the desktop for you, including reading menus, icons, dialog boxes, what you type, and more. To run Narrator, select Start | Programs | Accessories | Accessibility | Narrator. When you first start it, Narrator will interpret the following message, as it appears on the screen:

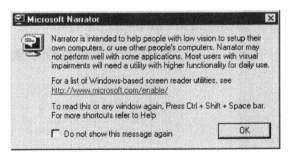

Click OK to close the message box. The Narrator configuration setting box will also be open on your desktop. Experiment with the settings, including those in this box (see Figure 9-7).

Open WordPad and create or edit a document.

FIGURE 9-6

The desktop with
Magnifier

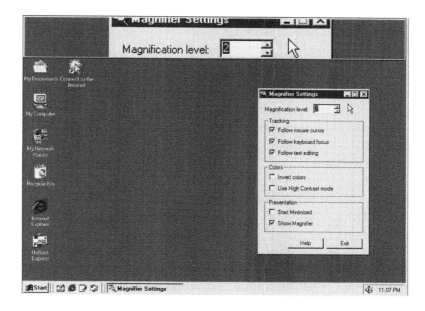

When you have finished experimenting with Narrator, close all open windows
and return your desktop to the settings you prefer.

FIGURE 9-7

The Narrator
configuration
box with Voice
Settings

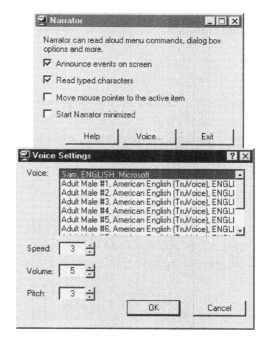

LAB ANALYSIS TEST

1. Your team leader on the rollout team is questioning the value of all the time the team members have spent in the test lab. He is curious to know if you have learned enough to solve some of their actual desktop problems. He has asked you how you would configure a Windows 2000 Professional computer so that each new user on that computer had the standard set of shortcuts on the desktop and the corporate wallpaper on the background. Explain how you would do this.

   _____

   _____

2. Samantha from the accounting department has called you. Theirs was one of the first departments to receive the new Windows 2000 Professional computers. After a month without problems, she logged on this morning and received a message that her profile is corrupted and she should call the administrator. She is sure that a second message said that none of her work can be saved, and she's afraid to log off. She also is worried that she does not have her normal shortcuts on the desktop. What will you tell Samantha, and what will you do to correct the problem?

   _____

   _____

3. You have carefully configured local policies on the Windows 2000 computers in the shipping department. When you tested these policies in the test lab they worked, but you now notice that not all the policies have taken effect on the computers in shipping. What could be the problem?

   _____

   _____

4. Harry, the staff supervisor in the accounting department, is a very orderly person. He keeps his physical work area neat and tidy at all times. He has removed most of the icons from his desktop. He would like a way to quickly open the general ledger application without cluttering his desktop. What solution can you offer Harry?

   _____

   _____

5. Marissa in sales needed a visual aid. You helped her to test the options available to her, and she selected the Narrator utility. She is delighted, but her co-workers in neighboring cubicles have complained that the voice is annoying. What would you try next?

   _____

   _____

KEY TERM QUIZ

Use the following vocabulary terms to complete the sentences below. Not all the terms will be used.

> Accessibility Options
>
> Default User
>
> Group Policy
>
> High Contrast
>
> Local Policy
>
> Magnifier
>
> NTUSER.DAT
>
> Quick Launch bar
>
> Roaming profile
>
> User Profile

1. The name of the profile given to a user at their first logon is _____.

2. The group of settings that are saved on a computer to be applied at each start up and refresh period is called the _____.

3. When your computer is a member of a domain, the group of settings that are saved in the domain and applied at startup, logon, and refresh are called collectively _____.

4. The _____, located on the Taskbar, holds program icons that you can single-click to start.

5. Someone with a slight visual impairment may benefit from the _____ utility.

LAB WRAP-UP

In this lab you tested several methods of configuring and troubleshooting user profiles and the desktop environment. You began by creating a custom default profile. Then you purposely corrupted a user profile in order to see how and if Windows 2000 handles this problem, which you eventually corrected. You modified local policy and tested the settings on two users. You also added a program icon to the Quick Launch bar, and finally you tested several Accessibility Options.

LAB SOLUTIONS FOR CHAPTER 9

In this section, you'll find solutions to the lab exercises, Lab Analysis Test, and Key Term Quiz.

Lab Solution 9.01

Step 1. No additional instructions are required for this step.

Step 2. By now you know how to create a user account through Computer Management | Users And Groups or through Control Panel | Users And Passwords. In Lab Exercise 4.01 in Chapter 4 of this lab manual, the solution included using Computer Management, while Exercise 9-1 in the *MCSE Windows 2000 Professional Study Guide* provided the steps for using Control Panel | Users And Passwords. In this step, since you are only creating a single user, consider using Users and Passwords.

Step 3. Log on as Newdefault. Clear the checkbox in the lower left-hand corner of the Getting Started window so that it does not open every time this user logs on, then close it. Use the Desktop properties to modify the appearance of the Desktop. For instance, we selected the Rose scheme to have a scheme that is distinctive. On the job, if your corporate logo is available as a bitmap file, you would probably add it as wallpaper on the Background page. In addition to the Display properties, you would also add the standard drive mappings that are required by all the users of this computer.

Step 4. Our favorite way to open the System applet is to right-click on My Computer and select Properties. In System Properties, click on the User Profiles tab. In the list of profiles stored on this computer, select *computername*\Newdefault and click Copy To. In the Copy To dialog box click the Browse button. Browse to C:\DOCUMENTS AND SETTINGS\DEFAULT USER. Click OK. In the Copy To dialog box click Change under Permitted To Use. In the Select User or Group dialog box select Authenticated Users, and click OK. Click OK to close the Copy To dialog box. A confirm copy message box will open stating that the current contents of this directory will be deleted. Click Yes. After that box closes, you will be back in System Properties User Profiles. Notice that the Default User is not listed. This is normal because it is a special profile that we do not normally modify. Click OK to close the System Properties box.

Step 5. No additional instructions are required for this step.

Lab Solution 9.02

Step I. You can add a shortcut to any program, file, folder, computer, etc., you wish. Here are instructions for creating a shortcut for Windows Explorer: Right click on an empty spot on the desktop and select New | Shortcut. In the Create Shortcut dialog box click the Browse button and browse to *%systemroot%*\EXPLORER (the one with the computer icon), then click OK. Ensure that the path resembles C:\WINNT\EXPLORER.EXE (the drive and directory name may be different, but the file name should be the same). Click Next. In the Type A Name For The Shortcut box type Windows Explorer, and then click Finish.

You may create a file any way you wish. Here are instructions for creating an RTF (Rich Text Document) file: Right-click on an empty spot on the desktop and select New | Rich Text Document.

You may create a folder any way you wish. Here are instructions for creating a folder named Personal on the desktop: Right-click on an empty spot on the desktop and select New | Folder.

To configure the Folder Options to Show Hidden Files And Folders, open My Computer or Windows Explorer, then select Tools | Folder Options | View. In the Advanced Settings, list select Show Hidden Files And Folders and then deselect the check box by Hide File Extensions For Known File Types. Click OK.

To arrange the icons on your desktop by name, right-click on an empty spot on the desktop and select Arrange Icons | By Name.

To apply a different scheme to the desktop, open Display, select Appearance, select a different scheme, then click OK. The new scheme will be applied to your desktop.

Log off.

Step 2. To remove the Hidden attribute, right-click on the file and select Properties. At the bottom of the General tab locate the Hidden attribute and deselect it (remove the check from the box). Click OK to close the NTUSER.DAT Properties.

The instructions for corrupting the file are complete.

Step 3.

1. The file, folder, and shortcut created earlier are not on the desktop.
2. The folder view options are not set to show hidden files.
3. The desktop is not configured to use the scheme the user selected at the last logon.

Steps 4 and 5. No additional instructions are required for these steps.

Step 6. None of the changes survived.

Lab Solution 9.03

Steps 1 through 3. No additional instructions are required for these steps.

Step 4. In the Policy list, double-click on Hide Specified Control Panel Applets, select Enabled, click the Show button, then in the Show Contents window (see below) click Add, then in the Add Item box enter **Display**. Click OK three times to return to the Local Policy snap-in.

Step 5. Your completed table should match Table 9-3. Open the Start menu to see if Network and Dial-up Connections has been removed from the settings. Look in Start | Programs to see if personalized menus have been disabled. Look on the Desktop to see if My Network Places has been removed. Right-click on My Documents as an attempt to change the path in the Target box.

TABLE 9-3	Policy	Enabled? (Yes/No)
Policy Status Table (filled out)	Remove Network & Dial-up Connections from Start Menu	Yes
	Disable personalized menus	Yes
	Hide My Network Places icon on desktop	No
	Prohibit user from changing My Documents path	Yes
	Hide specified control panel applets: Display	Yes

Step 6. Before logging off, all policies except the Hide My Network Places Icon On The Desktop should have taken effect. After logging off, this policy also will take effect.

Steps 7 and 8. No additional instructions are required for these steps.

Lab Solution 9.04

Steps I and 2. No additional instructions are required for these steps.

Lab Solution 9.05

Step I. Log on as a non-administrator user. Select Start | Settings | Control Panel | Accessibility Options. Select Display and click to place a check to select Use High Contrast. Click OK to close Accessibility Options.

   To change the color scheme go back into Accessibility Options, click Display, click Settings. Switch from White on Black to Black on White. Click OK twice. If neither of these options works for you or the user you are helping, go back into Accessibility Options and experiment with custom color combinations. When you are done, return your desktop to the settings you wish to continue working with. If you turn off Accessibility Display options, you may have to rearrange the objects on your desktop.

Step 2. Click Start | Programs | Accessories | Accessibility | Magnifier. This will run the Magnifier lens, which will appear as a horizontal area at the top of the screen that acts like an optical lens, magnifying the area of the desktop that is in the immediate vicinity of the mouse pointer. The message that appears informs you that this utility is designed to help people with slight visual impairment. Higher power magnification programs are available. If you would like to learn more about them, check out www.microsoft.com/enable and select the link labeled Visual Impairments. After you have experimented with the Magnifier, including creating or editing a document in WordPad, close all open windows and return your desktop to the settings you prefer.

Step 3. Select Start | Programs | Accessories | Accessibility | Narrator. Read the Microsoft narrator message, and then click OK to close the box.

Experiment with the settings in the Narrator configuration box. You will find that you can even choose from several voices—male and female. The default voice is Sam, English. After you have selected settings, open WordPad and create or modify a document.

ANSWERS TO LAB ANALYSIS TEST

1. First, you would create a new user (not a real person), log on as that user, then make all the necessary changes to the desktop. Log off; log back on as an administrator and open the System Properties applet. In the User Profiles tab sheet select the profile of the new user and then copy it over the Default User profile. Log off. The next time a user logs on to this computer for the first time, they will receive this profile.

2. First, tell Samantha to save her data to folders outside the profile folders. You can give her some guidance on this. If she has access to a file and print server, you can show her how to save her documents to a share on the server, or simply direct her to save to another folder on her local hard drive. If you do the quick repair method you practiced in Lab Exercise 9.02, she will only get her Desktop shortcuts back if they were part of the Default User Profile. It will probably be a quicker solution to solve the problem using that method, then help Samantha recreate the shortcuts she needs on her desktop.

3. The most likely cause of this is if the test lab computers were in a workgroup, but the computers in the shipping department are members of a domain. Therefore, higher-level domain group policies are overriding the local policies you set.

4. Add the general ledger application icon to the Quick Launch bar.

5. Suggest a set of headphones for Marissa. Her sound card is likely to have a connector for earphones. If it does not, install one that does. (Ok. This question isn't exactly fair, but neither is life. We threw this in just to remind you that your own common sense is still required.)

ANSWERS TO KEY TERM QUIZ

1. Default User

2. Local Policy

3. Group Policy

4. Quick Launch bar

5. Magnifier

MICROSOFT CERTIFIED SYSTEMS ENGINEER

10

Configuring Multi-language Support and Using Windows Installer

LAB EXERCISES

Y ou have now worked with several methods of managing the desktop. In this chapter you will explore the support that Windows 2000 provides for multiple languages and multiple locations. Then you will shift gears away from configuring the desktop to installing applications onto desktop computers—in particular, you will work with the Windows Installer technology. This is a technology in Windows 2000 that manages application installations, modifications, repairs, and uninstalls. In order to be installed by the Windows Installer service, an application must first be "prepacked" in a file with an MSI extension that contains both the files to be installed and the necessary instructions for performing the installation, including any necessary registry changes, file copy locations, etc.

LAB EXERCISE 10.01

Removing Multiple Language Support

20 Minutes

In Exercise 10-1 of the *MCSE Windows 2000 Professional Study Guide* you added new system level language support to your computer for an additional language. This system locale added a language group, which essentially consists of character set and font files, to support user and input locales. The user locales control how numbers, currency, dates, and times are displayed and depend on the installed system locales, or languages. The input locales control how input from a keyboard or speech-to-text software is interpreted, using one of the installed languages (system locales).

When you did Exercise 10-1 you observed the new system locale that was made when you selected it for your user locale setting. You saw that you had new Numbers, Currency, Time, and Date settings. Finally, you modified your Input Locales setting to add the new locale and configured it so that you could switch between the locales. You tested this ability by opening a Notepad document and entering it in both locales. Now you would like to return your Regional Options to the way they were before that lab, because sometimes you are left with a distorted system font.

Learning Objectives

By the end of this lab, you'll be able to

- Remove a system (locale) language
- Remove an input locale.

Lab Materials and Setup

The materials you need for this lab are:

■ A PC with Windows 2000 installed

cross Reference *As a pre-requisite for this lab exercise, read the section titled "Configuring Support for Multiple Languages or Multiple Locations" and complete Exercise 10-1 in Chapter 10 of the MCSE Windows 2000 Professional Study Guide.*

Getting Down to Business

In the following steps you will remove the changes you made to Regional Options in Exercise 10-1 in the *MCSE Windows 2000 Professional Study Guide.*

Step 1. Open the Regional Options applet in Control Panel and return your Locale to the Locale in effect before you did Exercise 10-1. If you are in the United States, this was English (United States). Leave the Regional Options dialog box open.

Step 2. Select the Numbers, Currency, Time, and Date tabs in turn and confirm that they have returned to appropriate settings for the locale. Leave the Regional Options dialog box open.

Step 3. Select the Input Locales tab and remove the Input language you added in the exercise. Leave the Regional Options dialog box open.

Step 4. Return to the General tab and in the Language settings for the system clear the check box by the language you added in Exercise 10-1. Click OK to close the Regional Options dialog box. You will be prompted to restart your computer. Select Yes to restart.

Step 5. Log on with the account you used when you modified the Regional Options settings. Is your desktop back to the way it was before you did Exercise 10-1? If not, read the following lab hint.

lab

Hint

On our test computers, completing Exercise 10-1 from Chapter 10 of the MCSE Windows 2000 Professional Study Guide left us with a very small, hard-to-read system font, even after we returned the Regional Options to their previous settings. We were finally able to correct this when we selected a different Display Scheme.

LAB EXERCISE 10.02

Examining Windows Installer Files

20 Minutes

Although you have completed Exercise 10-2 in the *MCSE Windows 2000 Professional Study Guide,* you are still curious about the Windows Installer files. You have now created a Windows Installer file, and you know that a Windows Installer file has an MSI extension and contains all the files and instructions for installing a single application. You would like to learn a little more about both this file format and the Installer service itself.

Learning Objectives

By the end of this lab, you'll be able to

- Identify MSI files
- Use summary information to identify the application in a MSI file.

Lab Materials and Setup

The materials you need for this lab are:

- A PC with Windows 2000 installed

cross

Reference

To best prepare for this lab exercise, read the section titled "Installing Applications by Using Windows Installer Packages" and complete Exercise 10-2 in Chapter 10 of the MCSE Windows 2000 Professional Study Guide.

Getting Down to Business

In the following steps you will examine the properties of a Windows Installer (MSI) file.

Step 1. Log on to your lab computer as Administrator (or a member of the local Administrators group). Use the Search program to find all files on your local hard drive(s) with an MSI extension.

Step 2. When the search is completed you should have found at least a few MSI files, as shown in Figure 10-1, although you will probably not have these exact same files. If you completed Exercise 10-2 in the *MCSE Windows 2000 Professional Study Guide* the TESTAPP.MSI file will be listed. If you installed any programs using MSI files you will see MSI files listed in the %SYSTEMROOT%\INSTALLER folder. These are renamed copies of the MSI files that were used to install programs.

Step 3. Select one of the files and open the Properties menu for it.
   On the General tab page notice the Type Of File and the Opens With information, as seen in Figure 10-2.

Step 4. Click on the Security tab. One way to restrict a user's ability to install an application is to grant permissions on the MSI file to only those who need to install the application. However that will only restrict access to that one file.

FIGURE 10-1

Search Results
with MSI files

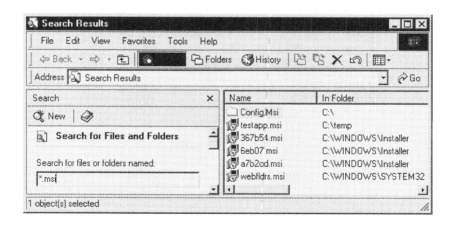

FIGURE 10-2

General
Properties of
a MSI file

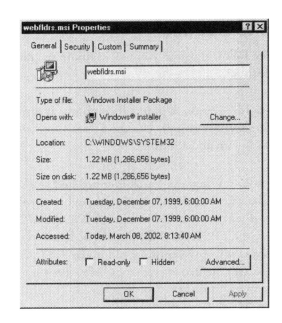

Another, more powerful way to control software installation on a user's computer
is through Group Policy. The Windows Installer policies are located under both
Computer Configuration and User Configuration in Administrative Templates |
Windows Components. There are other important Group Policy nodes that are
used in centralized control of applications; they are the Software Settings nodes
under both Computer Configuration and User Configuration.

lab
ⓗint   *Using group policy to control application installation is beyond the scope
of this book and the 70-210 exam. If you would like to learn more, use the
Help program from within the Group Policy Editor console and look for the
Help topic "Work with applications."*

Step 5. Click on the Custom tab. This is information you can optionally store
with any file to further identify it.

Step 6. Click on the Summary tab. This is the summary information for the file.
The Title field will contain either the name of the application, or in some cases, will
just identify it as an Installer file, identified as Installer Database or Microsoft Windows
Installer Database. The Subject field may contain the application name, and the Author

FIGURE 10-3

Summary
information for
an MSI file

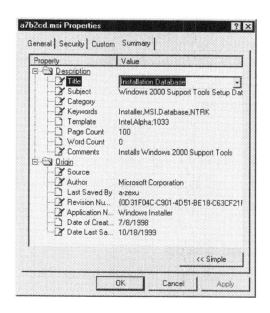

field should identify the vendor of the software. Figure 10-3 shows the Advanced view of the Summary information for the MSI file that was used to install the Windows 2000 Support Tools. If your summary page does not resemble this page, you are looking at the Simple view; click on the Advanced button to access the advanced view.

When you have explored the properties of any MSI files found, close the Search Results window.

LAB EXERCISE 10.03

Testing a New Windows Installer Package   20 Minutes

In Exercise 10-1 in the *MCSE Windows 2000 Professional Study Guide* you used WinInstall to package an application. On the job, you would probably have done this on a computer dedicated to this purpose. This would be a computer configured with the same operating system and applications as the computers on which the packaged application will be installed. To create the package (the MSI file), you installed the program on your computer. Therefore, if you are going to use that same computer to test how the MSI file works, you will have to remove all the changes made to it by the manual installation you did for the sake of creating the package.

Learning Objectives

By the end of this lab, you'll be able to

- Prepare a computer as a test bed for a Windows Installer package
- Install an application with a Windows Installer package file (MSI)
- Uninstall an application after a Windows Installer installation.

Lab Materials and Setup

The materials you need for this lab are:

- A PC with Windows 2000 installed

cross Reference

This lab requires that you read the section titled "Installing Applications by Using Windows Installer Packages" and complete Exercise 10-2 in Chapter 10 of the MCSE Windows 2000 Professional Study Guide.

Getting Down to Business

In the following steps you will first clean up your lab computer to remove all changes that were made to it in Exercise 10-2. Then you will install the test "application" using the MSI file you created in Exercise 10-2. Finally, you will uninstall the application.

Step 1.   Log on to your lab computer as Administrator (or a member of the local Administrators group). Using the instructions that begin with Step 9 in Exercise 10-2 in the *MCSE Windows 2000 Professional Study Guide* as a guide, remove the changes made to your lab computer when you created the MSI package.

Step 2.   Use My Computer or Windows Explorer to locate the MSI package file you created in Exercise 10-2 and double-click the file.

Step 3. Confirm that the files, folders, and registry entry you removed in Step 1 have been recreated by the Windows 2000 Installer package. When you are finished, close all open windows.

LAB EXERCISE 10.04

Removing an Application

15 Minutes

Once you have installed an application with Windows Installer, you can use the Add/Remove Programs applet to remove the application. You are now going to uninstall the application you installed in the last lab.

lab

Hint *In an Active Directory domain, if you use Group Policy to trigger a Windows Installer installation, it will be "self-healing," meaning that once an application has been installed using both of these technologies, if the application becomes damaged, it will automatically be repaired by having the damaged components replaced. This is transparent to the user. NOTE: Understanding how to use Group Policy for Windows Installer applications is beyond the scope of the Windows 2000 Professional exam, and of this book. Learn more about Group Policy by searching on "group policy" in the Windows 2000 Help. Another good resource is the "Deployment Planning Guide" that is installed when you install the Windows 2000 Support Tools. The guide is located under Start | Programs | Windows 2000 Support Tools | Deployment Planning Guide.*

Learning Objectives

By the end of this lab, you'll be able to

- Use Add/Remove Programs to uninstall a Windows Installer installed application
- Verify that the application has been completely removed.

Lab Materials and Setup

The materials you need for this lab are:

■ A PC with Windows 2000 installed

Getting Down to Business

In the following steps you will use the Add/Remove Programs applet to uninstall the application you installed in the previous lab exercise. Then, you will verify that all files, folders, and registry entries for that application have been removed.

Step 1. Open the Add/Remove Programs applet. Notice that any applications you have installed with Windows Installer are listed in the Change/Remove Programs sheet (see Figure 10-4). Select the Test Application, and click Remove.

Step 2. When asked if you are sure you want to remove the application, click Yes. When the application is removed it will no longer be listed in Add/Remove Programs. At that point, close the Add/Remove Programs window.

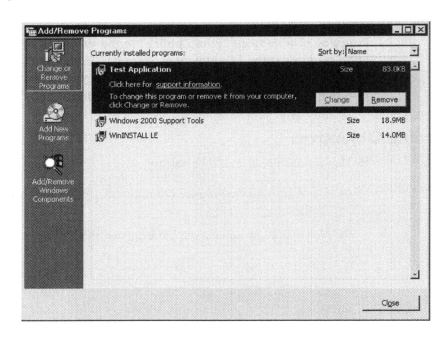

FIGURE 10-4

Add/Remove
Programs applet

Step 3. Verify that the program was removed by looking in the Program Files folder for this application's folder, and using REGEDIT to confirm that the registry entry has been removed.

Step 4. When done, close all open windows.

LAB EXERCISE 10.05

Installing the Windows 2000 Support Tools

15 Minutes

Microsoft creates a Resource Kit for most of their products. A Resource Kit consists of administrative/support level documentation as well as software utilities useful to administrators and other support professionals. Although the full Resource Kit is a separate product, Windows 2000 Professional and Server come with a subset of the Resource Kit called Support Tools. You have decided to install this version of the Resource Kit on your lab computer so that you can use some of these utilities.

Learning Objectives

By the end of this lab, you'll be able to

■ Install the Windows 2000 Support Tools from the Windows 2000 CD.

Lab Materials and Setup

The materials you need for this lab are:

■ A PC with Windows 2000 installed

■ The Windows 2000 Professional CD or the contents of the SUPPORT folder

Getting Down to Business

In the following steps, you will install the Windows 2000 Support Tools, reboot your computer, and then verify that the tools have been installed.

Step 1.   Log on to your lab computer as Administrator (or a member of the Administrators group). Insert the Windows 2000 Professional CD, or request the location of the SUPPORT folder, if your instructor has copied this to a network share.

Step 2.   If you are using the CD, and AutoPlay opens the Windows 2000 wizard, select Browse This CD. Otherwise, use My Computer or Windows Explorer. In any case, browse to the \SUPPORT\TOOLS folder and read the SREADME.DOC file. It is always a good habit to read the "read me" files that come with your software. If we have not made that point earlier, it is about time we did!

Follow the instructions in the SREADME.DOC file and run the Support Tools master setup program. When the Support Tools Setup Wizard appears, follow the instructions to add the Support Tools and, when prompted, provide your name and company, and select the Typical installation. There will be a short wait while the Installation Progress page appears, as shown in Figure 10-5, after which you can click Finish on the Completing page.

FIGURE 10-5

Windows 2000
Support Tools
Setup Wizard
installation
progress

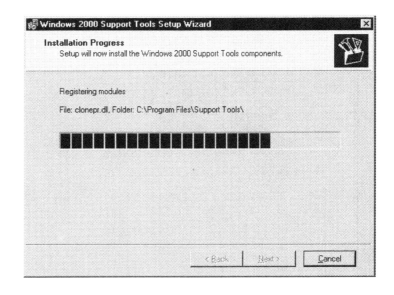

Step 3. After the reboot, log on to your lab computer as Administrator (or a member of the Administrators group). Verify that the Windows 2000 Support Tools shortcut has been added to your Start | Programs menu, as shown in Figure 10-6.

Step 4. Take a few minutes to get an overview of the tools in the Support Tools. You can do this through the Tools Help shortcut. When you are finished, close all open windows on your desktop.

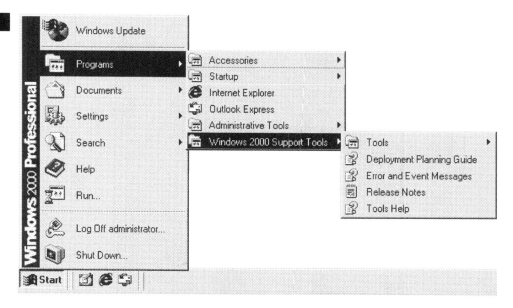

FIGURE 10-6

Start Menu with Support Tools displayed

LAB ANALYSIS TEST

1. The manager of the Hong Kong sales office has ordered the English version of Windows 2000 for the computers in their office because they do business in English. However, they want to be able to display the Chinese numeric and currency symbols. They also want to be able to read and write documents in other languages. He is concerned that he must order the Multi-Language version. What can you tell him?

_____

_____

2. To receive the "Designed for Windows 2000" logo, an application must meet several requirements, including providing an MSI package file for installing the application. However, you have a required application that does not have an MSI file. What options do you have to install this application?

_____

_____

3. One of your co-workers was not able to participate in the lab tests of WinInstall Lite. He is not sure what the packaging process is all about. Since you tested WinInstall in the lab, explain the process to him.

_____

_____

4. You have created an MSI package on a test computer. What steps should you take before testing this package on that same computer?

_____

_____

5. The Windows 2000 desktop computers you support belong to an Active Directory domain. What implications does this have for software deployment with Windows Installer and MSI packages?

_____

_____

KEY TERM QUIZ

Use the following vocabulary terms to complete the sentences below. Not all of the terms will be used.

> character set
>
> currency
>
> Input Locale
>
> Language Group
>
> MSI file
>
> System Locale
>
> User Local
>
> Windows Installer
>
> WinInstall
>
> Windows 2000 Support Tools

1. Support for a system level language is known as a/an _____.

2. _____ controls how numbers, currency, dates, and times are displayed and formatted.

3. A/an _____ controls how input from a keyboard or speech-to-text application is interpreted based on one of the installed languages.

4. Windows Installer installs applications by using a prepackaged _____.

5. The subset of the Windows 2000 Professional Resource Kit included on the Windows 2000 CD is the _____.

LAB WRAP-UP

In the lab exercises in this chapter you removed the multiple language support that you added when you did Exercise 10-1 in the *MCSE Windows 2000 Professional Study Guide.* You examined the Windows MSI installer files. You tested the MSI package file you created in Exercise 10-2 in the *MCSE Windows 2000 Professional Study Guide.* You removed an application that had been installed by Windows Installer, and finally, you installed the Windows 2000 Support Tools. These five fairly short lab exercises are designed to help you better understand two Certification Objectives for the Windows 2000 Professional exam 70-210.

You are now ready to move on to the study of implementing, managing, and troubleshooting network protocols and services.

LAB SOLUTIONS FOR CHAPTER 10

In this section, you'll find solutions to the lab exercises, Lab Analysis Test, and Key Term Quiz.

Lab Solution 10.01

Steps 1 through 5.   No additional information is required for these steps.

Lab Solution 10.02

Step 1.   Select Start | Search | For Files and Folders. In the Search for files or folder name text box enter the following: *.**MSI**. Leave the Containing text box blank, and ensure that Local Hard Drives is selected in the Look In: box. Click Search Now.

Step 2.   No additional information is needed for this step.

Step 3.   In the Search Results window, right-click on one of the MSI files and then select Properties.

Step 4 through 6.   No additional information is required for these steps.

Lab Solution 10.03

Step 1.

1. Use My Computer or Windows Explorer to delete the folder W2K PRO TEST Application (under the C:\PROGRAM FILES folder).
2. Use the Registry Editor to remove the Registry key W2K Pro Test App located under HKEY_LOCAL_MACHINE\SOFTWARE.

Step 2.   Using My Computer or Windows Explorer browse to the C:\TEMP folder. To execute the package, simply double-click on the MSI file.

Step 3.   No further instructions are needed for this step.

Lab Solution 10.04

Steps 1 through 4. No further instructions are needed for these steps.

Lab Solution 10.05

Step 1. No additional information is needed for this step.

Step 2. Using My Computer or Windows Explorer browse to d:\SUPPORT \ TOOLS (where *d:* is the drive letter of your CD-ROM drive) on the Windows 2000 Professional CD-ROM. To execute the package, simply double-click on the file named 2000RKST. The Windows Installer service will then install the application. You will see the Installer Wizard on your screen.

Steps 3 and 4. No additional information is needed for these steps.

ANSWERS TO LAB ANALYSIS TEST

1. You can tell him that his users will be able to read and write documents in other languages, although the user interface will be in English. He can install the appropriate Language Groups to support the locales they need for their numeric and currency symbols. They will also be able to read and edit documents in other languages in their English version.

2. You could choose to install this application without using an MSI package, but this will leave Windows Installer out of the loop, and you will lose some of the benefits of installing with an MSI package. A better choice is to create an MSI package by using either WinInstall Lite (free with Windows 2000) or another third-party product, including the retail version of WinInstall.

3. Basically, a program like WinInstall is said to repackage an application. You should start with a computer configured with the same operating system that you expect to be installed on the target computers, but otherwise, very clean. You run WinInstall in Discover mode, in which it takes a "before snapshot" of the computer, recording the existing folder and file structure, and the registry structure. It records information about these objects so that it can detect any changes you make after you run this discovery. Next, you install your application(s) and configure the application(s) with any customization that is required. Finally, you run the repackage program (WinInstall in this case) to discover the changes made to the computer. This is called an "after

snapshot." Based on the differences recorded, it will build a package (an MSI file) that can be distributed to the computers that need the application(s). When executed, the MSI file will cause the Windows Installer service to run and install the application.

4. Before testing the MSI package on the computer on which you created it, you will need to uninstall the application, removing all folders, files, and registry changes made when the application was installed.

5. With an Active Directory domain, administrators can use Group Policy to deploy the MSI packages.

ANSWERS TO KEY TERM QUIZ

1. System Locale

2. User Locale

3. Input Locale

4. MSI file

5. Windows 2000 Support Tools

MICROSOFT CERTIFIED SYSTEMS ENGINEER

11

Implementing, Managing, and Troubleshooting Network Protocols and Services

LAB EXERCISES

As a desktop support analyst you are not expected to have the level of knowledge required of a network support person. However, you may find yourself needing to help a user solve a problem trying to connect to network resources. To that end, in the first three lab exercises in this chapter, you will practice using some of the utilities that can aid you in troubleshooting network problems for your desktop users. Then you will practice setting up a VPN connection.

LAB EXERCISE 11.01

Using Pathping to Find an Internet Bottleneck

30 Minutes

Beginning with Windows 2000, you can use Pathping, a great new utility that combines Ping and Tracert capabilities, while providing more information than either command. It first performs a route trace (the Tracert function), then it pings each router in turn to determine where a problem may exist. Pathping will report the degree of packet loss at each router along the way, allowing you to determine which routers are not functioning properly. Use this utility when you are unable to reach a remote computer on an *intranet* (a private network using Internet technologies) or on the Internet. It is also useful when you find a connection that is extremely slow.

Remember that Pathping is only available in TPC/IP for Windows beginning with Windows 2000. If you are working with an older version of Windows, use Tracert and Ping. When you do this lab, you will see that it takes several minutes for Pathping to complete its calculations. When you want to quickly check connectivity between hosts, you will still use Ping. When you want to simply see a trace of a route between hosts, you will still use Tracert.

lab
Hint

An intranet is a private network using Internet technologies. As such, we usually think of it as being a routed network, as well as one that may be using web pages and browsers, FTP, and other Internet technologies. In the context we use here, it is a routed network. That is where Pathping shines—in detecting which router may be the bottleneck.

Learning Objectives

By the end of this lab, you'll be able to

- Run the Pathping command
- Analyze the result of the Pathping command to find a bottleneck in a routed network.

Lab Materials and Setup

The materials you need for this lab are:

- A PC with Windows 2000 installed
- Internet access

cross
Reference

*To best prepare for this lab exercise, read the section titled "Configuring and Troubleshooting the TCP/IP Protocol" in Chapter 11 of the **MCSE Windows 2000 Professional Study Guide.***

Getting Down to Business

In the following steps you will run the Pathping command, then analyze the output to determine where a bottleneck may lie in the path between you and www.osborne.com.

Step 1.   Log on to your lab computer as Administrator (or a member of the local Administrators group). Open a command prompt and enter the following command:

```
PATHPING -n WWW.OSBORNE.COM
```

Figure 11-1 shows the results after the Tracert portion of the Pathping command ran, while calculating the statistics for each router. This takes over 5 minutes. The final result of running the command is shown in Figure 11-2. The output from this command is normally more verbose, showing the result of a DNS name resolution for each router. Using the –n parameter avoids this name resolution. This was run from a computer in our office in Minnesota. The result will be very different for you, since you will be running this from a different location.

FIGURE 11-1

Pathping while computing statistics for each router

```
C:\WINNT\System32\cmd.exe - pathping -n www.osborne.com
Microsoft Windows 2000 [Version 5.00.2195]
(C) Copyright 1985-2000 Microsoft Corp.

C:\>pathping -n www.osborne.com

Tracing route to www.osborne.com [198.45.24.130]
over a maximum of 30 hops:
  0  10.0.0.11
  1  64.122.56.1
  2  64.122.32.201
  3  4.0.246.29
  4  4.24.6.201
  5  4.24.5.245
  6  4.0.1.197
  7  4.24.9.34
  8  4.24.146.74
  9  209.252.96.10
 10  216.43.64.2
 11  209.255.255.70
 12  198.45.24.244
 13  198.45.24.130

Computing statistics for 325 seconds...
```

FIGURE 11-2

Pathping results after computation of statistics

```
Command Prompt
Computing statistics for 325 seconds...
               Source to Here   This Node/Link
Hop  RTT    Lost/Sent = Pct   Lost/Sent = Pct  Address
 0                                             10.0.0.11
                                0/ 100 =  0%   |
 1   30ms    1/ 100 =  1%      1/ 100 =  1%   64.122.56.1
                                0/ 100 =  0%   |
 2   27ms    0/ 100 =  0%      0/ 100 =  0%   64.122.32.201
                                0/ 100 =  0%   |
 3   37ms    0/ 100 =  0%      0/ 100 =  0%   4.0.246.29
                                0/ 100 =  0%   |
 4   25ms    1/ 100 =  1%      1/ 100 =  1%   4.24.6.201
                                0/ 100 =  0%   |
 5   30ms    1/ 100 =  1%      1/ 100 =  1%   4.24.5.245
                                0/ 100 =  0%   |
 6   27ms    1/ 100 =  1%      1/ 100 =  1%   4.0.1.197
                                0/ 100 =  0%   |
 7   50ms    1/ 100 =  1%      1/ 100 =  1%   4.24.9.34
                                0/ 100 =  0%   |
 8   46ms    1/ 100 =  1%      1/ 100 =  1%   4.24.146.74
                                0/ 100 =  0%   |
 9   118ms   1/ 100 =  1%      1/ 100 =  1%   209.252.96.10
                                0/ 100 =  0%   |
10   109ms   0/ 100 =  0%      0/ 100 =  0%   216.43.64.2
                                0/ 100 =  0%   |
11   144ms   0/ 100 =  0%      0/ 100 =  0%   209.255.255.70
                                0/ 100 =  0%   |
12   136ms   0/ 100 =  0%      0/ 100 =  0%   198.45.24.244
                                0/ 100 =  0%   |
13   105ms   0/ 100 =  0%      0/ 100 =  0%   198.45.24.130

Trace complete.

C:\>_
```

Step 2. Examine the result of running the Pathping command on your lab computer, then answer the following questions:

1. How many hops (router-to-router communication) in total were displayed?

_____

2. How many hops showed zero lost packets?

_____

3. How many hops showed lost packets?

_____

4. Which hop (identify it by the IP address) was the slowest link?

_____

lab
ⓘint *Try the command again without the –n parameter. You will then see the name of each router in the path. To learn more about Pathping, search on "Pathping" in the Windows 2000 Help.*

LAB EXERCISE 11.02

Using Nslookup to Troubleshoot DNS Problems

15 Minutes

Most of the applications we use to connect to other computers allow us to select a computer name, not an IP address (at the internetwork layer) or (worse yet) a MAC (physical or network interface layer) address. This is because most of us are better at remembering names than long numbers. Therefore, your computer must resolve the name of a server before it can communicate with it. This is true whether you are connecting to a file and print server or to a web page. In the case of resources that are part of the DNS domain namespace, your computer performs DNS name resolution to find the IP address of the server to which it should send the packets of information.

Nslookup lets you troubleshoot DNS problems by allowing you to query DNS name servers and see the result of the queries. In using Nslookup you are looking for problems such as a DNS server not responding to clients, DNS servers not resolving names correctly, or other general name resolution problems. Nslookup has two modes: *interactive* and *non-interactive*. In interactive mode, Nslookup has its own command prompt, a greater than sign (>) within the system command prompt. You enter this mode by typing **nslookup** without any parameters or **nslookup** followed by a hyphen and the name of a name server. In the first instance, it will use your default name server, and in the second instance, it will use the name server you specify. In interactive mode you enter commands at the nslookup prompt, and you must enter the **exit** command to end interactive mode and return to the system command prompt. In non-interactive mode, when you enter the Nslookup command plus command line parameters for using one or more Nslookup subcommands, the response is sent to the screen, and you are returned to an active command prompt. This is good for a quick test. In this lab you will use non-interactive mode.

Learning Objectives

By the end of this lab, you'll be able to

- Run the Nslookup command
- Analyze the result of the Nslookup command.

Lab Materials and Setup

The materials you need for this lab are:

- A PC with Windows 2000 installed
- TCP/IP configured with a Preferred DNS name server
- Internet access
- An alternate DNS name server IP address to use in Step 2

cross
Ceference

For an overview of Nslookup, read the section titled "Nslookup" in Chapter 11 of the **MCSE Windows 2000 Professional Study Guide.**

Getting Down to Business

In the following steps you will run the Nslookup command in non-interactive mode to determine if your default name server can resolve a name.

Step 1. Log on to your lab computer as Administrator (or a member of the local Administrators group). Open a command prompt and enter the following command:

NSLOOKUP WWW.OSBORNE.COM

In the above command, www.osborne.com is the name of the server to find. When we run this command, we see the following result:

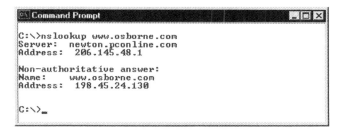

If you are connected to the Internet and able to browse web sites, you should have similar, but not identical, results. The Server name and Address in the first and second lines of the output are the name and IP address of the DNS server that responded to your request. This is a DNS name server that your computer is configured to query when it is doing name resolution. Your results for these two lines should be different, unless you happen to use the same name server we use (not very likely). The second group of lines shows the result of the query. It is a non-authoritative answer because the name server queried was not authoritative for the zone that holds this server name. It had to query other name servers to find the name for us. If the name server had queried for this name previously, it may have had this name and address in its name cache, an area of memory where it saves the result of queries. You can see that www.osborne.com is located at 198.45.24.130. This shows us that name resolution is working, so if we are having a problem with this connection, it is not a name resolution problem. Perhaps the server www.osborne.com is offline, or a critical link or router between it and the Internet has failed. This is information you could pass on to your network administrator or to your ISP.

lab
ⓗint

In Step 1 you ran the Nslookup command with only one parameter, the name of the server you are trying to resolve. When you do this, it uses your preferred DNS name server, as listed in your Internet Protocol properties for your network connection. You can also choose to tell it which name server to query by providing the name or address of a name server as the second parameter. We like the first method as a quick and easy test, because it tells you if the DNS server that your client queries by default can resolve the name. You would only specify the DNS server when the first command has failed, and you want to see if another DNS server would work. Now, we are definitely getting into territory that is beyond the scope of the 70-210 exam and of this book. To learn more about Nslookup, search on "Nslookup" in the Windows 2000 Help.

Step 2.   Now try providing the Nslookup command with the address of an alternate DNS server, as shown in the command below:

```
NSLOOKUP WWW.OSBORNE.COM 209.166.160.36
```

Alternatively, you can use an address provided to you by your instructor, in which case substitute it for the IP address in the command above.

lab
ⓗint

For more information on Internet domain names, check out the following web sites: www.internic.net, www.icann.org, and www.iana.org. You will find good information and lots of "light reading" on these sites.

Step 3.   Run the same command you used in Step 1, only query for the address of www.microsoft.com. When we ran this command we had the following result:

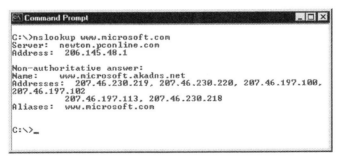

This is an example of a name that is aliased to several IP addresses—6 in fact. This is also a successful result, and would mean that if you cannot connect to www.microsoft.com, the problem is probably not with DNS, unless these addresses are wrong!

lab
ⓗint　*To learn more techniques, search www.microsoft.com/technet for the article "How to Troubleshoot Basic TCP/IP Problems."*

LAB EXERCISE 11.03

Using Netdiag

30 Minutes

Netdiag is a command line utility that comes with the Windows 2000 Support Tools, on the Windows 2000 CD. Netdiag performs a series of tests on the state of your network client, such as examining DLL files, looking at the output from tests, and checking the system registry. It works with TCP/IP or IPX/SPX.

When you run Netdiag, it first checks to see which network protocols or services are running, and then performs the appropriate tests, drawing on over two dozen tests. To use Netdiag, you must first install the Support Tools. Once they are installed, you can run Netdiag from a command prompt. Run it without any command line parameters to have it perform all the tests appropriate for your network configuration. The results will be displayed on the screen in the command shell, and will also be written to a file called NETDIAG.LOG saved in the root of the system drive. You could run this command on a computer, and collect this file (copy it to a central location) in order to document the network configuration of a computer.

Learning Objectives

By the end of this lab, you'll be able to

- Run the Netdiag utility
- Analyze the output of the Netdiag utility.

Lab Materials and Setup

The materials you need for this lab are:

- A PC with Windows 2000 installed
- The Windows 2000 Support Tools (as installed in Lab Exercise 10-05)

Getting Down to Business

In the following steps you will run the Netdiag command and analyze the results.

Step 1. Log on to your lab computer as Administrator (or a member of the local Administrators group). At the command prompt enter the following command:

```
NETDIAG
```

The output from this command can be too large for your screen buffer, therefore you will open the Netdiag log file to see the output.

Step 2. Use Notepad to open the NETDIAG.LOG file that was saved in the root of your system drive. Since our operating system was installed on drive C:, that is the system drive. The contents of the file will be similar to the following:

```
Computer Name: LABCOMPUTER1
    DNS Host Name: LABCOMPUTER1
    System info : Windows 2000 Professional (Build 2195)
    Processor : x86 Family 6 Model 3 Stepping 0, AuthenticAMD
    List of installed hotfixes :
        Q147222
Netcard queries test . . . . . . . : Passed
Per interface results:
    Adapter : Local Area Connection
        Netcard queries test . . . : Passed
        Host Name. . . . . . . . . : LABCOMPUTER1
        IP Address . . . . . . . . : 192.168.131.66
        Subnet Mask. . . . . . . . : 255.255.255.0
        Default Gateway. . . . . . : 192.168.131.254
        Primary WINS Server. . . . : 192.168.131.253
        Dns Servers. . . . . . . . : 206.145.48.1
        IpConfig results . . . . . : Failed
            Pinging the Primary WINS server 192.168.131.253 -
```

```
not reachable
        AutoConfiguration results. . . . . . : Passed
        Default gateway test . . . : Passed
        NetBT name test. . . . . : Passed
        WINS service test. . . . . : Passed
Global results:
Domain membership test . . . . . . : Passed
    Dns domain name is not specified.
    Dns forest name is not specified.
NetBT transports test. . . . . . : Passed
    List of NetBt transports currently configured:
        NetBT_Tcpip_{F58CD8EF-B7F0-48AB-B336-6C21AD59009E}
    1 NetBt transport currently configured.
Autonet address test . . . . . . : Passed
IP loopback ping test. . . . . . : Passed
Default gateway test . . . . . . : Passed
NetBT name test. . . . . . . . . : Passed
Winsock test . . . . . . . . . . : Passed
DNS test . . . . . . . . . . . . : Passed
Redir and Browser test . . . . . : Passed
    List of NetBt transports currently bound to the Redir
        NetBT_Tcpip_{F58CD8EF-B7F0-48AB-B336-6C21AD59009E}
    The redir is bound to 1 NetBt transport.
    List of NetBt transports currently bound to the browser
        NetBT_Tcpip_{F58CD8EF-B7F0-48AB-B336-6C21AD59009E}
    The browser is bound to 1 NetBt transport.
DC discovery test. . . . . . . . : Skipped
DC list test . . . . . . . . . . : Skipped
Trust relationship test. . . . . : Skipped
Kerberos test. . . . . . . . . . : Skipped
LDAP test. . . . . . . . . . . . : Skipped
Bindings test. . . . . . . . . . : Passed
WAN configuration test . . . . . : Skipped
    No active remote access connections.
Modem diagnostics test . . . . . : Passed
IP Security test . . . . . . . . : Passed
    IPSec policy service is active, but no policy is assigned.
The command completed successfully
```

By analyzing the output from the Netdiag command, we see that when Netdiag pinged the address of the WINS server it did not receive a response. If you had results like this, you would contact the network administrator and tell them about the result. Perhaps the WINS server is down, or that service may have been moved to another server. Several tests were skipped because they did not apply to the current configuration of this computer. The first 5 skipped tests were skipped because they are tests that are only appropriate for a computer that is a member of a Windows domain. The last one that was skipped was because this computer did not have a WAN connection (modem). It accesses the Internet through the LAN.

lab
⒣int
If you are curious about all available Netdiag tests, at the command prompt type netdiag ? *and press Enter. A list of available switch settings will appear.*

LAB EXERCISE 11.04

Configuring Incoming and Outgoing VPN Connections

30 Minutes

Some of your mobile users will need to connect to the corporate intranet while traveling. Previously, these same users dialed-in directly to a remote access server. They used a simple dial-up connection, which is a connection that uses the telephone network. This was secure enough, but was very expensive in long distance charges. These users all now have an ISP that they can use to connect to the Internet, still using dial-up connection, but using local phone numbers in each city to which they travel. Allowing them to connect to the corporate network over the Internet will save many thousands of dollars in long distance charges each month, but it will not be secure, unless additional steps are taken.

The network team has decided that Virtual Private Network (VPN) Connections are the answer. In a VPN connection, hosts, client, and server connect over a public network. Their communications are encapsulated, and because of this we often talk about creating a tunnel through the public network. Furthermore, security measures, such as encryption and authentication of the tunnel, can be applied to the communications. You have learned that Windows 2000 offers several options in communications and security protocols (such as IPSec) that can be combined to make a secure VPN solution. You do not have to know the details of all of these options for the 70-210 exam, however, you do need to have overview knowledge, and you must have practice in enabling the client side of VPN communications. In your company, the Server Support Group has configured a VPN server that can be accessed over the Internet by these users. You are going back into the lab to practice configuring an outgoing VPN connection for your mobile users.

cross
Reference   *To best prepare for this lab, read the entire section titled "Connecting to Computers by Using Dial-up Networking" in Chapter 11 of the* **MCSE Windows 2000 Professional Study Guide.**

Learning Objectives

By the end of this lab, you'll be able to

- Set up your computer to accept an incoming dial-up connection
- Set up an incoming VPN connection
- Set up a dial-up connection to the Internet
- Set up an outgoing VPN connection.

Lab Materials and Setup

The materials you need for this lab are:

- A PC with Windows 2000 installed
- An Internet connection
- The IP address of a VPN server (optional)

Getting Down to Business

It is not likely that you will have an address of a VPN server to which you may connect over the Internet. Nor are you likely to have a modem on your lab computer (if it is a classroom lab). We have written the following steps for both sides of the VPN connection, so that you can see and do all the steps required to create a VPN. You are not expected to be able to connect to your own VPN server from the client on the same machine. If you set this up on two separate computers, each with their own Internet connection and IP address, you can connect to the other student's VPN server. In the first step, you configure a pseudo-server (your lab computer) to accept incoming VPN connections. Because this is done on a Windows 2000 Professional computer and not on an Internet server, the procedure for creating a VPN server is different than what would actually be done on a Windows 2000 server. This first step is optional if your instructor has given you the IP address of a VPN server to which you can connect.

In the second step you configure a client computer (your same lab computer) to connect to the Internet via a dial-up connection to an ISP. This provides the underlying, but insecure, network between the client and server.

In the third step you create a VPN connection over this dial-up connection. A desktop support person would only have to perform the second and third steps on client computers.

Step 1. Log on to your lab computer as Administrator (or a member of the local Administrators group). Open the Network Connection Wizard and use the Incoming Dial-up Connection Entry Form (Table 11-1) to complete the wizard and configure incoming dial-up connections.

After completing the wizard, you should now have an incoming connection in the Network and Dial-up Connections folder, as shown in Figure 11-3.

lab
Warning *If you are doing these labs on your home computer, your personal firewall (We sure hope you have one!) will have to be configured to allow incoming traffic before you can actually use the incoming connection. If you make such a change to your firewall, be sure to change back to more secure settings after you complete the lab so that you will not be open to an intruder.*

TABLE 11-1	Page	Setting
Incoming Dial-up Connection Entry Form	Network Connection Type	Accept Incoming Connections
	Devices for Incoming Connections (if this page appears)	Modem
	Incoming Virtual Private Connection	Allow Virtual Private Connections
	Users Allowed To Connect	Select Users Permitted To Connect
	Networking Components	Keep The Default
	Completing	Name The Connection

FIGURE 11-3

Incoming
Connections icon
in Network and
Dial-up
Connections

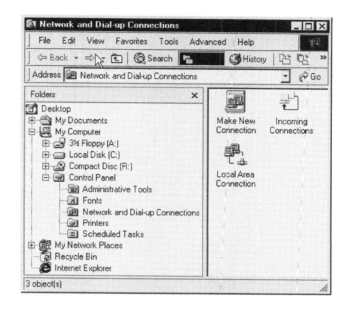

Step 2. Use the New Connection Wizard to configure an outgoing connection using the Outgoing Dial-up Connection Form (Table 11-2).

After you have completed the Network and Dial-up Connection, if you configured an Internet Connection through a locally connected modem, you will have a new icon in the Network and Dial-up Connections folder, similar to that in Figure 11-4. If you connect to the Internet through your LAN, there will not be a new icon here.

TABLE 11-2

Outgoing Dial-up
Connection Entry
Form

Page	Setting
Network Connection Type	Dial-up to the Internet
Internet Connection Wizard	Complete with appropriate information to connect to your ISP

FIGURE 11-4

Outgoing Dial-up
Connections icon
in Network and
Dial-up
Connections

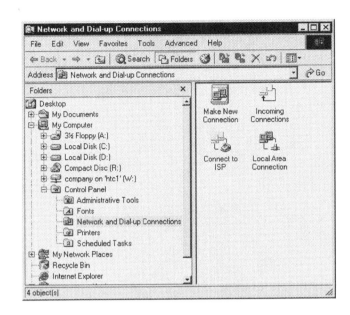

Step 3. Use the New Connection Wizard to configure the outgoing VPN connection using the Outgoing VPN Connection Entry Form (Table 11-3).

When you have completed the Network Connection Wizard, the Initial Connection message box will appear:

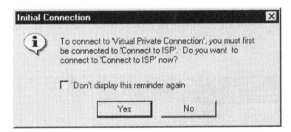

TABLE 11-3	Page	Setting
Outgoing VPN Connection Entry Form	Network Connection Type	Connect to a private network through the Internet
	Public Network	Automatically dial this initial connection
	Destination Address	The IP address of the VPN server

If you actually have a dial-up connection to the Internet, and have configured the VPN connection with an actual IP address of a VPN server, select Yes, but otherwise, select No. The Network and Dial-up Connections folder will now contain a VPN icon, as shown in Figure 11-5.

Step 4.   To connect to the VPN server, double-click on the VPN icon. This will start the Connection Virtual Private Connection dialog box:

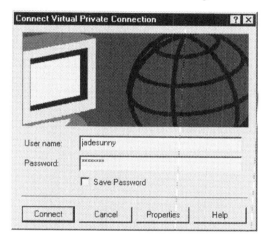

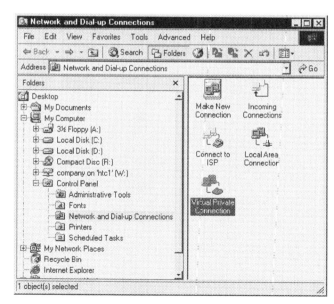

FIGURE 11-5

VPN Connection icon in Network and Dial-up Connections

Enter the username and password of a user who is authorized to use this VPN connection. There will be a delay after you select the Connect button, after which, the following message signals a successful connection:

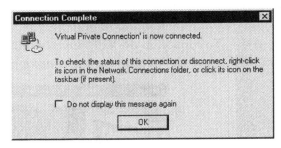

If you make a successful connection, open the command prompt and enter the following command:

```
IPCONFIG /ALL
```

The listing will show an IP address and configuration for three devices: your LAN network card, the modem (PPP device), and the VPN connection.

LAB ANALYSIS TEST

1. Like most companies rolling out a new operating system to the desktop, your organization has been doing this in stages. Therefore you still have users who are using Windows 98. You have just received a call from one of those users who is complaining that an Internet connection to a web site she needs to access for her work is extremely slow. This is hindering her work and making her late with reports she compiles after accessing this site. How can you help her?

   _____

   _____

2. You would like to gather all the network configuration information you can from a computer using a single command. Which command will you use?

   _____

   _____

3. In your test lab, you ran the Nslookup command, querying on the name www.osborne.com. However, the result was an error message, stating that the DNS request timed out, and that it could not connect to a server at XXX.XXX.XXX.XXX (the IP address of your computer's preferred DNS name server). Furthermore, it said that default servers are not available. What does this tell you? What action will you take next?

   _____

   _____

4. One of your co-workers is concerned that the result of the Netdiag command showed that several tests were skipped. He believes this may indicate a problem with the network configuration. What can you tell him?

   _____

   _____

5. Sarah Smith, the manager of the merchandise control department, has users who travel and connect to the network through a remote access server using simple dial-up connections. She is wondering what the value is of using VPNs over Internet connections. Please provide the explanation you would give Sarah.

   _____

   _____

KEY TERM QUIZ

Use the following vocabulary terms to complete the sentences below. Not all of the terms will be used.

> dial-up connection
>
> DNS domain namespace
>
> encapsulation
>
> IP address
>
> MAC address
>
> name server
>
> Nslookup
>
> Pathping
>
> tunnel
>
> VPN

1. The _____ command is time-consuming, but worthwhile when you need to find the source of a failure or bottleneck when a connection over a routed network fails or is extremely slow.

2. The telephone network is the underlying technology that we use for a/an _____.

3. In order to resolve DNS host names to IP addresses, a computer's Internet Protocols (TCP/IP) advanced properties must include the IP address of at least one _____.

4. The _____ command allows you to determine if a failure to connect is due to a name resolution problem.

5. Properly configured, a/an _____ connection provides security when you need to connect to a private network over the Internet.

LAB WRAP-UP

In this chapter you worked on implementing a network protocol by configuring VPN connections. VPNs are becoming increasingly important in business, and you will find yourself setting them up frequently. You also focused on troubleshooting some common network problems. You worked with three important tools: Pathping, Nslookup and Netdiag, and you will find, as you get deeper into your real-world work, that these three tools will become almost second nature to use. They are so fundamental to discovery of basic network problems that you will be glad you took the time to become familiar with them.

In the next chapter you will move on to work with security and user accounts.

LAB SOLUTIONS FOR CHAPTER 11

In this section, you'll find solutions to the lab exercises, Lab Analysis Test, and Key Term Quiz.

Lab Solution 11.01

Step 1.   Select Start | Programs | Accessories | Command Prompt. At the command prompt enter the following:

```
PATHPING-n WWW.OSBORNE.COM
```

Step 2.   Answers will vary, depending on the routers between you and www.osborne.com.

Lab Solution 11.02

Step 1.   Select Start | Programs | Accessories | Command Prompt. At the command prompt enter the following:

```
NSLOOKUP WWW.OSBORNE.COM
```

Step 2.   Select Start | Programs | Accessories | Command Prompt. At the command prompt enter the following:

```
NSLOOKUP WWW.OSBORNE.COM 209.166.160.36
```

Step 3.   Select Start | Programs | Accessories | Command Prompt. At the command prompt enter the following:

```
NSLOOKUP WWW.MICROSOFT.COM
```

Lab Solution 11.03

Step 1.   Select Start | Programs | Accessories | Command Prompt. At the command prompt enter the following:

```
NETDIAG
```

Step 2.   No further instructions are needed for this step.

Lab Solution 11.04

Step 1. If your modem has not been configured, the Location Information dialog box will open, in addition to the Network Connection Wizard, as shown in Figure 11-6.

If this page appears, complete the information, then click OK. This will, in turn, result in the appearance of the Phone and Modem Options page. If that page appears, ensure that a location is selected, then click OK. Then return to the Network Connection Wizard.

1. In the Welcome to the Network Connection Wizard page, click Next.

2. On the Network Connection Type page select Accept Incoming Connections, then click Next.

3. On the Devices for Incoming Connections page (if it appears) select the modem you will use.

4. On the Incoming Virtual Private Connection page select Allow Virtual Private Connections, then click Next.

5. In the Users Allowed To Connect box on the Allowed Users page, select (place a check in the check box) all the users who you wish to allow to connect, then click on the properties button for one of them. This allows an administrator to change the password for the user and to set callback options. Leave the Properties settings at the default, then click OK. Back in the Allowed Users page, click Next.

<table>
<tr>
<td>

FIGURE 11-6

The Location
Information page

</td>
<td>

</td>
</tr>
</table>

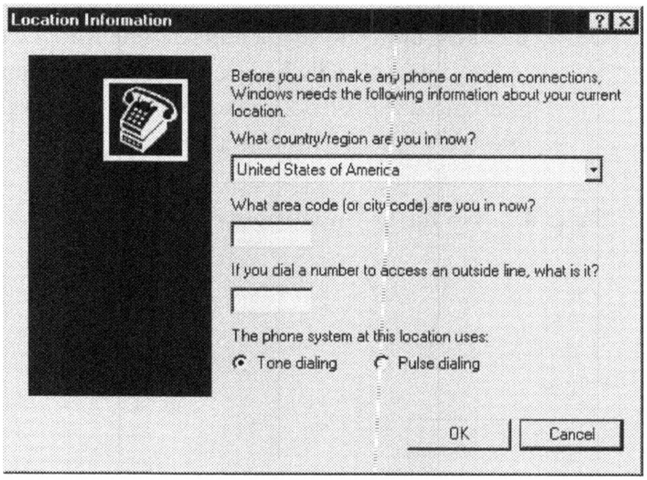

6. In the Networking Components page, leave the default settings and click Next. On the Completing page, name the connection (the default is Incoming Connections), then click Finish.

Step 2.

1. In the Welcome to the Network Connection Wizard page, click Next.

2. On the Network Connection Type page, select Dial-Up To The Internet, then click Next.

3. The Internet Connection Wizard will open. Your choices here will depend on the settings for your ISP. When you have finished the Internet Connection Wizard, do not have it connect to the Internet immediately.

Step 3.

1. In the Welcome to the Network Connection Wizard page, click Next.

2. On the Network Connection Type page, select Connect To A Private Network Through The Internet, then click Next.

3. On the Public Network page, select Automatically Dial This Initial Connection.

4. On the Destination Address page, enter the Host name or IP address of the VPN server, then click Next.

5. On the Connection Availability page, select For All Users, then click Next.

6. On the Completing page, name the connection. The default name is Virtual Private Connection. Click Next. The Initial Connection message box will open. If you actually have a dial-up connection to the Internet and have configured the VPN connection with an actual IP address of a VPN server, select Yes. Otherwise, select No.

Step 4. No further instructions are needed for this step.

ANSWERS TO LAB ANALYSIS TEST

1. Well, don't dust off your red cape, yet. You may not be a hero in this case, at least not without help, and you are not likely to produce fast, dramatic results. Run the Tracert command on this user's computer, using the fully qualified domain name (such as www.osborne.com) of the server to which she is trying to connect. The router (hop) showing the longest length of time (measured in milliseconds) is the router with a possible bottleneck. Report your findings to your network administrator or to your ISP. On your Windows 2000 computers, you can run the Pathping command, which gives you more information, measuring packet loss at each router.

2. If you have installed the Windows 2000 Support Tools, you can use the Netdiag command, which will run several tests on the network configuration of a computer. The output is saved in a file, named NETDIAG.LOG.

3. This error tells you that when your computer (as a DNS client) sent a DNS query to the IP address of the Preferred DNS name server, it did not get a response. Furthermore, the default server's error indicates that it tried any additional DNS servers that were configured in the client's Advanced Internet Protocol (TCP/IP) properties, and did not get a response from any of them. You should contact your network administrator. Using a little common sense, if these are all valid DNS name server addresses, it is not likely that they will all be down at the same time. However, there may be a network component (probably a router or network segment) between this client computer and the DNS servers it is trying to query. Since this is your test lab, it may actually be isolated from the rest of the corporate intranet.

4. Tell your co-worker that Netdiag only runs tests that are appropriate for the configuration it detects. If it skips tests, this is an indication that the test would not be appropriate. If a test fails, then you have reason for concern since it only runs commands that are appropriate for the configuration.

5. The old method of connecting using a dial-up connection to a remote access server is expensive when people are dialing from locations outside your calling area. By giving the users dial-up connections to a national ISP, they can use a local number to gain access to the Internet in each of the cities to which they travel. For security, your company provides one or more VPN servers on the corporate intranet (also connected to the Internet), and the client's connection is made secure by the creation of a VPN connection over the Internet connection to the IP address of the VPN server.

ANSWERS TO LAB ANALYSIS TEST

1. Pathping

2. dial-up connection

3. name server

4. Nslookup

5. VPN

MICROSOFT CERTIFIED SYSTEMS ENGINEER

12

Implementing, Monitoring, and Troubleshooting Security and User Accounts

LAB EXERCISES

Support professionals who have worked with Windows 9x and Windows NT in the past, while new to Windows 2000, often find themselves saying, "Where is…?" When this question involves a setting for controlling the desktop, security, logons, and/or user rights, the answer is Group Policy. Now, just where in Group Policy you find a setting is another story. Previously, in Lab Exercise 9.03 in Chapter 9, you worked with the Administrative Templates in local policy. In the labs in this chapter you will test security account password policies and both enable and test security account lockout policies. Then you will look at user rights, which are set at the computer level. Finally, you will use policies to disable Encrypting File System (EFS) on a computer.

LAB EXERCISE 12.01

Testing Account Security Policies

45 Minutes

Group policy is the central change and configuration management tool in Windows 2000. The real power of group policy is felt in an organization with an Active Directory domain and member computers that are running Windows 2000 or newer versions of Windows. Organizations with support people who fully understand group policy, and who implement it after careful planning, will gain the most from having their Windows 2000 desktops in an Active Directory domain.

In your organization, you have learned that most policies will be set in group policy at the domain level. However, your group has decided to spend time in the test lab today working with local policies in the hope that this will help you to get a better understanding of the bigger picture—Group Policy set at the domain level. In this lab you will test the Account Security Password Policies you set in Lab Exercises 12-1 and 12-2 in the *MCSE Windows 2000 Professional Study Guide.*

Learning Objectives

By the end of this lab, you'll be able to

- Understand what is meant by "password complexity requirements"
- Test the effect of combining password policies
- Test for success and failure with compliant and non-compliant passwords.

Lab Materials and Setup

The materials you need for this lab are:

- A PC with Windows 2000 installed
- Successful completion of Lab Exercise 4.01 in this lab manual
- Successful completion of Exercises 12-1 and 12-2 in the *MCSE Windows 2000 Professional Study Guide*
- An Internet connection

cross
Reference

To best prepare for this lab exercise, read the section titled "Implementing, Configuring, Managing, and Troubleshooting Local Group Policy" in Chapter 12 of the **MCSE Windows 2000 Professional Study Guide.**

Getting Down to Business

In the following steps, you will first confirm that you successfully completed lab Exercise 12-2 in the *MCSE Windows 2000 Professional Study Guide* by examining your Security Account Password settings using the Group Policy Editor. Then you will research the effect of setting password complexity requirements.

Step 1. Log on as Administrator (or a member of the Administrators group). Open the Group Policy Editor and verify that the policies you set in Exercise 12-2 in the *MCSE Windows 2000 Professional Study Guide* "Forcing More Secure Passwords" have taken effect. The Local Settings column lists settings that exist in local group policy (or simply "local policy"). The Effective Settings column lists the policy settings that have taken effect—both from local group policy and from group policy set at the site, domain, or organizational unit level, if your computer is a member of an Active Directory domain. Your Password Policy settings should appear as shown in Figure 12-1 unless your locally set policy has not taken effect yet, or your lab computer is a member of a domain. In the latter case, conflicting policies set at the Site, Domain, or Organizational Unit level will override your Local Computer Security policies. Once you have confirmed the settings, close the Group Policy Editor.

Step 2. One of the settings that you configured in Exercise 12-2 in the *MCSE Windows 2000 Professional Study Guide* was Passwords Must Meet Complexity Requirement. Research what this setting means by pointing your Internet browser to www.microsoft.com/technet and searching for the document titled "Password must meet complexity requirements." Read this document, then describe the password complexity requirements of this policy in the space provided below.

_____

_____

_____

_____

_____

_____

_____

Local Account
Password Policies

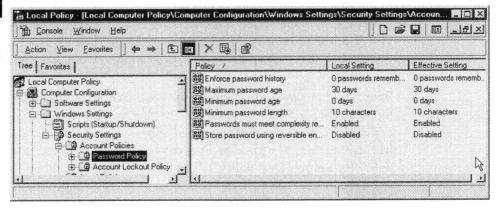

Step 3. In addition to the above complexity requirement, Exercise 12-1 in the *MCSE Windows 2000 Professional Study Guide* had you set a maximum password age of 30 days, and a minimum password length of 10 characters. Describe how these might be combined with the complexity requirement, and provide a sample password that meets all these requirements.

_____

_____

_____

lab
Hint   *When is Password Policy enforced? What about existing accounts with old, non-compliant passwords? The Password Policy is enforced whenever a password is created for a new user or changed for an existing user. A user whose password does not presently comply will not be required to make the password comply until he or she attempts to change it. This is a good reason for limiting the age of a password. If you change the Password Policy, users will eventually be required to comply when their password expires and they have to change passwords.*

Step 4. Reset the password of one of the users, using a password that does not comply with the Password Policy. If the policy set in Exercise 12-1 was not overridden, use one that is shorter than 10 characters and does not meet the complexity requirements. If you are unsure of how to reset a password, search for the topic "Change a User's Password" in Windows 2000 Help. When you attempt to change the password to one that does not comply with the Account Password Policy, you will receive the following message:

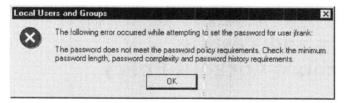

Yes, we insist on using the phrase "reset password," because that is the phrase most often used in practice. However, to reset a password you actually select Set Password when you right-click on a user in Local Users and Groups. The Help topic that explains how to do this is "Change a User's Password." Is this confusing?

Here's some context: You are working on the help desk, and you get a call that a user has forgotten his password. You can't go look it up for him (without special hacker tools, and we don't want to go there), so the best you can do for this person is offer to reset this password. Perhaps you both agree on what it should be, then someone with the correct permissions can "reset" the password for the user. This is a frequent task of administrators, and is most often done on a user's domain user account.

Keep in mind that a domain user account is most often the only account a user has. They get access to their local Windows 2000 computer through its membership in the domain and the fact that a domain user is a member of the Domain Users group. This group is, in turn, a member of the local Users group on each and every Windows NT, Windows 2000, and Windows XP computer that is a member of the domain.

Step 5.   Now reset the password using the password you created in Step 3. Close all open windows and log off.

Step 6.   Log on as the user for whom you reset the password.

LAB EXERCISE 12.02

30 Minutes

Enabling and Testing the Account Lockout Policy

Another important group of security settings is Account Lockout. Many organizations have used this setting in their Windows NT domains, and we are glad to see it supported by policies in Windows 2000. Once again, you will go back to the test lab and test this on a Windows 2000 Professional computer, knowing that your organization will apply it at the domain level. Although in your Active Directory domain the domain administrators will actually implement this policy, you will find it valuable to experiment with this policy on a smaller scale in the lab. One thing you will notice is that you are reminded to set all three policies under Account Lockout.

If you select only one of the three, you will be prompted with a box containing suggested value changes for the other two when you click OK in its setting box.

Learning Objectives

By the end of this lab, you'll be able to

- Enable the Account Lockout Policy
- Cause a refresh of group policy
- Test Account Lockout Policy
- Remove a lockout from an account.

Lab Materials and Setup

The materials you need for this lab are:

- A PC with Windows 2000 installed

cross
Reference   *To best prepare for this lab exercise, read the section titled "Implementing, Configuring, Managing, and Troubleshooting Local Group Policy" in Chapter 12 of the **MCSE Windows 2000 Professional Study Guide.***

Getting Down to Business

In the following steps, you will set the three options of Account Lockout Policy. You can start with any one of them—the instructions below have you start with Account Lockout threshold. No matter which one you start with, if one or both of the other two do not have viable settings, it will suggest settings. In the lab, we have you set the number of invalid lockout attempts to 3, and just accept the suggestions for the other two settings. After you have set policy, you will run the SECEDIT command to force an immediate refresh of security policy. Then, you will test the effect of the new set of policies by attempting to log on four times with a bad password. You will see the error messages generated by these attempts so that you will understand these messages when users report them to you.

Step 1.   Log on as Administrator (or a member of the Administrators group). Open the Group Policy Editor focused on the local computer policy. Use the entry form in Table 12-1 to enable and define the Account Lockout Policy. You can start

TABLE 12-1	Policy	Setting
	Account Lockout Threshold	3 invalid logon attempts
Account Lockout Policy Entry Form	Account Lockup Duration	30 minutes
	Reset Account Lockup Lockout Counter After	30 minutes

with any of the three policies. We started with the account lockout threshold because that was the only one for which we were not going to accept the suggested settings.

The Local Security Policy Setting dialog box for account lockout threshold is shown in Figure 12-2 with the value changed to 3.

Click OK to enable the account lockout threshold, which will cause the Suggested Value Changes dialog box to appear (Figure 12-3). When you click OK on this box the suggested setting will be applied. If you would like to alter these settings, you may do so in the Group Policy Editor. After making these changes close the Group Policy Editor.

Step 2. Computer Configuration policy is refreshed at an interval. The default for Windows 2000 computers, except domain controllers, is to update this in background every 90 minutes, with a random offset of 0 to 30 minutes. To cause an immediate refresh of group policy, enter the following command from a command prompt:

```
secedit /refreshpolicy machine_policy
```

FIGURE 12-2

Account lockout threshold

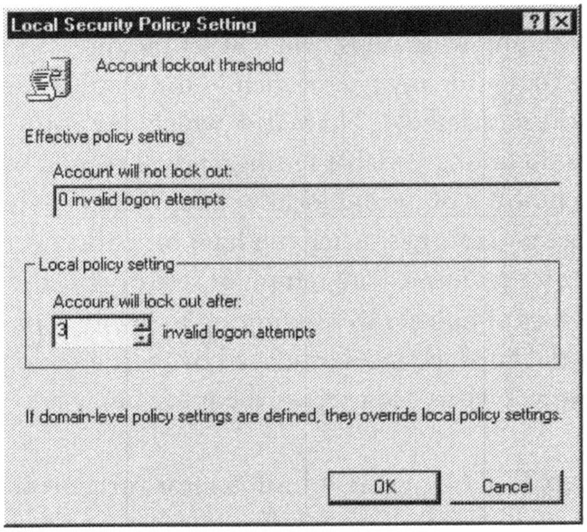

FIGURE 12-3

Suggested Value
Changes dialog
box

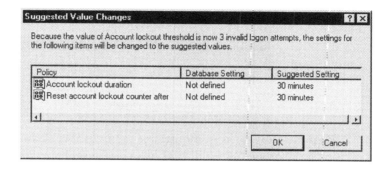

Although this command can easily be run from Start | Run, we prefer to open a command prompt so that we can see the output sent to the screen from this command as shown here:

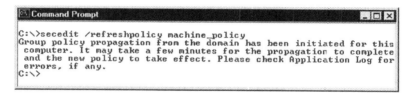

Step 3. Verify that group policy was applied by using Group Policy Editor to check the effective group policy settings. You can also open the Application Log in Event Viewer, and look for an event with a source of SceCli and an Event ID of 1704 at the time at which you ran the SECEDIT command. This is the event that signals the successful application of security policy.

Step 4. Next, test the effectiveness of this policy and see what messages are generated when a user exceeds the number of invalid logon attempts.

Log off.

Test the new policy by attempting to log on four times with the wrong password as another user (*not* Administrator, who cannot be locked out). The first three times you should see this message:

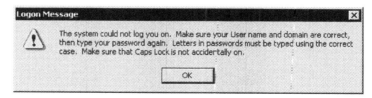

On the fourth attempt you should see this message:

Step 5. Log on as Administrator (or a member of the Administrators group). Open the properties for the user who was locked out. There will be a check by Account Is Locked Out, as shown in Figure 12-4. This is the only time anyone can modify this setting. Clear the check box now.

Step 6. Log off and then log back on as the user whose account was locked out.

Account lock out

lab
Hint

This often goes hand-in-hand with the task of resetting a user's password. A user who forgets a password will try several guesses, and if account lockout is enabled, they will call for help when they are locked out or when they get tired of guessing. Remember, in this lab you are working with a Windows 2000 Professional computer and the local accounts. If your computer is a member of a domain, this policy will be set at the domain level. In a domain, users normally log on with Domain accounts, and it would be the Domain account that would become locked out. In most organizations, users then call the help desk and someone would remove the account lock out and reset the password on the user's domain account. It has been estimated that this one problem accounts for 60% to 80% of the calls to help desks. Although we don't know the source of that estimate, we are sure it is not an urban myth. Our experiences, and those of our students and clients, tell us that this is a very realistic number.

Step 7. Disable Account Lockout Policy.

LAB EXERCISE 12.03

Exploring User Rights Assignment

45 Minutes

The next group of policy settings you will work on are those that control user rights (or *privileges*) to perform certain system-wide functions on a computer. This may include being permitted to log onto a computer or having the right to install device drivers on a computer. Most of these same rights existed in Windows NT, and some of us, in our first months of learning Windows 2000, thought longingly of the simplicity of setting user rights in Windows NT. Yes, it was right there in User Manager (or User Manager for Domains) on the Policy menu. Gee, weren't you born knowing that? We tend to forget that it was not exactly intuitive to find these settings on that menu either. It is just that we learned it, and then we knew it, and it worked for us for several years. But we also had to learn how to use several other tools and methods in other places to control other important settings.

Now many of these scattered settings have been brought together to be centrally controlled in Group Policies. Yes, there are hundreds of individual group policy settings, but at least now you know exactly where to start digging for the buried treasure—powerful settings that let you control and manage the desktop once you master them. Yes, these settings are best implemented in a Domain environment, but once again, we are using the mini-environment of our test lab Windows 2000 Professional computers to look at more of these settings. This is what you will explore in this lab.

Learning Objectives

By the end of this lab, you'll be able to

■ Understand the capabilities of key User Rights settings.

Lab Materials and Setup

The materials you need for this lab are:

■ A PC with Windows 2000 installed

cross
Reference

To best prepare for this lab read the section "User Rights Assignments" in Chapter 12 of the **MCSE Windows 2000 Professional Study Guide.**

Getting Down to Business

Several of the user rights are only assigned to the operating system itself, or are available for programmers to access during software development. But there are several other user rights that are important for support people to understand. In the following steps you will research these key user rights, completing a table in which you research the effective settings for these rights on your lab computer. These settings define the users or groups that have been assigned each right.

lab
Hint

If your computer is a member of a workgroup, and if you have not modified the local policy settings, your answers will match those in the solution for this step. If your computer is a member of a Windows 2000 domain, you may have different effective settings, due to group policies having been set at the Site, Domain, or Organizational Unit (OU) level. By default, there is only one domain level Group Policy Object (GPO), the Default Domain Policy, which would affect a Windows 2000 Professional member computer. Most organizations will decide to create additional GPOs, most of which will be applied at the OU level. You are not expected to memorize all the hundreds of group policy settings for the 70-210 exam. However, for the exam and on-the-job, the settings in Table 12-2 may come in handy.

Step 1.   Log on as Administrator (or a member of the Administrators group). Open the Group Policy Editor focused on the local computer policy. Open the User Rights Assignment node, which can be found in Computer Configuration | Windows Settings | Security Settings | Local Policies. Complete Table 12-2, which contains a User Rights Assignments Worksheet, by recording the Effective Settings for the listed User Rights.

Some of the settings have several user or group names listed. For those settings, double-click on the single policy to open the Local Security Policy Setting dialog box, as shown in Figure 12-5. This is much easier to read!

TABLE 12-2	Policy	Users/Groups
Effective User Rights Form	Act As Part Of The Operating System	
	Back Up Files And Directories	
	Change The System Time	
	Load And Unload Device Drivers	
	Log On Locally	
	Manage Auditing And Security Log	
	Remove Computer From Docking Station	
	Restore Files And Directories	
	Shut Down The System	
	Take Ownership Of Files Or Other Objects	

FIGURE 12-5

Local Security
Policy Setting
dialog box

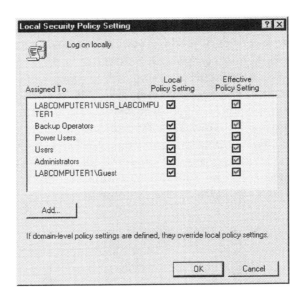

lab

Hint *We have used many terms that you may eventually need to learn if you study the Windows 2000 Active Directory domains. In brief: a domain is an administrative grouping of users, groups, computers, and other objects within a single security boundary. When you create a domain on a Windows 2000 server the domain objects are stored in a central, multi-mastered directory called the Active Directory. An organizational unit (OU) is an administrative grouping of users, groups and computers within a domain. A Group Policy Object (GPO) contains group policy settings. For more information on these and other terms, see the "Glossary" section in the MCSE Windows 2000 Professional Study Guide.*

LAB EXERCISE 12.04

Applying and Testing Auditing

45 Minutes

You have no doubt heard the Microsoft statement that Windows 2000 brings together the best parts of the Windows 9*x* user interface and the stability of the Windows NT platform. We have worked with Windows NT for several years, and believe this is true. One of the many valuable features of Windows NT that lives on in Windows 2000 is the *auditing* function. This is enabled through Audit Policy and when enabled and configured, certain selected events will be recorded in the Security log, which is viewable from Event Viewer. Auditing is a very resource-intensive activity that is usually done very selectively on servers in an organization. Setting too many auditing functions on a computer will negatively affect the performance of the computer, diminishing its effectiveness as a desktop or server computer. You are less likely to turn on auditing on a Windows 2000 Professional desktop than on a server. And on a server you would be extremely selective, because of the possible performance degradation that can occur. However, once again, it is good practice to work with auditing at the desktop level to gain some understanding of how it works. And you never know, you may find a very good use for it on a user's desktop. In this lab exercise, you will apply auditing to account logon events. Once configured, you will test it by causing some logon events to fail.

cross
Reference
To best prepare for this lab, read the entire section titled "Auditing" and complete Exercise 12-3 in Chapter 12 of the **MCSE** *Windows 2000* **Professional Study Guide.**

Learning Objectives

By the end of this lab, you'll be able to

- Understand Windows 2000 auditing
- Enable auditing for account logon events
- Test auditing for account logon events.

Lab Materials and Setup

The materials you need for this lab are:

- A PC with Windows 2000 installed

Getting Down to Business

In the following steps you will turn on auditing to catch account logon failures. Then you will attempt to log on with an invalid password. This should result in an event being logged to the Security event log, which you will verify after you log on successfully.

Step 1. Log on as Administrator (or a member of the Administrators group). Open the Group Policy Editor focused on the local computer policy. Select the Audit Policy named Audit Account Logon Events and configure it to only audit failures as shown in Figure 12-6. Close out of all dialog boxes and windows.

lab
ⓘint

Did you notice that there are two policies for logons? In addition to the audit policy you used here, Audit Account Logon Events, there is a similar one called Audit Logon Events. The first focuses on where the account exists, while the second one focuses on where the user actually logs on. If your computer is in a domain, and you want to detect all logon failures at this computer, whether the user is using a domain account or a local account, then use the second policy, Audit Logon Events.

Step 2. Log off and attempt to log on with an incorrect password. Then log on correctly as Administrator (or a member of the local Administrators group).

Step 3. Open the Event Viewer and search for the failed logon event (event #681) in the Security log, as shown in Figure 12-7. Log off when you are finished.

Audit account
logon events
settings

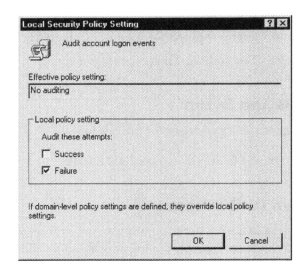

Event properties
display

lab

Warning   *You must be logged on as a member of the Administrators group (that includes Administrator) in order to view the Security event log. While access to the Security event log is restricted, the Application and System event logs can be viewed by anyone in the Users group.*

LAB EXERCISE 12.05

Disabling EFS (Encrypting File System)

45 Minutes

You have studied Encrypting File System (EFS), the technology built into Windows 2000 that allows you to encrypt files on a file-by-file basis on an NTFS volume. By now you have practiced several tasks involving EFS. All that remains is to learn how to disable EFS. Why would you want to disable EFS? Some organizations have high security standards that might require a more robust form of encryption than that used by EFS. To disable EFS, remember that no one can encrypt files (using EFS) on a computer if the computer does not have at least one recovery agent. The recovery agent is an account that can use its private recovery keys to remove encryption from files that were encrypted by another person. This is done in the case of a user who loses his private key or certificate. All you do to disable EFS is remove all recovery agents from a computer. But what happens if you already had files encrypted on your computer? Will they remain encrypted? You will have to do the lab to find out for sure.

To best prepare for this lab, read the entire section titled "Encrypting Data on a Hard Disk by Using EFS" and complete Exercises 12-4 through 12-8 in Chapter 12 of the **MCSE Windows 2000 Professional Study Guide.**

Learning Objectives

By the end of this lab, you'll be able to

- Disable EFS on a computer
- Understand the implications of disabling EFS.

Lab Materials and Setup

The materials you need for this lab are:

- A PC with Windows 2000 installed

Getting Down to Business

In the following steps, you will first create a directory, copy files into the directory, then encrypt the directory. You will then disable EFS, and finally, test the effect of having EFS disabled.

Step 1. Log on as Administrator (or a member of the Administrators group). Use Windows Explorer to create a folder on your hard drive. Copy a few files into this folder, then access the Advanced Attributes in the properties for the folder and encrypt it. Figure 12-8 shows the Applying Attributes message box that displays a progress bar while your files are being encrypted. This was a folder with many, many files and subfolders. Notice that the time remaining is 54 minutes. It can be very time consuming to encrypt a great deal of data at once. When the Applying Attributes message box closes, close Windows Explorer.

FIGURE 12-8

Applying
Attributes

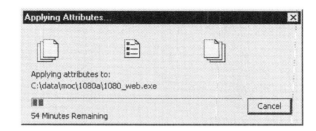

Step 2. Open the Group Policy Editor focused on the local computer policy. Remove all encrypted data recovery agents.

Step 3. Refresh policy on your computer.

Step 4. Open Windows Explorer and view the folder you created and encrypted in Step 1. Is it still encrypted?

_____

Are you able to open an encrypted file?

_____

Are you able to remove the encrypted attribute from the folder and its contents?

_____

Step 5. Select a folder that does not have encryption turned on and attempt to encrypt the folder.

Were you successful? Explain below:

_____

LAB ANALYSIS TEST

1. Your company is in an industry that has been affected by a new law requiring more stringent security measures than previously required. A committee has been appointed to write a document describing the measures that will be taken to comply with the new law. One of the committee members has called to ask you if Windows 2000 has a means of enforcing a strict password policy. How will you answer him?

_____

_____

2. A manager is concerned that the company has decided on a strict account lockout policy by which users will be locked out of their domain accounts for one hour after just three failed logon attempts. He is concerned about the productivity of his users with this policy enforced. What can you tell this manager?

_____

_____

3. Another member of your desktop support team, Carmella, is actually a trainee. Windows 2000 is the first version she has worked with as a support person. She is having a problem grasping the differences between permissions and user rights. How will you explain the difference to her?

_____

_____

4. One of your users suspects that someone has been in his office after hours. No items have been taken, but things have been physically rearranged, as if someone was sitting at his computer. The domain administrators have not detected any sign of an intruder or mischief on their servers, but they have decided to watch the activity on this computer. What auditing setting would you recommend for this computer to discover when and if someone is using this computer after hours?

_____

_____

5. You are configuring Windows 2000 Professional on a laptop for an executive who would like to encrypt some of his sensitive data. Describe how you will help him with this.

_____

_____

KEY TERM QUIZ

Use the following vocabulary terms to complete the sentences below. Not all the terms will be used.

Account Lockout Policy

Account Security Policies

Audit Policy

Encrypting File System (EFS)

Group Policy Editor

load and unload device drivers

log on locally

Password Policy

recovery agent

User Rights

1. Administrators use the _____ to modify group policy settings.

2. Someone installing a new network card in a computer needs to have the _____ user right.

3. _____ is the Windows 2000 technology that will allow you to provide greater protection for your sensitive data on an NTFS partition simply by using a special attribute.

4. _____ should be used sparingly, because using too many of these settings can affect the performance of a computer.

5. If you receive a call from a user who says she can no longer even attempt to log on to her computer, a/an _____ was set, and you will have to access the properties of her account and make a change so that the she can log on.

LAB WRAP-UP

With this chapter, you finished your focused exploration of Windows 2000 Professional by working with Security settings in Local Group Policy. The purpose of this book is two-fold. First, of course, to help you prepare for Microsoft Exam 70-210; second, to help you acquire confidence in your ability to make Windows 2000 Professional function effectively for you. This lab took you through testing of Security Account Password Policies and enabling and testing the Security Account Lockout Policy. You went on to explore User Rights Assignment, Disabling EFS support, and applying and testing Auditing.

This has been quite a journey for you through these 12 chapters. This lab manual has provided you with 50 lab exercises which, if you used them in conjunction with the many exercises in the *MCSE Windows 2000 Professional Study Guide,* have given you a genuine hands-on experience in working with Windows 2000 Professional. As each iteration of Windows makes its way into the marketplace, there are new concepts to learn, old concepts to adapt, different ways of doing familiar tasks, familiar techniques that are no longer available, and many other capabilities to master. Our hope is that this lab manual has been interesting and useful to you. We certainly worked to make it so. Good luck in taking the test and in your future endeavors.

LAB SOLUTIONS FOR CHAPTER 12

In this section, you'll find solutions to the lab exercises, Lab Analysis Test, and Key Term Quiz.

Lab Solution 12.01

Step 1.　If you created and saved an MMC console with the Group Policy Editor focused on Local Security policies, open that console now. Otherwise, use the GPEDIT.MSC command, as instructed in Exercise 12-1 in the *MCSE Windows 2000 Professional Study Guide.* Browse to Local Computer Policy | Computer Configuration | Windows Settings | Security Settings | Account Policies | Password Policy to view the settings in the content pane similar to those in Figure 12-1.

Step 2.　The complexity requirements are:

- A password must not contain all or part of a user's name.
- A password must be at least 6 characters in length.
- A password must contain characters from 3 of the following 4 categories:

  - English upper case characters (A to Z)
  - English lower case characters (a to z)
  - Base 10 numeric characters (0 to 9)
  - Non-alphanumeric characters (such as !, $, #, %)

Step 3.　When all the password policy settings are combined the users will have to have passwords comply with all the complexity requirements, but rather than a minimum of 6 characters (part of the complexity requirement), they will have to be at least 10 characters in length. These passwords will also expire in 30 days. An example of a password that meets both the complexity and length requirements of the Password Policy configured in Exercise 12-1 is: 10sPi9ffy1.

Step 4.

1. Open the Computer Management console. Right-click on My Computer, then select Manage.

2. In the Computer Management console, browse to Computer Management |
   System Tools | Local Users and Groups | User, and double-click on Users
   in the tree pane so that a list of users appears in the contents pane.

3. Right-click on one of the users (do not pick Administrator). Select Set
   Password. In the New Password and Confirm Password text boxes enter
   a password that does not conform with the effective password policy.

Steps 5 and 6.   No further instructions are needed for these steps. Step 5 is a repeat
of Step 4, only using a password that meets the requirements.

Lab Solution 12.02

Steps 1 through 6.   No further instructions are required for these steps.

Step 7.   Using Group Policy Editor, Open the Account Lockout Policy node
in Computer Configuration | Windows Settings | Security Settings | Account Policies.
Double-click on the Account Lockout Threshold and set it to 0 (zero). Click OK,
and the Suggested Value Changes dialog box will open. Click OK to accept the
suggested values.
    After making these changes close the Group Policy Editor.

Lab Solution 12.03

Step 1.   Answers may vary if the lab computer is a member of a domain. Table 12-3
contains the settings on our lab computer, which was a member of a workgroup.

Lab Solution 12.04

Step 1.   In the Group Policy Editor, open Audit Policy in Local Computer Policy |
Computer Configuration | Windows Settings | Security Settings | Local Policies.
Double-click on the policy Audit Account Logon Events.

Step 2.   No further instructions are needed for this step.

TABLE 12-3		

Policy	Users/Groups
Act As Part Of The Operating System	No one is assigned this right
Back Up Files And Directories	Administrators, Backup Operators
Change The System Time	Power Users, Administrators
Load And Unload Device Drivers	Administrators
Log On Locally	Computername\IUSR_*Computernam, Backup Operators, Power Users, Users, Administrators, Computername*Guest
Manage Auditing And Security Log	Administrators
Remove Computer From Docking Station	Power Users, Users, Administrators
Restore Files And Directories	Administrators, Backup Operators
Shut Down The System	Administrators, Users, Power Users, Backup Operators
Take Ownership Of Files Or Other Objects	Administrators

Effective User Rights Form Completed

Step 3. Open Event Viewer by entering EVENTVWR.MSC in the Start | Run box (or use your favorite method). In Event Viewer, select Security, and look for an event 681 that occurred at the time of your failed logon.

Lab Solution 12.05

Step 1. Using Windows Explorer, create a new folder on a local drive. Copy some files into the folder. Right-click on the folder, select Properties, and then click on the Advanced button. In the Advanced Attributes dialog box select Encrypt Contents To Secure Data (see Figure 12-9), and then click OK.

Click OK in the Properties dialog box for the folder. This will cause the Confirm Attribute Changes dialog box to appear, as shown in Figure 12-10. Select Apply Changes To This Folder, Subfolders And Files, then click OK. The Applying Attributes message box will appear with a progress bar, and you should notice some disk activity while the files are being encrypted.

Step 2. Open Local Computer Policy | Computer Configuration | Windows Settings | Security Settings | Public Key Policies | Encrypted Data Recovery Agents. Right-click on each recovery agent and select Delete.

FIGURE 12-9

Advanced
Attributes

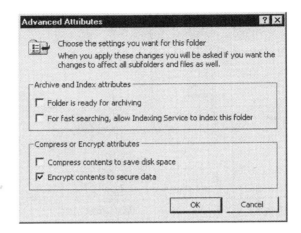

Step 3. To cause an immediate refresh of group policy security settings, enter the following command from a command prompt:

```
secedit /refreshpolicy machine_policy
```

Step 4. The files are still encrypted.

Yes, I can open and read the encrypted file (as long as I am the person who encrypted the file).

Yes, I can remove the encrypted attribute from the folder and its contents.

Step 5. No, I was not successful, because there can be no EFS encryption if there are no recovery agents. I received the error message in Figure 12-11 and had to cancel the operation.

FIGURE 12-10

Confirm
Attribute
Changes

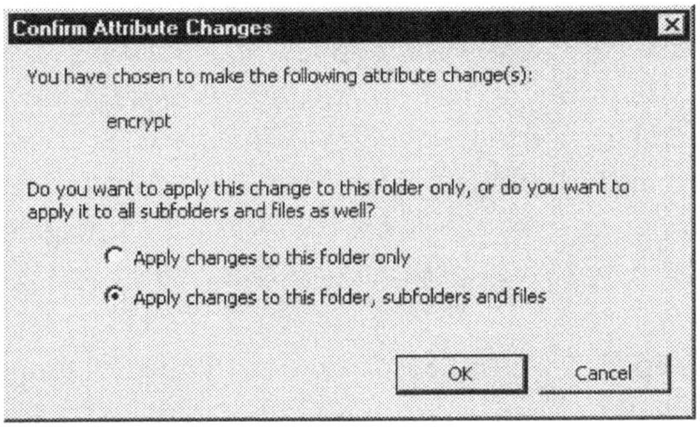

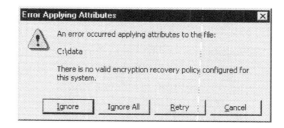

FIGURE 12-11

Error Applying
Attributes

ANSWERS TO LAB ANALYSIS TEST

1. I would tell the caller that Windows 2000 has several policy options for enforcing passwords including length, age, uniqueness, complexity, and account lockout after a configurable number of failed logon attempts. I would have to take a closer look at the specific password requirements of the law to know if these settings would be sufficient.

2. You can tell the manager that the users can call the help desk and an administrator will unlock their domain user account. In reality, the hope is that they will get better at remembering their passwords!

3. Permissions are attached to objects. They allow or deny users or groups to take particular action on an object. An example of permission is the read permission. Permissions are managed through the properties of an object. User rights are specific privileges assigned to users or groups to perform system-wide functions, such as logon locally or load and unload device drivers. User rights are assigned through local or domain level group policy.

4. The domain administrator can turn on both success and failure for the Audit Logon Events Policy. This will detect all logons that occur at this computer, regardless of whether they are logging on with a local account or a domain account. In addition, auditing access to files on the local computer and/or selected servers will detect what they are accessing. However, be careful with this setting and be selective about the folders or files you choose to audit. This can cause the security log file to grow quickly, and it will also consume some system resources. Once the mystery is solved, the auditing should be turned off—at least for file and folder access.

5. Answers will vary somewhat. Since he is an executive, let's make it as simple as possible for him. Find out what files he needs to encrypt and create one or more folders just for these files, then turn on the Encryption attribute found in the Advanced Attributes of the Properties dialog box for each of these folders. Be sure to apply changes to the folder, its subfolders, and files. If this is successful, you will also be confirming that encryption is enabled on his computer. It is turned on by default, but we never take anything for granted. Show him how he encrypts a file by simply copying it into this folder. Tell him that when he opens a file in an application, it is automatically decrypted. When he saves it back to one of the encrypted folders, it will be encrypted again. Finally, warn him that if he tries to encrypt an existing folder with many files, it may take as much as several hours to complete all encryption.

ANSWERS TO KEY TERM QUIZ

1. Group Policy Editor
2. load and unload device drivers
3. Encrypting File System (EFS)
4. Audit Policy
5. Account Lockout Policy

INDEX

M

T

INTERNATIONAL CONTACT INFORMATION

AUSTRALIA
McGraw-Hill Book Company Australia Pty. Ltd.
TEL +61-2-9417-9899
FAX +61-2-9417-5687
http://www.mcgraw-hill.com.au
books-it_sydney@mcgraw-hill.com

CANADA
McGraw-Hill Ryerson Ltd.
TEL +905-430-5000
FAX +905-430-5020
http://www.mcgrawhill.ca

**GREECE, MIDDLE EAST,
NORTHERN AFRICA**
McGraw-Hill Hellas
TEL +30-1-656-0990-3-4
FAX +30-1-654-5525

MEXICO (Also serving Latin America)
McGraw-Hill Interamericana Editores S.A. de C.V.
TEL +525-117-1583
FAX +525-117-1589
http://www.mcgraw-hill.com.mx
fernando_castellanos@mcgraw-hill.com

SINGAPORE (Serving Asia)
McGraw-Hill Book Company
TEL +65-863-1580
FAX +65-862-3354
http://www.mcgraw-hill.com.sg
mghasia@mcgraw-hill.com

SOUTH AFRICA
McGraw-Hill South Africa
TEL +27-11-622-7512
FAX +27-11-622-9045
robyn_swanepoel@mcgraw-hill.com

**UNITED KINGDOM & EUROPE
(Excluding Southern Europe)**
McGraw-Hill Education Europe
TEL +44-1-628-502500
FAX +44-1-628-770224
http://www.mcgraw-hill.co.uk
computing_neurope@mcgraw-hill.com

ALL OTHER INQUIRIES Contact:
Osborne/McGraw-Hill
TEL +1-510-549-6600
FAX +1-510-883-7600
http://www.osborne.com
omg_international@mcgraw-hill.com

New Offerings from Osborne's
How to Do Everything Series

How to Do Everything with Your Palm™ Handheld, 2nd Edition
ISBN: 0-07-219100-7
Available: Now

How to Do Everything with Your Scanner
ISBN: 0-07-219106-6
Available: Now

How to Do Everything with Your Visor, 2nd Edition
ISBN: 0-07-219392-1
Available: October 2001

How to Do Everything with Photoshop Elements
ISBN: 0-07-219184-8
Available: September 2001

How to Do Everything with Your Blackberry
ISBN: 0-07-219393-X
Available: October 2001

How to Do Everything with Digital Video
ISBN: 0-07-219463-4
Available: November 2001

How to Do Everything with MP3 and Digital Music
ISBN: 0-07-219413-8
Available: December 2001

How to Do Everything with Your Web Phone
ISBN: 0-07-219412-X
Available: January 2002

How to Do Everything with Your iMac, 3rd Edition
ISBN: 0-07-213172-1
Available: October 2001

HTDE with Your Pocket PC & Handheld PC
ISBN: 07-212420-2
Available: Now

 OSBORNE
www.osborne.com

www.ingramcontent.com/pod-product-compliance
Lightning Source LLC
Chambersburg PA
CBHW080351060326
40689CB00019B/3964